Florida Atlas & Gazetteer

Grid numbers refer to detailed map pages

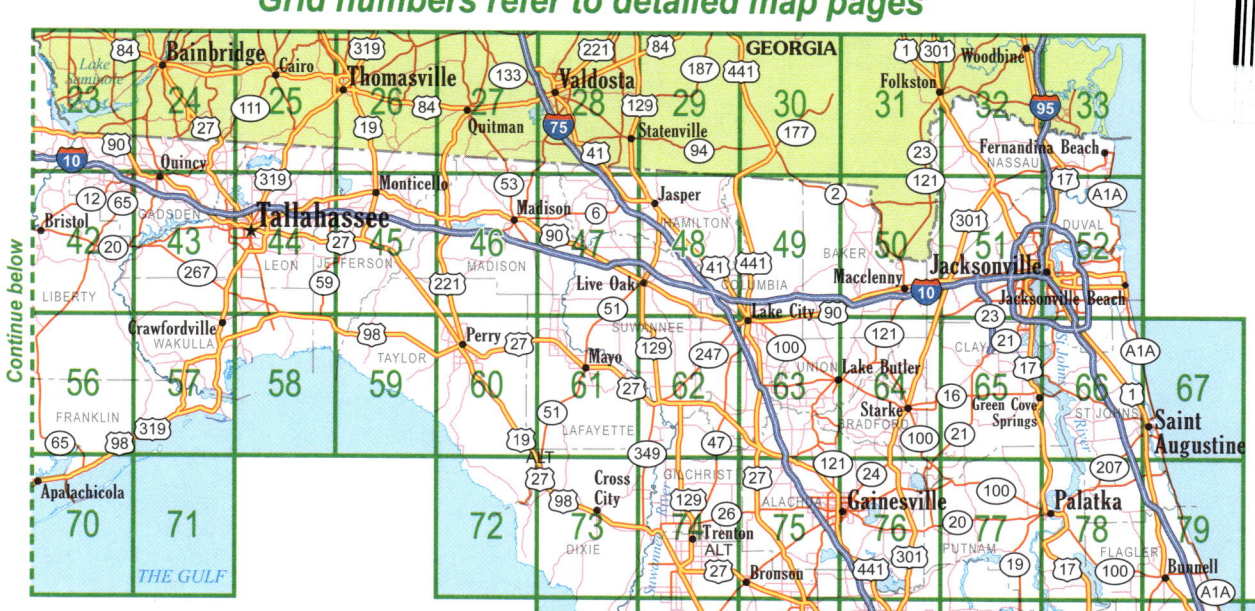

Table of Contents

THE ATLAS
- Detailed Topo Maps 15–159
- Index of Placenames 2–6
- Legend .... Inside Front Cover

THE GAZETTEER
- Introduction 7
- Campgrounds 13–14, 160
- Family Outings 8–10
- Fishing 12
- Outdoor Adventures 10
- Recreation Areas 11–12

No portion of this atlas may be photocopied, electronically stored or reproduced in any manner without written permission from the publisher.

Important Notices

Garmin has made reasonable efforts to provide you with accurate maps and related information, but we cannot exclude the possibility of errors or omissions in sources or of changes in actual conditions. GARMIN MAKES NO WARRANTIES OF ANY KIND, EITHER EXPRESS OR IMPLIED, INCLUDING THE WARRANTIES OF MERCHANTABILITY AND FITNESS FOR A PARTICULAR PURPOSE. GARMIN SHALL NOT BE LIABLE TO ANY PERSON UNDER ANY LEGAL OR EQUITABLE THEORY FOR DAMAGES ARISING OUT OF THE USE OF THIS PUBLICATION, INCLUDING, WITHOUT LIMITATION, FOR DIRECT, CONSEQUENTIAL OR INCIDENTAL DAMAGES.

Nothing in this publication implies the right to use private property. There may be private inholdings within the boundaries of public reservations. You should respect all landowner restrictions.

Some listings may be seasonal or may have admission fees. Please be sure to confirm this information when making plans.

Safety Information

To avoid accidents, always pay attention to actual road, traffic and weather conditions and do not attempt to read these maps while you are operating a vehicle. Please consult local authorities for the most current information on road and other travel-related conditions.

Do not use this publication for marine or aeronautical navigation, as it does not depict navigation aids, depths, obstacles, landing approaches and other information necessary to travel these waters safely.

California Prop 65 Warning

⚠ WARNING: Cancer and Reproductive Harm - www.p65warnings.ca.gov

FOURTEENTH EDITION

Copyright © 2026 Garmin Ltd. or its Affiliates. All rights reserved.
2 DeLorme Dr. Suite 200, Yarmouth, Maine 04096
www.garmin.com/DeLormeAtlas
Printed in Canada.

Index of Placenames

A

Abe Springs 41 C7
Aberdeen 141 A7
Achan 107 D5
Acline 128 B4
Adam 75 D6
Adams 47 B8
Adams Beach 60 D1
Adamsville 90 B4; 105 D8
Agricola 115 A6
Agricola Station 115 A6
Alachua 93 A7
Aladdin City 150 C3
Alafaya 101 A6
Alafaya Woods 93 D6
Alamana 93 A7
Alaqua Lakes 92 C4
Alcoma 108 D3
Alderene Park 92 B4
Aldermans Ford 106 D3
Alexander Springs 85 D6
Alford 21 D8
Allandale 87 C5
Allanton 54 B3
Allenhurst 94 C3
Allentown 16 C4
Alliance 22 D3
Alligator Point 57 C8
Alpine 116 B3
Alpine Heights 19 C6
Altamonte Springs 92 D4
Altha 41 A7
Alton 61 B7
Altoona 92 A1
Alturas 107 D8
Alva 130 C1
Amelia City 52 A3
American Beach 52 A3
Anastasia 67 C5
Anclote 104 A3
Anclote Key 104 A2
Andalusia 78 C3
Andover 147 C6
Andrew 43 C7
Andrews 31 C1; 74 C2
Andytown 146 A3
Angel City 103 C5
Anglers Park 154 C4
Anglevillas 119 D8
Ankona 127 A5
Anna Maria 112 C4
Anona 104 D2
Anthony 83 B7
Antioch 106 B2
Apalachicola 70 A1
Apollo Beach 113 A7
Apopka 92 D2
Aqui Esta 128 A4
Araquey 66 C4
Arcadia 122 B2
Archbold 123 C8
Archer 75 C6
Ards Crossroads 20 A4
Argyle 19 C8
Argyle Forest 65 A7
Ariel 94 C3
Aripeka 97 B5
Arlington 52 C1; 89 B8
Armstrong 78 A3
Arno 75 A5
Arran 57 A8
Arrant Settlement 20 B1
Arredondo 75 B8
Arundel 127 D5
Ashmore 57 B7
Ashton 101 D6
Ashville 27 D5
Astatula 91 C8
Astor 85 C6
Astor Farms 92 B4
Astor Park 85 C6
Athena 60 C3
Atlantic Beach 52 C4
Atlantic Blvd Estates 52 C2
Atlantis 141 A7
Auburn 18 B2
Auburndale 107 B7
Aucilla 45 B7
Audubon 103 B5
Aurantia 94 C2
Aurora 110 A4
Avalon Beach 35 A7
Ave Maria 137 C7
Avoca 47 A8
Avon Park 116 B2
Avon Park Lakes 116 B2
Avondale 85 B5; 51 C8
Ayers 97 B7
Azalea Park 101 A5
Azalea Terrace 52 D2

B

Babson Park 108 D2
Bagdad 16 D4; 35 A8
Bahama Beach 53 A6
Bahia Oaks 83 C6
Bahia Shores 112 A4
Bahoma 21 B6
Bailey 46 A1
Baird 115 B5
Bairs Den 124 B1
Baker 17 C8; 53 A8
Baker Settlement 20 B2
Bakers Mill 48 A1
Bakerstown 85 A6
Bakersville 66 C3
Bal Harbour 147 D7
Baldwin 51 C5
Ballard Pines 111 C7
Ballentine Manor 113 D5
Balm 114 A1
Bamboo 91 B5
Barber Quarters 125 B6
Barberville 85 C7
Barcola 107 D6
Bardin 77 A8
Barefoot Beach 136 C2
Barker Store 20 A2
Barrineau Park 15 D7
Barth 15 C8
Bartow 107 D6
Barwal 141 C7
Bascom 22 A3
Basinger 124 A4
Baskins 104 D3
Bass 62 A4
Bass Haven 66 C1
Bassville Park 91 B7
Basswood Estates 125 B6
Battle Ground Forks 39 A5
Baum 44 A3
Baxter 50 A2
Bay City 69 A8
Bay Harbor 54 A1
Bay Harbor Islands 147 D7
Bay Hill 90 C2; 100 B2
Bay Lake 77 C5; 99 B6; 100 C2
Bay Pines 104 D3
Bay Point 157 C5
Bay Ridge 92 C2
Bay Springs 15 C7
Bay View 38 B2
Bayard 66 A2
Bayhead 60 C2
Bayonet Point 96 C4
Bayou Crossing 20 C2
Bayou George 40 D2
Bayport 97 A5
Bayshore 129 C6
Bayshore Gardens 113 D5
Bayshore Manor 129 D6
Bayview 53 A8; 104 C4
Bayway 11 C4
Baywood 77 A7
Beach Haven 35 C5
Beach Highlands 38 C1
Beachville 62 C2
Beachwood 52 D2
Beacon Beach 54 B1
Beacon Hill 54 C4
Beacon Hills 52 C2
Beacon Square 96 D4
Bealsville 106 C4
Bean City 132 D3
Bear Hollow 124 B1
Beattys Corner 106 C2
Beauclerc Gardens 52 D1
Beaver Creek 17 B7
Beck Hammock 93 C6
Becker 33 D5
Beckhamtown 76 B4
Bee Ridge 113 D8
Beeghly Heights 51 B8
Bel Marra 141 B8
Belair 44 C1
Belandville 17 A6
Bell 74 A2
Bellair 65 A8
Belle Glade 133 D5
Belle Glade Camp 132 D4
Belle Isle 100 B4
Belle Meade 142 B4
Belleair 104 C3
Belleair Beach 104 C2
Belleair Bluffs 104 C2
Belleair Shores 104 C2
Belleview 83 D8
Belleview Heights 83 D8
Bells Mill 21 D6
Bellview 35 B5
Bellville 47 A5
Bellwood 102 A3
Belmont 48 B3
Belmore 65 D6

Belspur 120 A3
Benbow 131 B8
Benbow No 2 131 C8
Benbow No 3 131 C8
Bennett 40 C2
Bennett Field 86 C2
Benson Junction 93 B5
Benton 49 B5
Bereah 116 B1
Beresford 85 D8
Berkeley 97 B5
Berrydale 16 B4
Bertha 93 D5
Bessemer 126 D1
Bessent 50 D3
Bethany 114 D1
Bethel 44 D1
Bethlehem 20 A3
Bethune Beach 94 A2
Betts 40 A4
Beulah 34 A4; 100 A2
Bevell Place 98 B4
Bevens 89 A8
Beverley Terrace 120 A2
Beverly 56 D1
Beverly Beach 79 C7
Beverly Hills 51 B8; 89 A7
Beville Heights 75 B8
Bevilles Corner 90 D4
Big Coppitt Key 157 D5
Big Hammock 37 B8
Big Pine 157 C5
Big Scrub 84 D3
Biggar 136 A2
Biltmore 51 C8
Biltmore Beach 53 A7
Bimini 78 D4
Bird Island 72 A1
Biscayne Park 147 D6
Biscayne Village 51 B8
Bithlo 101 A4
Black Creek 44 A3
Black Curve 42 C3
Black Diamond 89 A7
Black Hammock 52 A2
Black Point 79 D5
Black Rock 33 D6
Blackman 18 A1
Blacks Ford 66 B2
Blacks Still 48 B3
Blake 86 C4
Bland 63 C7
Blanton 98 B2
Blitchton 82 B4
Blitchville 74 B2
Blocker 44 A1
Bloomingdale 106 D2
Blountstown 41 B8
Blowing Rocks 134 A4
Bloxham 43 C5
Blue Gulf Beach 38 C2
Blue Heron Pines 129 B5
Blue Lake 98 C4
Blue Lakes Ridge 92 A2
Blue Mountain Beach 38 C2
Blue Springs 47 B6
Bluefield 126 B1
Bluewater Bay 37 B7
Bluff Springs 16 A1
Bluffton 85 C6
Boardman 76 D2
Boca Ciega 112 A3
Boca Del Mar 141 C7
Boca Grande 128 C1
Boca Harbour 141 B8
Boca Pointe 141 C7
Boca Raton 141 C8
Boca West 141 C7
Boden 93 B7
Bogia 16 B1
Bohemia 35 B7
Bokeelia 128 C2
Bon Ami 56 A1
Bon Terra 79 C6
Bonaventure 102 D4
Bonifay 20 C4
Bonita Shores 136 C2
Bonita Springs 136 C3
Bonnie 107 D5
Bookertown 93 B5
Bostwick 78 A1
Bottoms Fishery 57 B8
Boulogne 31 C1
Bounds Crossing 20 C1
Bowden 52 D1
Bowling Green 115 B7
Boyd 60 A1
Boyette 106 D2
Boynton Beach 141 A8
Brackridge 52 D2
Braden Castle 113 C6
Bradenton 113 D6
Bradenton Beach 112 D4

Bradford 21 D6
Bradfordville 44 A2
Bradley 114 A4
Bradley Junction 115 A5
Branchborough 98 D3
Branchton 106 A1
Branchville 24 D3
Brandon 106 C1
Branford 62 C1
Brannonville 40 D1
Bratt 15 A7
Breezewood 83 D8
Brent 35 B6
Brentwood 52 C1
Brewster 115 A5
Brickdale 16 C1
Brickyard 55 C8
Bridgeport 78 A2; 104 B4
Bridges 115 D6
Brighton 124 B3
Brightsville 51 C6
Briny Breezes 141 A8
Bristol 42 B1
Broad Branch 41 C5
Broadview Park 147 B6
Broadwater 112 A4
Brock Crossroad 21 D5
Bronson 75 D5
Brooker 64 D1
Brooklyn 51 C8
Brookridge 97 A6
Brookside 119 A6
Brooksville 97 A8
Broscan 72 B4
Broward Estates 147 A6
Brown 63 C7
Browns Farm 140 A2
Browns Still 63 C7
Brownsdale 16 B1
Brownsville 35 B5; 147 D5
Browntown 21 A7
Brownville 122 B3
Broxson 36 A1
Bruce 39 B5
Bruceville 84 B1
Bruing 105 A7
Bryant 133 B5
Bryceville 51 C5
Bucell Jct 60 B2
Buchanan 115 D7
Buck Siding 56 D1
Buckhead Ridge 125 C6
Buckhorn 57 B7; 59 A5
Buckingham 129 D8
Buckingham West 75 B7
Buckville 61 A5
Buda 75 A5; 93 C7
Buena Vista 22 B4; 100 C2
Buenaventura Lakes 100 C4
Buffalo Bluff 77 C8
Bunche Park 147 C5
Bunker 38 C3
Bunker Hill 114 C2; 137 C8
Bunnell 79 D5
Burbank 83 B8
Burnetts Lake 75 A7
Bushnell 90 D3
Butler Beach 67 D5
Byrd 78 B3
Byrneville 16 A1

C

Cabbage Grove 45 D6
Cadillac 75 A6
Cairo 40 C3
Caleb 51 D6
Callahan 51 A6
Callaway 54 A2
Calphos 89 A8
Cambon 51 C7
Cameron City 93 C6
Camp Echockotee 65 A8
Camp Mack 108 C4
Camp Ocala 85 C5
Camp Palm 69 B6
Camp Roosevelt 83 C7
Campbell 100 D3
Campbell Woods 89 B6
Campbellton 21 A7
Camps 97 A7
Camps Still 48 B2
Campton 18 B2
Campville 76 B3
Cana 126 B3
Canaan 93 C6
Canal Point 133 B5
Canaveral Acres 102 B3
Candler 84 D1
Canning Town 17 B8
Canova Beach 111 A6
Cantonment 15 D8

Cape Canaveral 103 C5
Cape Coral 136 A1
Cape Haze 128 B1
Capitola 44 B3
Capps 45 B6
Captiva 135 A6
Cara 83 A5
Carbur 60 C3
Cardwell 133 C5
Carlson 90 B2
Carlton 126 A3
Carlton Village 91 A6
Carnestown 143 C8
Carol City 147 C5
Carraway 77 A7
Carrabelle 57 D5
Carrabelle Beach 56 D4
Carters Corner 107 B6
Carters Crossing 107 B6
Carrollwood 105 B6
Carters 107 B6
Carver 90 D3
Carver Heights 141 C7
Carver Manor 51 C8
Carver Village 141 D7
Cary 51 B7
Carysfort Yacht Harbor 155 B5
Caryville 20 C3
Casa Blanco 45 A6
Casa Cola 66 C4
Cassadaga 93 A6
Casselberry 93 D5
Cassia 92 B3
Cassia Station 92 B3
Castle Hill 99 A8
Catawba 89 D8
Caxambas 142 C4
CC Trail 141 A7
Cedar Creek 84 B2
Cedar Creek Estates 89 A5
Cedar Grove 54 A1
Cedar Hammock 113 D5
Cedar Hills 51 D8
Cedar Hills Estates 51 D8
Cedar Island 60 D1
Cedar Key 80 C4
Cedar Point 52 B3
Celebration 100 C2
Center Hill 91 D5
Center Park 52 D3
Center Ridge 19 B7
Centerville 44 A2
Central City 56 A1
Central Telemetry 103 B5
Century 16 A1
Century Village 134 C3
Cerny Heights 35 B5
Cerrogordo 20 B2
Chain O Lakes 92 A2
Chaires 44 B3
Chaires Crossing 44 B3
ChampionsGate 100 D1
Chancey 47 D5
Chantilly Acres 75 A7
Chapel Hill 141 A8
Chapman 105 A7
Charleston Park 130 C2
Charlotte Beach 128 A2
Charlotte Harbor 128 A4
Charlotte Park 128 A4
Chaseville 52 C1
Chason 41 A6
Chassahowitzka 89 C5
Chatham 148 A1
Chatmar 82 D3
Chattahoochee 23 C6
Cherry Lake 46 A3; 91 A5
Chester 33 D6
Chestnut Hill Ranches 83 B5
Cheval 105 A6
Chiefland 74 D2
Childs 123 B8
Childs Station 123 B8
Chipley 21 C6
Chipola 41 A7
Chipola Park 41 D6
Chipola Terrace 22 B3
Chobie Dock 111 D7
Choctaw 38 C3
Choctaw Beach 37 B8
Chokoloskee 143 D8
Christmas 101 A8
Chuluota 93 D7
Chumuckla 16 C2
Chumuckla Springs 16 B1
Cinco Bayou 37 B5
Cisky Park 91 C6
Citra 76 D3
Citronelle 89 A6
Citrus Center 131 B6
Citrus Hills 89 B7
Citrus Park 105 B6
Citrus Springs 89 A7
City Point 102 B3
Clair-Mel City 105 C8

Clara 73 A5
Clarcona 92 D3
Clark 75 A5
Clarksville 41 B6; 66 A3
Clarkwild 106 B1
Clay Island 91 D8
Clay Sink 98 B4
Clayno 64 C2
Clear Springs 18 A4; B2
Clearwater 104 C3
Clearwater Beach 104 C2
Clermont 99 A7
Cleveland 129 A5
Clewiston 132 C1
Clifton 93 C5
Cliftonville 63 B8
Clinch 75 C8
Clinton Heights 98 C2
Clio 42 C3
Cloud Lake 134 D4
Cluster Springs 19 B6
Coachman 104 C3
Cobb Cross Roads 21 A6
Cobbtown 16 B3
Cocoa 102 C4
Cocoa Beach 103 C5
Cocoa West 102 C3
Coconut 136 B2
Coconut Creek 141 D6
Cody 44 C4
Codys Corner 86 A1
Coker 115 C7
Coleman 90 C4
College Park 51 C8; 66 D4; 141 C7
College Station 40 D1
Collier Park 141 D7
Collins Mill 21 A6
Collins Park Estates 127 A5
Columbia 62 B4
Combee Settlement 107 B5
Compass Lake 40 A4
Compass Lake in the Hills 21 D8
Conant 91 A5
Conch Key 159 C6
Concord 24 D4; 44 A4
Confer 92 A1
Conner 84 B1
Connersville 85 B7; 107 C7
Conrad 85 C8
Conrock 97 A8
Conway 101 A5
Cooglers Beach 97 A5
Cook 54 A2
Cooks Hammock 61 C5
Cooper City 147 B5
Cooper L Hills Estates 77 B6
Cooper Lake 105 A7
Coopertown 150 A2
Copeland 143 C8
Copeland Settlement 76 B2
Coquina Gables 67 D5
Coral Cove 120 B2
Coral Gables 151 A5
Coral Gardens 127 C6
Coral Manor 141 D7
Coral Springs 141 D5
Coral Terrace 151 A5
Corey 44 C2
Cork Academy 106 B2
Corkscrew 137 B6
Cornwell 124 A3
Coronet 106 C4
Cortez 112 D4
Cortez Plaza 113 D6
Cosme 105 A6
Cosmo 52 C2
Cosson Mill 19 C6
Cottage Hill 16 D1
Cotton Plant 83 C5
Cottondale 21 C8
Couch 40 C3
Council 136 C3
Country Estates 146 B4
Country Walk 150 B3
County Club Acres 141 B7
Courtenay 102 B4
Cove 54 A1
Cove Springs 104 A3
Cow Camp 73 A8
Cow Creek 93 B8
Cox 22 D3
Cox Corner 107 D7
Crackertown 81 D8
Craggs 74 A4
Crandall 33 C5
Crawford 51 A6
Crawfordville 57 A8
Creels 56 D2
Creighton 94 B1
Crescent Beach 79 A5
Crescent City 78 D2
Crescent City Station 78 D2
Crestview 18 C2

2

Crewsville 116 D1
Cromanton 54 A1
Crooked Lake Park 108 D2
Croom 98 A2
Croom-A-Coochee 98 A2
Cross Bayou 104 D4
Cross City 73 B7
Cross Creek 76 D2
Crossley 77 C5
Crossroads 47 B7
Crow 21 C6
Crown Point 100 A2
Crows Bluff 85 D8
Crystal Beach 104 B3
Crystal Lake 39 B8; 107 B6; 141 D7
Crystal River 89 A5
Crystal Springs 106 A3
Cubitis 122 B2
Cudjoe Key 157 C7
Cummings 119 A7
Cumpressco 98 C4
Cunningham Estates 98 D2
Curlew 104 B3
Curry Ferry 20 A2
Curtis 74 A2
Curtis Mill 57 B6
Cutler Ridge 150 C4
Cutlers 89 B5
Cypress 22 C4
Cypress Creek 48 A3
Cypress Gardens 107 C8
Cypress Harbor 141 D7
Cypress Lake 136 A2
Cypress Lake Estates 86 D1
Cypress Lakes 134 C3
Cypress Point 78 A1
Cypress Quarters 125 B7

D

Dade City 98 C2
Dade City North 98 C2
Dahlberg 132 D4
Dahoma 51 B6
Daisy Lake 85 D8
Dalhousie Acres 92 B1
Dalkeith 55 B6
Dallas 90 A4
Dame Point Manor 52 C2
Dames Point 52 C2
Dana 63 C8
Dana Point 37 B7
Dania 147 B7
Danks Corner 83 D7
Danville 63 B8
Darby 97 C8
Darlington 19 A8
Darsey 24 D4
Davenport 108 A1
Davie 147 B6
Davis Shores 67 D5
Day 61 A5
Daysville 75 B8
Daytona Beach 86 B4
Daytona Beach Shores 87 C5
Daytona Highridge Estates 86 C3
Daytona Park Estates 86 D2
De Funiak Springs 19 C7
De Leon Springs 85 C8
De Leon Springs Heights 86 C1
De Soto City 116 D4
Deanville 85 A8
DeBary 93 B5
Deem City 140 C2
Deep Creek 49 C5; 121 D8
Deep Lake 143 B8
Deer Park 105 A7; 110 B2
Deerfield Beach 141 C7
Deerland 18 C3
Deerwood Club 52 D2
Dekle Beach 60 D1
Del Rio 105 B8
DeLand 86 D1
DeLand Highlands 86 D1
Delespine 102 B3
Dell 61 A6
Dellwood 22 B4; 104 C4
Delray Beach 141 B8
Delray Gardens 141 B7
Delray Shores 141 B7
Delta 134 C2
Deltona 93 A5
Delwood Beach 53 A8
Denaud 130 C2
Denham 105 A7
Dennet 46 A1
Denver 78 D2
Desoto Lakes 120 A3
Destin 37 C6
Devils Garden 131 D7
Dewey Park 51 D8
Dickert 47 C7
Dinner Island 78 C4
Dinsmore 51 B8
Direyo Park 54 A1
Dismal Key 143 D6
Dixie 98 B1

Dixie Heights 119 C8
Dixie Ranch Acres 125 A6
Dixietown 74 A1
Dixon 19 C7
Dixonville 16 A4
Doctor Phillips 100 B2
Doctors Inlet 65 A7
Dogtown 24 D2
Dogwood Estates 97 A8
Dona Vista 91 B8
Doral 146 D4
Dorcas 18 C4
Douglass Crossroads 20 D1
Dover 106 C2
Dowling Park 47 D6
Drew Park 105 C6
Drexel 97 D7
Drifton 45 B6
Drury 91 C6
Dublin 92 C1
Duck Key 159 C6
Duette 114 C3
Dukes 63 C8
Dummitt Grove 94 C4
Dundee 108 B1
Dune Allen Beach 38 C2
Dunedin 104 B3
Dunedin Isles 104 B3
Dunedin Marina 104 B3
Dunes Road 141 B7
Dunn Creek 52 B1
Dunnellon 82 D3
Dupont 106 C2
Dupont Center 79 A5
Dupree Gardens 97 D7
Durant 106 C2
Durant Estates 75 B8
Durbin 66 B3
Durham 41 B8
Dutton Still 98 B3
Duval 52 B1
Dyal 31 D2

E

Eagle Island 118 D2
Eagle Lake 107 C7
Eales Nest 91 B6
Ealum 19 B5
Earleton 76 A3
Early 55 B5
Early Bird 82 B4
East Camp 56 A4
East Dunbar 129 D6
East Lake 104 B4
East Mandarin 66 A1
East Mayport 52 C4
East Milton 16 D4
East Mims 94 D3
East Naples 142 A3
East Palatka 78 B1
East Pensacola Heights 35 B6
East Silver Springs Shore 84 D2
East Tampa 105 D8
Eastgate 113 D6; 120 D3
Eastlake Weir 84 D2
Eastpoint 70 A2
Eastport 52 B1
Eastwood 107 B8
Eaton Park 107 B6
Eatons Beach 91 A5
Eatonville 92 D4
Eau Gallie 111 A5
Ebb 46 C1
Ebenezer 63 B6
Ebro 39 B6
Econfina 40 B2; 59 A6
Eddy 49 A8
Eden 127 B6
Edgar 77 C5
Edgeville 121 A7
Edgewater 94 A1
Edgewater Gulf Beach 53 A6
Edgewater Junction 94 A1
Edgewood 51 C8; 100 B4
Edison 106 D4
Eggleston Heights 52 C1
Eglin Village 37 B6
Egypt Lake 105 B7
Ehren 97 D7
El Chico 157 C5
El Destinado 44 A1
El Jobean 128 A2
El Portal 147 D6
Elder Springs 93 C5
Eldora 94 A3
Eldorado 91 C7
Eldorado Estates 89 C7
Eldred 127 A5
Eldridge 85 B7
Eleanor 21 A6
Electra 84 C2
Eleven Mile 69 A7
Elfers 96 D4
Elkton 78 A3
Ellaville 21 A8; 47 C6
Ellenton 113 C6

Ellerbee 64 A2
Ellerslie 98 C3
Ellinor Village 86 B4
Ellis 22 A2
Ellisville 63 B5
Ellsworth Junction 91 C8
Ellzey 81 A7
Eloise 107 C8
Eloise Woods 107 B8
Elwood 66 C2
Elwood Park 113 D6
Emathla 91 A6
Emeralda 91 A6
Emporia 85 C7
Enchanted Park 51 D7
Englewood 52 D1; 120 D2
Enon 15 C6
Ensley 35 A5
Enterprise 93 B5
Eridu 45 C7
Erie 113 C7
Escambia 35 A7
Escambia Farms 18 A1
Espanola 79 C5
Estero 136 B3
Estiffanulga 41 C8
Esto 21 A5
Ethel 92 B3
Eucheeanna 19 D8
Eugene 73 B7
Eureka 84 A1
Eustis 91 B8
Eva 99 C7
Evans Pines 111 C6
Everglades City 143 D8
Evergreen 31 C3
Evinston 76 D2
Ewell 107 D5
Ezell Camp 60 D1

F

Facil 48 C3
Fair Gate 141 D6
Fairbanks 76 A1
Fairfield 83 A6
Fairlane Estates 93 C5
Fairview 49 B6; 78 A2
Fairview Shores 100 A4
Fairvilla 100 A3
Fairyland 102 D4
Fakahatchee 143 D7
Falmouth 47 C7
Fanlew 44 D4
Fanning Springs 74 C1
Farm Hill 15 D8
Farmdale 54 B3
Farmton 93 B8
Fatio 93 A5
Favorета 86 A2
Feather Sound 104 C4
Federal Point 78 A2
Fedhaven 108 D4
Felda 137 A7
Felda Station 137 A8
Felicia 89 A8
Felkel 44 A3
Fellowship 83 B5
Fellowship Park 65 B8
Fellsmere 119 A5
Fenholloway 60 B3
Fern Crest Village 147 B6
Fern Park 92 D4
Fernandina Beach 33 D7
Ferndale 91 D8
Ferry Pass 35 A6
Fidelis 16 A4
Fiftone 51 D5
Fiftymile Bend 145 D5
Fincher 26 D1
Fish Creek 72 A2
Fish Hawk 106 D2
Fisher Corner 41 C6
Fisher Island 151 A7
Fishermens Village 128 A3
Fivay Junction 97 C6
Five Points 20 C3; 49 D5
Flagler Beach 79 D7
Flamingo 100 C4; 153 C5
Flamingo Bay 135 A7
Fleming Island 65 B8
Flemington 76 D1
Fletcher 74 A1
Florahome 77 A6
Floral Bluff 52 C1
Floral City 90 C1
Floral Shores 90 C1
Florence 43 A7; 66 C2
Florence Villa 107 B8
Floresta 141 C7
Florida Beach 39 D6
Florida City 150 D2
Florida Gardens 134 D2
Florida Highlands 83 D5
Florida Hills 92 A3
Florida Ridge 119 C8
Floridale 17 D6
Floridana Beach 111 C7
Floridatown 35 A7
Floritan 108 C1

Flowers Still 41 B8
Flowersville 18 A4
Foley 60 B2
Footman 102 C4
Fordville 120 A4
Forest City 92 D3
Forest Corners 84 C2
Forest Grove 75 A6
Forest Highlands 18 C4
Forest Hills 85 D7; 104 A4
Forest Island Park 136 B2
Forest Lakes Park 84 D2
Fort Basinger 124 A4
Fort Basinger Station 124 A4
Fort Braden 43 B6
Fort Caroline 52 C2
Fort Centre 131 A6
Fort De Soto 112 B3
Fort Drane 83 A5
Fort Drum 118 C3
Fort Florida 92 B4
Fort Gadsden 56 C1
Fort Gates 78 D1
Fort George 52 B3
Fort Green 115 B5
Fort Green Springs 115 C5
Fort Hamer 113 C7
Fort King Acres 98 D2
Fort Kissimmee 117 C6
Fort Lauderdale 147 A7
Fort Lonely 113 B6
Fort Lonesome 114 A3
Fort Mason 91 B8
Fort McCoy 84 A1
Fort McRee 35 C5
Fort Meade 115 A7
Fort Myers 129 D6
Fort Myers Beach 136 B1
Fort Myers Shores 129 C8
Fort Myers Villas 136 A2
Fort Ogden 122 D1
Fort Peyton 66 D4
Fort Pierce 119 D8; 127 B8
Fort Pierce North 119 D8
Fort Pierce Shores 127 B8
Fort Pierce South 119 D8
Fort Taylor 159 D3
Fort Union 47 B8
Fort Walton Beach 37 B5
Fort White 62 C4
Fortymile Bend 149 A7
Fountain 40 B3
Fountain Heights 107 C5
Fountainbleau 84 B1
Four Corners 104 C4
Four Mile Village 38 C1
Four Points 44 B1
Four Seasons 136 D3
Fowlers Bluff 80 A4
Fox Town 47 A5
Foxleigh 113 D7
Foxs Corner 105 A5
Francis 77 B8
Franjo 150 C4
Franklin 69 A8
Franklintown 52 A3
Franwood Pines 141 B7
Freemont 24 D3
Freeport 38 B3
Fremd Village Padgett Island 133 B5
Frink 41 C6
Frog City 150 A1
Frontenac 102 B3
Frostproof 116 A2
Fruit Cove 66 A1
Fruita 127 C6
Fruitland 78 D1
Fruitland Park 91 B5
Fruitville 120 A3
Fuller Heights 107 C5
Fullers 100 A2
Fullers Earth 113 C6
Fullerville 85 D7
Fussells Corner 107 B6

G

Gaberonne 35 B7
Gabriella 93 D6
Gainesville 76 B1
Galliver 17 C8
Galloway 106 B4
Galt City 35 A8
Gandy 105 D5
Gandyville 16 A1
Garden City 18 B2; 51 B8
Garden Cove 154 C4
Garden Grove 97 B7
Garden Isles 141 D7
Gardens of Gulf Cove 128 A2
Gardenville 105 D8
Gardner 44 B3; 122 A3
Garnier 37 B5
Gary 105 C7
Gaskin 19 A7
Gaskins 41 C7
Gaskins Still 55 B6
Gasparilla 128 B1
Gateway 136 A3

Gator Creek Estates 120 B4
Geneva 93 C7
Genoa 48 C3
Georges Lake 77 A6
Georgetown 85 A5
Georgiana 102 D4
Gibson 43 A8
Gibsonia 107 A5
Gibsonton 105 D8
Gifford 119 B7
Gilberts Mill 21 D6
Gilchrist 129 C6
Gillette 113 C6
Gilmore 52 C2
Gladeview 147 D6
Glass 21 B7
Glen Ridge 134 D4
Glen Saint Mary 50 D3
Glencoe 87 D5
Glendale 19 B7
Glenwood 33 D6; 54 A1; 85 D8
Glidden Park 119 D8
Glimpse of Glory 66 C4
Godfrey Road 141 D6
Godleys Bluffs 70 A2
Golden Beach 147 C5
Golden Gate 127 C6; 142 A4
Golden Gates Estates 143 A6
Golden Glades 147 C6
Golden Hills 83 B5
Golden Lakes 134 C3
Goldenrod 93 D5
Goldstein 105 B7
Golf 141 B7
Golfview 134 D3
Gomez 127 D7
Gonzalez 35 A5
Good Hope 18 A1
Goodbys 52 D1
Goodland 143 C5
Goodno 131 C5
Gopher Ridge 78 B4
Gordon 19 B5
Gordonville 107 C7
Gotha 100 A2
Goulding 35 B5
Goulds 150 C4
Gowers Corner 97 C6
Graceville 21 A6
Grady 62 C1
Graham 64 D2
Grahamsville 84 B1
Gramercy Park 134 C3
Gramlin No 2 131 B8
Grand Crossing 51 C8
Grand Island 91 B8
Grand Park 51 C8
Grand Ridge 22 C4
Grandin 77 A5
Grandview 78 B1
Grant 111 C6
Grantham 40 A1
Grayton Beach 38 C2
Grayvik 155 A5
Green Bay 107 D5
Green Cove Springs 65 B8
Green Grove 76 B1
Green Meadow 146 B4
Green Point 70 A3
Green Pond 99 C6
Greenacres City 134 D3
Greenbriar 93 C5
Greenfield 49 C6; 52 C3; 97 C6
Greenhead 39 A8
Greenland 66 A2
Green-Mar Acres 150 B4
Greensboro 42 A3
Greenville 46 B1
Greenwood 22 B3
Gretna 24 D1
Griffin 107 B5
Griffin Park 97 C5
Griffins Corner 115 C8
Gritney 20 B3
Grosh 38 C1
Gross 31 C4
Grove City 128 A1
Grove Park 76 B3
Groveland 99 A6
Grovenor Estates 119 C7
Guilford 63 B8
Gulf Beach 34 D3
Gulf Beach Heights 34 C3
Gulf Breeze 35 C6
Gulf City 113 A7
Gulf Gate Estates 120 B2
Gulf Hammock 81 B8
Gulf Harbor 136 D3
Gulf Harbors 96 D3
Gulf Lagoon Beach 53 A7
Gulf Pine 105 A5
Gulf Pines 37 C8
Gulf Resort Beach 39 D6
Gulf Stream 141 B8
Gulfport 112 A4
Gun Club Estates 134 D3
Gunnals 75 D7

H

Hacienda Village 147 B6
Hague 75 A7
Haile 75 B6
Haines City 108 A1
Hainesworth 63 D7
Halcyon Shores 34 B4
Half Moon 75 D4
Halifax Estates 87 C5
Hall City 131 B5
Hallandale Beach 147 C7
Halsema 51 C6
Hamburg 46 A2
Hammond 85 A6
Hampton 64 D3
Hampton Beach 64 D2
Hampton Springs 59 B8; 60 B1
Hamptons at Boca Raton 141 C6
Hancock 78 A1
Hanna Lake 105 A7
Hanson 46 A4
Happy Valley 16 A1
Harbeson City 57 D5
Harbinwood Estates 43 A8
Harbor Bluffs 104 C2
Harbor East 141 C8
Harbor Oaks 87 C5
Harbor Palms 104 B4
Harbor Shores 91 B8
Harbor View 51 C8; 104 B3; 128 A4
Harbor Village 141 D7
Harbour Heights 128 A4
Hardaway 23 D8
Hardeetown 74 D2
Hardin Heights 23 D6
Harker 137 C8
Harlem 132 C1
Harlem Heights 100 A1; 136 A1
Harmony 109 A7
Harney 105 B8
Harold 17 D6
Harp 35 A7
Harper 36 B2
Harris 36 B4
Harrisburg 131 A5
Harrison 89 A7
Hart Haven 51 C7
Harvard 74 A3
Hasan 63 D7
Hastings 78 A2
Hatchbend 62 D2
Hathaway Mill 20 B3
Havana 24 D4
Haven Park 34 B4
Haverhill 134 D3
Hawley Heights 150 B4
Hawthorne 76 C3; 91 C6
Hayden 120 B2
Haynes 23 B5
Hays Place 56 D1
Heatherwood Estates 89 C8
Heathrow 92 C4
Hedges 52 A1
Heilbronn 64 B3
Helen 43 C8
Hell Gate 134 A3
Hells Half Acre 144 D1
Hen Scratch 123 A7
Henderson Mill 41 A8
Henrietta 44 C1
Heritage Hills 89 B6
Hernando 89 A8
Hernando Beach 97 B5
Hernando Ridge 98 B2
Hero 33 D5
Hesperides 108 D3
Hialeah 147 D5
Hialeah Gardens 147 D5
Hibernia 65 B8
Hickory Hammock Grove 100 A1
Hickory Hill 20 B1
Hicoria 123 C8
Hidden River 121 B5
High Bluff 56 D3
High Point 97 A6; 104 C4; 141 D7
High Springs 63 D5
Highland 64 A4
Highland Beach 141 C8
Highland City 107 C6
Highland Lakes 116 B2
Highland Park 108 D2
Highland View 55 D5
Highlands 51 B8
Highlands Park Estates 124 A1
Hiland Park 40 D1
Hilden 66 B3
Hildreth 62 C3
Hill 'n Dale 98 A1
Hillcoat 48 B1
Hillcrest Heights 108 D2
Hilliard 31 D1
Hilliardville 43 D8
Hillsboro Beach 141 D8
Hillsboro Pines 141 C6
Hillsboro Ranches 141 C6

3

Hilolo 118 D3
Hines 73 A6
Hinson 24 D4
Hinsons Cross Roads 20 D2
Hobbs Crossroads 20 A1
Hobe Sound 127 D7
Hobe Sound Station 127 D7
Hodgson 75 D7
Hog Valley 77 D6
Hogan 52 D2
Holden Heights 100 A4
Holder 89 A7
Holiday 104 A3
Holiday Harbor 52 C3
Holiday Hill 52 C2
Holiday Manor 107 A8
Holland 43 B6
Holland Crossroads 21 A5
Holley 36 B2
Hollister 77 B7
Holly Ford 52 B1
Holly Hill 86 B4
Holly Point 65 A8
Hollywood 147 B7
Hollywood Beach 39 D5
Holmes Beach 112 D4
Holmes Valley 39 A8
Holopaw 109 A7
Holt 17 C7
Homeland 107 D6
Homestead 150 D2
Homestead Base 150 D4
Homestead Ridge 44 A3
Homosassa 89 C5
Homosassa Springs 89 B6
Honeyville 55 B6
Honore 121 B5
Hooker Point 132 C1
Hooper 90 D1
Hopewell 46 C3; 106 C3
Hornsville 22 A4
Horseshoe 73 C5
Horseshoe Beach 73 D5
Hosford 42 C3
Houston 48 D2
Howard 150 B4
Howard Creek 55 D8
Howell Place 72 A2
Howey in the Hills 91 C7
Howey Height 91 D8
Hoyt 82 C4
Hucomer 94 A2
Hudson 20 B1; 96 C4
Hugh 64 A4
Hulaw 21 C6
Hull 122 C1
Hunter 77 B7
Hunters Creek 100 C3
Huntington 78 D2; 83 C8
Hyde Grove 51 D7
Hyde Park 51 D7; 58 A1; 120 A3
Hypoluxo 141 A8
Hypoluxo Village 141 A7

I

Iamonia 25 D7
Iddo 45 D8
Idylwild 75 B8
Ilexhurst 112 D4
Immokalee 137 B7
Indialantic 111 B6
Indian Ford 17 C5
Indian Harbour Beach 111 A5
Indian Lake Estates 108 C4
Indian Mound Village 93 B6
Indian River City 102 A3
Indian River Estates 127 A5
Indian River Shores 119 A8
Indian Rocks Beach 104 C2
Indian Shores 104 D2
Indian Spring Estates 104 D2
Indianola 102 C4
Indiantown 126 D2
Indrio 119 C3
Ingle 51 B5
Inglis 81 D8
Inlet Beach 38 D4
Innisbrook 104 A3
Intercession City 100 D2
Interlachen 77 B6
Inverness 90 B1
Inverness Highlands North 89 B8
Inwood 23 D5; 107 B7
Iola 55 A7
Iona 136 A1
Iowa City 93 D7
Irvine 76 D1
Islamorada 159 D7
Island Grove 76 D3
Islandia 155 A6
Isle of Palms 52 D3
Isle of Palms South 52 D3
Isleboro 87 D5
Isles of Capri 142 C4
Isleworth 100 B2
Istachatta 90 D1

Istokpoga 116 D4
Italia 31 D4
Ivan 43 D8
Izagora 20 A2

J

Jabo Camp 60 D1
Jack Lee Island 60 D1
Jackson Bluff 43 C5
Jacksonville 52 C1
Jacksonville Beach 52 C4
Jacksonville Heights 51 D7
Jacobs 21 B8
Jamestown 93 D6
Jamieson 24 D3
Jan-Phyl Village 107 B7
Jarrott 26 D1
Jasmine Estates 96 D4
Jasper 48 A1
Jay 16 A3
Jay Jay 94 D3
Jena 72 B4
Jennings 28 D3
Jensen Beach 127 B6
Jensen Place 42 D1
Jerome 143 C8
Jessamine 98 B1
Jessie Willies 145 B8
Jessie Willies Seminole Village 145 C8
Jewfish 154 C4
Johnson 77 C5; 108 A3
Johnson Crossroad 21 C5
Johnsons Beach 34 C4
Johnsons Corner 92 A2
Johnstown 64 B1
Jolly Corner 106 B1
Jones Corner 107 B7
Jonesboro 73 A5
Jonesville 75 B6
Joshua 122 B4
Joydon 107 B5
Jug Island 60 D1
Jumeau 90 C1
June Park 110 B4
Juniper 42 A3
Juno Beach 134 B4
Juno Isles 134 C4
Juno Ridge 134 B4
Jupiter 134 A3
Jupiter Inlet Beach Colony 134 A4
Jupiter Island 127 D7

K

Kalamazoo 93 B7
Kalon 43 A3
Kanapaha 75 C7
Kathleen 106 A4
Keaton Beach 60 D1
Keela 132 D2
Keene 51 B6
Keentown 114 C3
Kellys Mill 17 C7
Kenansville 110 D1
Kendall 151 B5
Kendall Green 141 D7
Kendall Lakes 150 B3
Kendall West 150 A3
Kendrick 83 B7
Kennedy Hill 106 C1
Kennedy Still 48 A2
Kenneth City 104 D4
Kenny 50 C2
Kensington Park 120 A3
Kent 51 A5
Kent Mill 21 D7
Kenwood 77 C6
Keri 137 A8
Kern 56 A1
Kerr City 84 A3
Keuka 77 B5
Key Biscayne 151 B7
Key Colony Beach 158 C4
Key Largo 154 D3
Key Largo Park 154 D3
Key West 156 D3
Keystone 105 A5
Keystone Heights 76 A4
Keysville 106 D3
Killarney 100 A1
Killarney Shores 52 D2
Killingsworth Crossroads 18 C3
Kinard 41 D6
Kincaid Hills 76 B1
Kings Ferry 31 C2
Kings Point 141 B7
Kings Road 141 B7
Kingsford 107 D5
Kingsland 141 B7
Kingsley 65 C5
Kingsley Beach 65 C5
Kingsley Village 64 C4

Kinsey 122 A2
Kirkwood 75 C8
Kissimmee 100 D4
Kissimmee Park 100 D4
Knights 106 B3
Knox Hill 20 D1
Koerber 19 C8
Kolokee 93 D7
Korona 79 D6
Kossuthville 107 B6
Kreftwood Estates 76 B1
Kuhlman 123 A8
Kynesville 21 C8

L

La Belle 130 C3
La Crosse 63 D7
La Grange 94 D3
La Grange Point 38 B2
LaBuena 50 D3
Lackawanna 51 D7
Lacoochee 98 B2
Lacota 84 B1
Lacymark 49 D5
Lady Lake 91 A5
Lafayette 44 B2
Laguna Beach 39 D5
Laird 39 C5
Lake Alfred 107 B8
Lake Alto Estates 76 A3
Lake Asbury 65 B7
Lake Ashby Shores 93 A7
Lake Bird 46 D1
Lake Buena Vista 100 C2
Lake Butler 63 B8
Lake Butter 100 A2
Lake Cain Hills 100 B3
Lake Charm 93 D6
Lake City 63 A5
Lake Clarke Shores 134 D3
Lake Como 78 D2
Lake Fern 105 A6
Lake Forest 51 B8
Lake Forest Hills 51 C8
Lake Forest Manor 52 C1
Lake Garfield 107 D7
Lake Geneva 76 A3
Lake Grove 55 A6
Lake Hamilton 108 B1
Lake Harbor 132 D3
Lake Hart 101 C6
Lake Helen 93 A6
Lake Jackson 43 A8
Lake Jem 92 C1
Lake Kathryn 85 D6
Lake Lindsey 89 D8
Lake Lorraine 37 B6
Lake Mack Park 92 A3
Lake Magdalene 105 B7
Lake Margaret Estates 78 D1
Lake Marian Highlands 109 D8
Lake Mary 93 C5
Lake McKenzie 41 A5
Lake Monroe 93 B5
Lake of the Hills 108 C1
Lake Panasoffkee 90 C3
Lake Park 134 B4
Lake Park Estates 51 C8
Lake Pasadena Heights 98 C2
Lake Pickett 101 A7
Lake Placid 123 B8
Lake Sarasota 120 A3
Lake Shipp Heights 107 C7
Lake Shore 51 D8
Lake Shore Estates 104 A4
Lake Suzy 121 D8
Lake View 93 C5
Lake View Point 43 B5
Lake Wales 108 C1
Lake Worth 134 D4
Lakeland 107 B5
Lakeland Highlands 107 C5
Lakemont 116 C3
Lakeport 131 A7
Lakes by the Bay 151 C5
Lakeside 44 C1; 65 A7
Lakeside Green 134 C3
Lakeside Park 63 B8
Lakeview 141 D7
Lakeview Estates 76 B1
Lakeville 129 C5
Lakewood 19 A5; 52 D1
Lakewood Estates 113 A5
Lakewood Park 119 C8
Lakewood Ranch 120 A3
Lamont 45 C7
Lanark Village 57 D5
Lancaster 47 D6
Land O'Lakes 97 D7
Landrum 89 C8
Lands End Ranch 77 C6
Lane Park 91 C7
Langmar 51 C7
Lansing 122 B2
Lantana 141 A8
Largo 104 C3
Larsen 52 D1
Lauderdale Lakes 147 A6

Lauderdale-by-the-Sea 147 A7
Lauderhill 147 A5
Laurel 120 C3
Laurel Grove 65 A8
Laurel Hill 18 A3
Laurel Villa 120 C3
Lawhons Mill 57 A8
Lawtey 64 B4
Layton 159 B7
Lealman 104 D4
Lebanon 82 D1
Lebanon Station 82 C1
Lecanto 89 B7
Lee 47 B5
Lee Cypress 143 C8
Leesburg 91 B6
Lehigh Acres 130 D1
Leisure City 150 D3
Leland 28 D1
Lely 142 A4
Lely Resort 142 B4
Lemon Bluff 93 B7
Lemon Grove 115 C8
Leno 66 D1
Leon Hamilton Place 148 C2
Leonards 41 B7
Leonia 19 A8
Leroy 83 C5
Lessie 31 C3
Lewis 41 D8
Liberty 19 B6; 42 D2
Liberty Point 132 B1
Lighthouse Point 127 B5; 141 D7
Lillibridge 114 A3
Lily 122 A1
Limestone 44 C4; 122 A2
Limestone Creek 134 A3
Limona 106 C1
Linadale 91 A7
Lincoln Estates 76 B1
Lincoln Park 90 D3
Linden 98 A4
Lindgren 150 C3
Lisbon 91 B7
Lithia 106 D2
Little Banana Patch 149 D6
Little Bare Beach 132 C2
Little Doctor Seminole Village 145 D8
Little Lake City 62 D2
Littman 43 A6
Live Oak 39 A6; 48 D1
Live Oak Island 58 B1
Lloyd 44 B4
Loch Lomond 141 D7
Lochloosa 76 C3
Lochmoor Waterway Estates 129 D5
Lock Arbor 93 C5
Lockhart 92 D3
Lockwood 101 A7
Lois 45 B6
Lokosee 118 A1
Long Beach Resort 53 A7
Long Branch 48 C4
Long Hammock 90 A3
Long Point 54 A1
Longbeach 112 D4
Longboat Key 113 D5
Longwood 37 B5; 93 C5
Lordland 93 C5
Loretto 66 A1
Lorida 117 D5
Lorraine 113 A7
Los Trancos Woods 75 A7
Lottieville 74 B2
Lotus 103 D5
Loughman 100 D2
Louise 64 D2
Lovedale 22 B4
Lovett 27 D6
Lowell 83 A6
Lower Grand Lagoon 53 A7
Lower Matecumbe Beach 159 B8
Lowry 42 B3
Loxahatchee 134 D1
Loyce 97 C7
Lucerne Park 107 B8
Luddersville 82 C3
Ludlam 151 A5
Lulu 63 A7
Lumberton 98 D3
Lundy 78 B1
Luraville 61 A6
Lutterloh 44 C1
Lutz 105 A7
Lyle Corner 107 C6
Lynchburg 107 B7
Lynn 84 C2
Lynn Haven 40 D1
Lynne 84 C2
Lyratta Dock 94 C2

M

Mabel 99 A5
Macclenny 50 D3
Macedonia 41 A8

Macom 40 A1
Macon 44 B1
Madeira Beach 112 A3
Madison 46 B4
Magnolia Beach 53 A8
Magnolia Gardens 51 C8
Magnolia Springs 65 B8
Maitland 92 D4
Majestic Oaks 83 D6
Majette 40 D2
Malabar 111 B6
Mallory Heights 22 C2
Malone 22 A3
Malore Gardens 75 B8
Manalapan 141 A8
Manasota 120 D4
Manasota Beach 120 D3
Manatee 113 D6
Manattee Road 74 C1
Manavista 113 C6
Mandalay 59 A5
Mandarin 66 A1
Mandeville 51 C6
Mango 106 C1
Mango Hill 106 C1
Mangonia Park 134 C3
Manhattan 114 C1
Manhattan Farms 120 C4
Manhatten 85 C6
Manhatten Beach 52 C4
Manning 64 A2
Manns Spur 50 D1
Mannville 77 B6
Marathon 158 C3
Marathon Shores 158 C4
Marco Island 142 C4
Marcy 126 C1
Margaretta 50 D2
Margate 141 D6
Margate Estates 141 D6
Marianna 22 C2
Maricamp 83 C7
Marietta 51 C7
Marineland 79 B6
Marion 48 B1
Marion Oaks 90 A2
Markham 92 C4
Marland 124 A2
Mart Law Seminole Village 145 C7
Martel 83 C6
Martin 83 B6
Marvina 106 D2
Mary Esther 37 B5
Marysville 41 D7
Masaryktown 97 B7
Mascotte 99 A6
Mason 63 B5
Matecumbe 159 D7
Matlacha 128 D3
Matoaka 113 D6
Mattox 50 D4
Maxcy Quarters 116 A2
Maxville 64 A4
Mayo 61 B6
Mayo Junction 47 D5
Maysland 46 A2
Mayport 52 C3
Maytown 94 B1
McAllaster Landing 40 C2
McAlpin 62 A1
McCaln 43 B8
McClellan 17 A6
McColskey 63 A6
McDavid 16 B1
McDonald 92 D1
McGregor 136 A1
McIntosh 76 D2
McIntyre 57 C6
McKinnon 15 C7
McMeekin 76 C4
McNeal 41 B8
McNeils 69 B5
McPherson 50 D4
Meadow Woods 100 C4
Meadowbrook Terrace 65 A8
Mecca 104 B4
Medart 57 B8
Medley 147 D5
Medulla 107 C5
Melbourne 111 B5
Melbourne Beach 111 B6
Melbourne Gardens 110 B4
Melbourne Shores 111 C6
Melbourne Village 111 B5
Meldrim Park 66 D2
Melrose 76 A4
Melrose Park 147 A6
Melton Manor 76 B1
Memphis 113 C6
Mercer 47 D7
Merediths 75 D5
Meridian 25 D5
Merrimac 92 C2
Merritt Island 102 C4
Mexico Beach 54 C4
Miami 151 A6
Miami Beach 151 A7
Miami Gardens 147 C6
Miami Lakes 147 C5
Miami Shores 147 D6

Miami Springs 147 D5
Micanopy 76 C1
Micanopy Junction 76 C2
Micco 111 D6
Miccosukee 44 A4
Mid Florida Lakes 91 B7
Middleburg 65 B6
Midway 43 B7; 61 B8; 93 C6; 106 B3
Midway Park 93 C5
Mikesville 63 C5
Mildred 125 B5
Miles City 143 A8
Millard 98 D3
Miller 63 C7
Miller Crossroads 20 A4
Millers Ferry 39 A6
Milligan 18 C1
Milltown 55 D5
Millview 34 B4
Millville 54 A1
Millwood 83 A6
Milton 16 D4
Mims 94 D2
Minehead 82 B4
Mineral Springs 16 B1
Minneola 99 A7
Minorville 100 A2
Mintons Corner 110 B4
Miramar 147 C5
Miramar Beach 37 C8
Miramar Terrace 51 D8
Mission Bay 141 C6
Mission City 87 D5
Mitchell Beach 112 A3
Mobile Gardens 128 A1
Modello 150 C3
Moffitt 115 D7
Mohawk 99 A8
Molasses Junction 66 D3
Molino 16 C1
Molino Crossroads 15 C8
Monarch 90 B4
Monet 134 B3
Monroe Station 144 D3
Monroes Corner 83 D7
Montague 83 C8
Monteocha 76 A1
Monticello 45 A6
Montivilla 45 A6
Montverde 91 D8
Montverde Jct 99 A8
Moon Lake Estates 97 C5
Moore Haven 131 B7
Moreland Park 90 B4
Morgan Place 56 B3
Morgantown 122 D1
Moricsville 106 A3
Morningside Park 100 B4
Morriston 82 B3
Morse Shores 129 D7
Moseley Hall 46 C2
Mosquito Grove 85 D7
Moss Bluff 84 D2
Moss Town 98 B2
Mossy Head 19 C5
Mott 132 D2
Moultrie 67 D5
Moultrie Junction 66 D4
Mount Carmel 16 A3
Mount Carrie 63 A6
Mount Dora 92 C1
Mount Enon 106 B4
Mount Homer 91 B8
Mount Olive 83 B5
Mount Pleasant 23 B8
Mount Plymouth 92 B2
Mount Plymouth Lakes 92 C2
Mountain Lake Station 108 C1
Muce 130 B3
Muddy Ford 36 B2
Mulat 35 A7
Mulberry 107 D5
Mullis City 105 B6
Munson 17 B6
Murdock 121 D7
Murray Hill 51 C8
Muscogee 15 D8
Mutual 74 A3
Myakka City 121 A7
Myakka Head 114 D4
Myrtis 63 B5
Myrtle Grove 35 B5
Myrtle Island 78 C3

N

Nalcrest 108 D3
Naples 142 A3
Naples Manor 142 B4
Naples Park 136 D3
Naranja 150 C3
Narcoossee 101 D6
Nash 45 B6
Nashua 77 C8
Nassauville 52 A2
National Gardens 86 A3

Navair 63 A5
Navarre 36 C2
Navarre Beach 36 C2
Navy Point 35 C5
Neals 74 A4
Neheb 93 D6
Neilhurst 65 A8
Neilson 116 B2
Neoga 78 C4
Neptune Beach 52 C4
Nevins 119 B8
New Berlin 52 C2
New Eden 101 D6
New Harmony 19 B5
New Home 19 D6; 20 A2; 39 A7; 41 C8
New Point Comfort 120 D2
New Port Richey 96 D4
New Port Richey East 96 D4
New River 64 C1
New Smyrna Beach 87 D5
New Upsala 93 C5
New York 16 B2
Newberry 75 B5
Newburn 47 D7
Newcastle 52 C1
Newco 63 A5
Newnans Lake Homesites 76 B2
Newnansville 63 D7
Newport 58 A2; 154 C3
Newport Station 58 A2
Newton 74 C4
Niceville 37 A7
Nichols 106 D4
Niles 69 A5
Ninemile Bend 133 D6
Nixon 40 C3
Nobleton 90 D1
Nocatee 122 C2
Nokomis 120 C3
Nokomis Beach 120 C3
Noma 21 A5
Noma Junction 21 A5
Norfleet 43 B8
Norland 147 C6
Norman 97 A7
Normandy 51 C7
Normandy Village 51 D7
North Andrews Gardens 147 A7
North Bay Village 147 D7
North Beach 119 A8
North Brooksville 97 A7
North DeLand 86 D1
North Fort Myers 129 D6
North Key Largo 155 B5
North Lauderdale 141 D6
North Meadowbrook Terrace 65 A7
North Miami 147 D6
North Miami Beach 147 C7
North Naples 136 D3; 142 A3
North Oak Hill 51 D7
North Palm Beach 134 B4
North Palm Beach Heights 134 B3
North Pompano Beach 141 D7
North Port 121 D6
North Redington Beach 104 D2
North River Shores 127 B5
North Ruskin 113 A8
North Sarasota 120 A2
North Shore 52 C1
North Tampa Heights 105 B7
North Weeki Wachee 97 A6
Northwood 51 B8; 75 B8
Norum 39 A7
Norwalk 77 D8
Norwood 51 C8
Nowatney 105 B7
Nubbin Ridge 17 B8
Nutal Rise 59 A5

O

O'Brien 62 B1
O'Neil 33 D6
Oak 83 B7
Oak Forest 90 D1
Oak Grove 15 A7; 18 A2; 23 D8; 69 A5; 89 C7; 98 A4; 115 D6
Oak Harbor 52 C5
Oak Hill 51 D8; 94 B2
Oak Hill Dock 94 B2
Oak Hill Estates 89 A7
Oak Hill Park 51 D7
Oak Knoll 114 C1
Oak Knoll Estates 44 A1
Oak Park 57 A7; 90 B4
Oak Ridge 100 B3
Oak Ridge Park 77 B5
Oak Run 83 D5
Oak Terrace 107 D5
Oakdale 22 C2
Oakhurst 51 C8

Oakhurst Acres 104 D2
Oakhurst Shores 104 D3
Oakhurst Terrace 104 D3
Oakland 100 A1
Oakland Park 91 B8; 147 A7
Oakwood Villa 52 C2
Ocala 83 C7
Ocala Highlands Estates 83 B7
Ocala Park Ranch 83 B6
Ocala Ridge 83 C6
Ocala Thoroughbred Acres 83 C5
Ocala Waterway 83 D6
Ocean Breeze Park 127 B6
Ocean City 37 B5
Ocean Ridge 141 A8
Ocheesee 41 A6
Ocheesee Gardens 23 D5
Ochlockonee 43 B8
Ochopee 144 B1
Ocoee 100 A2
Octahatchee 47 A6
Odena 69 A6
Odena Landing 69 A6
Odessa 105 A5
Ojus 147 C7
Okahumpka 91 C6
Okaloo 18 A3
Okeechobee 125 B7
Okeelanta 132 D4
Oklawaha 84 D1
Old Bay View 38 B3
Old Callaway 54 A1
Old Clark Field 86 C3
Old Duette 114 C3
Old Fernandina 33 D7
Old Henley Place 98 C3
Old Land Place 36 A1
Old Marco Junction 142 B4
Old Myakka 121 C4
Old Town 74 C1
Old Venus 123 D8
Oldsmar 105 B5
Olga 129 C8
Olive 35 A5
Olustee 49 D7
Olympia Heights 150 A4
Ona 115 D5
Oneco 113 D6
Opa-Locka 147 C5
Open Sands 39 D6
Orange 41 D8
Orange Bend 91 B7
Orange Blossom 91 D7
Orange Blossom Hills 90 A4
Orange Blossom Hills South 91 A5
Orange City 93 A5
Orange City Hills 93 A5
Orange Grove Villas 98 D2
Orange Heights 76 A3
Orange Hill Corners 21 D6
Orange Home 91 B5
Orange Lake 76 D2
Orange Mills 78 B2
Orange Mountain 99 A8
Orange Park 65 A8
Orange Springs 77 C5
Orange Terrace 104 D2
Orangedale 66 B1; 107 A6
Orangetree 137 D5
Orchid 119 A7
Orient Park 105 C8
Orienta Gardens 92 D4
Oriole Beach 35 C7
Orlando 100 A4
Orlovista 103 A3
Ormond Beach 86 B4
Ormond by the Sea 86 A4
Orsino 103 A5
Ortega 51 D8
Ortega Farms 51 D8
Ortega Forest 51 D8
Ortega Hills 51 D8
Ortega Terrace 51 D8
Ortona 86 B4; 131 B5
Osceola 93 C8
Oslo 119 C8
Osowaw Jct 118 C2
Osprey 120 C2
Osteen 93 B6
Otis 51 C6
Otter Creek 81 A7
Otter Sink Camp 80 A3
Overstreet 54 C4
Oviedo 93 D6
Owens Bridge 56 B2
Owls Head 38 A3
Oxford 90 A4
Oyster Lodge 16 A2
Ozello 89 B5
Ozona 104 B3

P

Pablo Keys 52 D3
Pace 16 D2; 35 A7
Packwood Place 94 A2

Padlock 48 D1
Page Park 136 A2
Pahokee 133 B5
Painters Hill 79 C7
Paisley 92 A2
Palatka 78 B1
Palatka Heights 78 B1
Palm 105 C8
Palm Aire 141 D6
Palm Bay 111 B5
Palm Beach 134 C4
Palm Beach Farms 134 D3
Palm Beach Gardens 134 B3
Palm Beach Isles 134 C4
Palm Beach Shores 134 C4
Palm Cay 83 D5
Palm City 127 C5
Palm Coast 79 C6
Palm Grove Colony 97 A5
Palm Harbor 104 B3
Palm Lake Park 127 B5
Palm River Shores 134 D3
Palm Shadows 93 C7
Palm Shores 111 A5
Palm Springs 134 D3
Palm Valley 66 A4
Palm View 113 C6
Palma Ceia 105 C6
Palma Sola 113 C5
Palma Sola Park 113 D5
Palmdale 131 A5
Palmetto 113 C5
Palmetto Bay 151 B5
Palmetto Estates 150 B4
Palmo 66 C2
Palmona Park 129 D5
Panacea 57 B8
Panacea Park 57 B8
Panacoochee Retreats 90 B3
Panama City 54 A1
Panama City Beach 53 A6
Panama Heights 40 A1
Panama Park 52 C1
Paola 52 C4
Paolita Station 145 D6
Paradise 75 A8
Paradise Beach 34 C3
Paradise Heights 92 D2
Paradise Palms 141 C7
Paradise Park 119 D8
Paradise Point 89 B5
Paradise Port 134 B3
Park Haven 147 C7
Park of the Palms 76 A4
Parker 54 A1
Parker Island 124 B1
Parkerville 17 C7
Parkland 141 C6
Parmalee 121 A6
Parramore 23 B5
Parrish 113 C7
Pasadena 112 A4
Pasadena Shores 98 C2
Pasco 97 C8
Pass a Grille 112 B3
Pass Station 65 C7
Patersonville 78 B1
Paxton 19 A5
Peace River Shores 122 D1
Peach Orchard 75 C6
Peacock Hammock 114 C3
Peaden 18 A2
Pearl Court 52 C1
Pebble Creek 105 A8
Pebbledale 107 C5
Pecan 78 B1
Pecan Park 52 A1
Peck 44 A3
Pedro 90 A3
Pelican Bay 136 D3
Pelican Lake 133 B5
Pelican Landing 136 C3
Pembroke 115 A7
Pembroke Pines 147 B5
Peniel 77 B8
Penney Farms 65 C7
Pennichaw 93 C6
Pennsuco 146 D4
Pensacola 35 B6
Pensacola Beach 35 C7
Peoria Siding 65 A7
Perdido Bay 34 C3
Perdido Heights 34 B3
Perkins 44 B2
Perky 157 C6
Perrine 150 B4
Perry 60 A1
Peterson 61 B6
Phifer 76 C2
Philips 52 C1
Phoenix Park 52 C1
Pickettville 51 C7
Picnic 114 A3
Picolata 66 C1
Piedmont 92 D3
Pierce 107 D5
Pierson 85 B7
Pine 15 A6
Pine Barren 15 C8
Pine Bluff 36 A1; 66 A1
Pine Castle 100 B4
Pine Dale 107 D5

Pine Forest 35 A5
Pine Grove 101 D6
Pine Hill Estates 75 B7
Pine Hills 92 A3; 100 A3
Pine Island 41 B8; 97 A5
Pine Island Center 128 D3
Pine Island Ridge 147 B5
Pine Lakes 92 A3
Pine Level 122 B1
Pine Log 39 B6; 57 C5
Pine Manor 136 A2
Pine Mount 62 A1
Pine Oaks Estates 82 D2
Pine Ridge 89 A7; 136 D3
Pine Run 83 D5
Pine Top 50 D2
Pine Tree Park 119 B7
Pinecraft 120 A3
Pinecrest 106 D3; 149 A5; 151 B5
Pineda 102 D4
Pinehurst Village 141 D7
Pineland 128 D3
Pineland Gardens 52 D2
Pinellas Park 104 D4
Pineola 90 D1
Pinesville 75 C6
Pinetta 46 A4
Pineville 15 B5
Pinewood 147 D6
Piney Grove 19 B7
Piney Point 113 B6
Pinkerton Pier 102 B3
Pinland 60 B2
Pioneer Park 150 A4
Pirate Harbor 128 B4
Pirates Cove 157 C6
Pirates Wood 62 B3
Pittman 20 A3; 92 A1
Pittsburg 116 B2
Placid Lakes 123 B7
Placida 128 B1
Plains 117 D6
Plant City 106 B3
Plantation 120 D4; 147 A5
Plantation Island 143 D8
Plantation Key Colony 159 D8
Platt 121 D8
Pleasant Grove 18 A4; 19 B8; 34 C4; 64 C3; 106 C2
Pleasant Ridge 19 D6
Plum Orchard 58 A3
Plummer 51 B7
Plummers 66 A1
Plymouth 92 D2
Poinciana 108 A3
Poinciana Park 119 B7
Poincianna Place 134 D2
Poinsettia Park 107 B8
Point Baker 16 D4
Point Brittany 112 A4
Point Pleasant 84 A3
Point Washington 38 C3
Polk City 107 A6
Polly Town 52 B1
Pomona Park 78 C1
Pompano Beach 141 D7
Pompano Park 141 D6
Ponce de Leon 20 C1
Ponce Inlet 87 D5
Pond Creek 18 C4
Ponte Vedra 52 D4
Ponte Vedra Beach 52 D4
Poplar Camp 56 A4
Poplar Head 21 C5
Pops Hammock Seminole Village 149 B7
Port Boca Grande 128 C1
Port Canaveral 103 B5
Port Charlotte 128 A3
Port Inglis 88 A3
Port La Belle 130 C4
Port Leon 58 A2
Port Lonesome 98 D3
Port Mayaca 133 A5
Port Orange 87 C5
Port Richey 96 D4
Port Royal 142 A3
Port Salerno 127 C6
Port Sewall 127 C6
Port St Joe 55 D5
Port St John 102 B3
Port St Lucie 127 B6
Port Sutton 105 C7
Port Tampa 105 D6
Portland 38 A2
Possum Bluff 77 C8
Postil 37 B7
Pouchers Corner 48 C3
Powell 97 B7
Poyner 99 C6
Prairie Junction 107 C5
Pretty Bayou 53 A8
Princeton 150 C3
Princetonian Park 150 C4
Progress Village 105 C8
Prosperity 20 B1
Providence 63 B6; 107 A5
Pumpkin Center 91 C6
Punta Gorda 128 A4
Punta Gorda Beach 120 D2

Punta Gorda Isles 128 A3
Punta Rassa 135 B8
Purvis Still 48 B3
Putnam Hall 77 A5

Q

Quail Heights 150 C4
Queens Cove 127 A8
Queens Park 127 C5
Quincy 43 A6
Quinlan 52 B1
Quintette 16 D1

R

Raiford 64 B2
Rainbow End Estates 82 C3
Rainbow Lakes 141 A7
Rainbow Lakes Estates 82 C3
Rainbow Ranch 77 C7
Raleigh 75 D7
Ramblewood East 141 D6
Rambo 21 A8
Ramsey Beach 34 B4
Ratliff 51 A7
Rattlesnake 105 D6
Rattlesnake Bend 65 B7
Ravenna Park 93 C5
Rawls 48 A1
Reams 46 B1
Reavills Corner 99 A8
Red Head 39 B6
Red Level 89 A5
Redbay 39 A5
Reddick 83 A6
Reddish Millsite 49 B7
Redington Beach 104 D2
Redington Shores 104 D2
Redland 150 C3
Reeves Field 48 D1
Regal Park 83 B6
Regent Park 136 D3
Relay 86 A1
Remington Park 65 B8
Remlap 105 D8
Renaissance 136 A3
Rerdell 98 A3
Resota Beach 40 C1
Reunion 100 D1
Rex 76 B3
Ribault Manor 51 C8
Rice Creek 78 A1
Riceland 75 B8
Rich Bay 24 D4
Richland 98 D3
Richloam 98 A3
Richmond 98 B4
Richmond Heights 150 B4
Richmond West 150 B3
Richter Crossroads 21 B6
Rideout 65 B7
Ridge Harbor 129 A5
Ridge Manor 98 A2
Ridge Wood Heights 120 B2
Ridgecrest 104 D3
Ridgewood 65 A7; 107 D6
Rio 127 B6
Rio Vista 105 D5
Riomar 119 B8
Rital 98 A2
River Bridge 119 A6
River Estates 82 D2
River Forest 85 D8
River Junction 23 D6
River Park 126 A4
Riverdale 98 D2; 98 B2
Riverside 51 C8; 92 A4
Riverside Acres 92 D3
Riverview 35 A6; 51 B8; 106 D1
Riviera Beach 134 C3
Rixford 48 C1
Roach 59 A8
Robinson Heights 76 B1
Robinswood 75 B8
Rochelle 76 C2
Rock Bluff 42 A2
Rock Creek 17 A7; 22 D2
Rock Harbor 154 D3
Rock Head 41 C5
Rock Hill 19 D7
Rock Island 143 A8
Rock Ridge 99 D5
Rockdale 150 B4
Rockledge 102 C4
Rocksprings 82 C4
Rockwell 102 D4
Rocky Creek 22 C2; 105 B6
Rocky Point 75 C8
Rodman 77 C7
Roeville 17 D5
Rolling Acres 98 A1
Rolling Hills 82 C4; 107 D5
Rolling Oaks 86 B6; 107 A5
Rolling Ranches 82 D4
Rollins Corner 41 B6
Romeo 82 B3

Rood 134 A2
Rose 44 C3
Rosedale 23 D7
Roseland 111 D7
Rosemary Beach 38 D4
Rosemont 92 D3
Rosewood 81 B5
Rotonda 128 B1
Rotunda-West 128 B1
Round Lake 21 D8
Roux Quarters 107 D7
Roy 78 B3
Royal 90 B3
Royal Highlands 89 D6
Royal Palm Beach 134 D2
Royal Palm Estates 134 D3
Royal Palm Hammock 143 C5
Royal Terrace 51 C8
Royals Crossroads 20 A1
Royster 107 D5
Rubonia 113 C6
Runnymede 101 D6
Runyon 132 C4
Ruskin 113 A7
Russell 65 B8
Russell Landding 65 B8
Ruthland 76 B1
Rutland 90 B2
Rutledge 75 B8
Rye 113 C8

S

Saddle Oak Club 83 C6
Safety Harbor 104 C4
Saint Andrew 53 A8
Saint Andrews Plaza 53 A8
Saint Augustine 67 D5
Saint Augustine Beach 67 D5
Saint Augustine Shores 67 D5
Saint Augustine South 67 D5
Saint Catherine 90 D3
Saint Cloud 101 D5
Saint Francis 85 D7
Saint George 104 B4
Saint James 57 C6
Saint James City 135 B8
Saint Joe Beach 54 C4
Saint Johns 66 A1
Saint Johns Park 51 D8; 78 D3
Saint Johns River Estates 92 B4
Saint Joseph 98 C1
Saint Josephs 93 B5
Saint Leo 98 C1
Saint Lucie 119 D8
Saint Marks 58 A2
Saint Nicholas 52 C1
Saint Peter 44 B2
Saint Petersburg 112 A4
Saint Petersburg Beach 112 A3
Saint Teresa 57 C7
Salem 60 D3
Salerno 127 C6
Salt Springs 84 A3
Salvista 129 D6
Sam Willie Seminole Village 145 D7
Samoset 113 D6
Sampson 64 C2; 66 B2
Samsula 86 D4
San Antonio 98 C1
San Blas 54 B1
San Carlos Park 136 B3
San Jose 52 D1
San Jose Forest 52 D1
San Mateo 52 B1; 78 C1
San Pablo 52 D3
San Pedro Junction 61 B6
Sanborn 57 B5
Sancassa 128 A1
Sand Cut 35 B5; 133 A5
Sand Hill 19 B6
Sandalfoot Cove 141 C6
Sandalwood 52 C2
Sanders Beach 35 C6
Sanders Park 141 D7
Sanderson 50 D1
Sandestin 38 D1
Sandy 121 B7
Sandy Point 62 C2
Sanford 93 B5
Sanford Farms 92 B4
Sanibel 135 B8
Sanlando Springs 92 D4
Sans Pareil 52 D2
Sans Souci 129 A5
Santa Clara 43 A6
Santa Fe 63 D7
Santa Fe Beach 76 A3
Santa Rosa Beach 38 C1
Santos 83 C7
Sapp 64 A2
Sarasota 120 A2
Sarasota Colony 124 D4
Sarasota Heights 120 A2
Sarasota Springs 120 A3
Saratoga 77 C8
Sargent 49 A7

Satellite Beach 111 A5
Satsuma 77 C8
Satsuma Heights 35 A5
Saunders 40 B3
Sawdust 42 A4
Saxton 64 B4
Saybrook 78 A4
Scanlon 59 A6
Sconiers Mill 19 D7
Scotland 43 A7
Scott Lake 147 C6
Scotts Ferry 41 D7
Scottsmoor 94 D2
Sea Ranch Lakes 141 D7
Seabreeze 86 B4
Seacoll 89 A8
Seagrove Beach 38 C3
Sears 130 D4
Seascape 37 C8
Seaside 38 C3
Sebastian 119 A7
Sebring 116 B3
Sebring Shores 116 C3
Sebring Southgate 116 D3
Secotan 60 A1
Seffner 106 C1
Selhaven 134 A3
Sellersville 17 A5
Selman 41 A8
Seminole 37 B8; 104 D3
Seminole Grove 77 C8
Seminole Hills 39 C5
Seminole Manor 141 A7
Seminole Shores 127 C6
Seminole Springs 92 B2
Seneca 92 B1
Senyah 85 A7
Seven Springs 97 D5
Seville 85 A7
Sewalls Point 127 C6
Shadeville 58 A1
Shadow Lawn Estates 75 B8
Shady 83 D6
Shady Grove 23 D5; 46 D1
Shady Hills 97 B6
Shady Rest 43 A7; 52 A2
Shaefer 47 D7
Shalimar 37 B6
Shamrock 73 B7
Shamrock Acres 89 A5
Shannon Wood 75 B7
Sharpes 102 B3
Sharpstown 41 C7
Shawano 140 A2
Shawnee 132 C1
Shaws Still 63 B7
Shell Bluff 78 C3
Shell Island 58 A2; 142 B4
Shell Point Village 136 A1
Shenks 76 A3
Sherman 125 B7
Sherman Grove 34 C4
Sherman Oaks 83 C5
Sherman Park 111 A5
Sherwood Forest 51 B8
Sherwood Park 141 B7
Shiloh 94 C3
Shilow 106 B3
Shiney Shore 120 C4
Shired Island 80 A2
Shore Acres 105 D5
Sidell 121 B7
Siesta Key 120 B2
Sills 22 A1
Silver Beach Acres 78 D1
Silver Beach Heights 91 A8
Silver Lake 91 B7
Silver Palm 150 B4
Silver Springs 18 B2; 83 B7
Silver Springs Shores 83 D8
Simmons Crossing 17 A5
Simsville 22 D2
Sinai 23 D6
Sink Creek 22 D3
Sirmans 46 C1
Sisco 78 C1
Sixmile Bend 133 D6
Sixmile Creek 105 C8
Skipper 57 B8
Sky Lake 100 B4
Skyline Heights 127 B6
Skyline Meadows 89 A7
Skytop 99 A8
Slade 47 D8
Slater 129 C6
Slavia 93 D6
Sloans Ridge 99 A5
Smallpox Tommies Seminole Village 149 A7
Smith 27 D8
Smith Creek 57 A5
Smith Crossroads 20 A3
Smyrna 20 B4
Sneads 23 C5
Snow Hill 93 C7
Snows Corner 106 B2
Snug Harbor 127 B6
Socrum 106 A4
Solana 47 B8
Sopchoppy 57 B6
Sorrento 92 B2
South Allapattah 150 C4

South Apopka 92 D2
South Bay 132 D4
South Beach 119 C8
South Bradenton 113 D5
South Brooksville 97 A8
South Clermont 99 B7
South Clewiston 132 C2
South Clinton Heights 98 C2
South Cocoa Beach 103 D5
South Daytona 86 C4
South Flomaton 16 A1
South Highpoint 104 C4
South Idylwild 75 B8
South Jacksonville 52 C1
South Masaryktown 97 B7
South Metro 52 D2
South Miami 151 A5
South Miami Heights 150 B4
South Mulberry 107 D5
South Palm Beach 141 A8
South Pasadena 112 A4
South Patrick Park 111 A5
South Patrick Shores 103 D5
South Pine Lakes 92 A3
South Ponte Vedra Beach 67 B5
South Port 108 A4
South Punta Gorda Heights 129 B5
South Sarasota 120 B2
South Side 76 D1
South Tampa 105 C8
South Titusville 102 A3
South Venice 120 D3
Southchase 100 C4
Southeast Arcadia 122 C2
Southfort 122 D1
Southgate 120 A2
Southmere 94 D1
Southport 40 D1
Southridge 52 D2
Southside Estates 52 C2
Southwest Ranches 146 B4
Southwest Venice 120 D3
Sparkman 122 D4
Sparr 83 A7
Spaulding 51 B7
Spivey 105 B6
Spray 46 A1
Spring Creek 58 B1
Spring Glen 52 C1
Spring Hill 17 C5; 43 C8; 63 D6; 97 B5
Spring Lake 98 B1; 116 D4
Spring Warrior Camp 59 C8
Springfield 52 C1; 54 A1
Springside 77 B8
Springville 48 D3
Spruce Creek 83 D6; 91 A5
Spuds 78 A3
Stacey Street 134 D3
Stanton 91 A6
Star 22 C3
Starke 64 C3
Starkes Ferry 91 A7
Starr 47 D7
Steckert 50 D3
Steele City 21 C8
Steinhatchee 72 B4
Stern 46 B1
Stevens Park 119 B7
Stock Island 156 D4
Stockade 52 D2
Stokes Ferry 89 A8
Storey Crossing 101 D8
Stuart 127 C5
Stuckey 99 A5
Sturkey 98 C4
Suburban Heights 75 B8
Sugar Junction 132 C1
Sugar Mill Estates 87 D5
Sugarloaf Shores 157 C6
Sugarmill Woods 89 C6
Sugarton 132 C1
Suggs Head 41 B6
Sulphur Spring 81 D8
Sulphur Springs 105 B7
Sumatra 56 B1
Summer Haven 79 B6
Summerfield 83 C7
Summerland Key 157 C7
Summerport Beach 100 B2
Sumner 81 B5
Sumterville 90 C4
Sun City 113 B7
Sun City Center 113 A8
Sun Garden 65 D8
Sun Lake Estates 91 A7
Sun N Sand Beaches 57 C8
Sun Valley 141 A7
Sunbeam 52 D2
Suncoast Estates 129 C6
Sunland Estates 93 C5
Sunland Gardens 119 D8
Sunniland 137 D8
Sunny Hills 40 A1
Sunnyland 120 B3
Sunnyside 39 D5; 91 C6
Sunrise 120 B3
Sunset 150 A4
Sunset Beach 105 C6; 112 A3
Sunset Harbor 91 A5

Sunset Point 154 D3
Sunshine Beach 112 A3
Sunshine Ranches 147 B5
Sunvale 124 A1
Surf 57 C7
Surfside 147 D7
Sutherlands Still 78 C1
Suwannee 48 C1; 80 A3
Suwannee River 74 C1
Suwannee Springs 48 C1
Suwannee Valley 48 C4
Svea 18 A4
Sweet Gum Head 20 A1
Sweetwater 42 A1; 51 D7; 115 D8; 150 A4
Switzerland 66 B1
Sycamore 42 A2
Sydney 106 C2
Sylvan Lake 92 C4
Sylvan Shores 123 A8
Sylvania 20 D4

Tacoma 76 C1
Taft 100 B4
Talisman 98 B2
Tallahassee 44 B1
Tallevast 113 D6
Talleyrand 52 C1
Tamarac 147 A6
Tamiami 150 A4
Tampa 105 C7
Tancrede 107 C5
Tangelo Park 100 B3
Tangerine 92 C1
Tang-O-Mar Beach 37 C8
Tarpon 105 B6
Tarpon Point 121 D5
Tarpon Springs 104 A3
Tarrytown 98 A4
Tatum 120 A3
Tatum Ridge 120 A3
Tavares 91 B8
Tavernier 154 D2
Taylor 50 B1
Taylor Creek 125 B7
Teasdale 78 A1
Tedder 141 D7
Tee and Green Estates 128 A4
Telegraph Estates 129 C8
Telogia 42 C3
Temple Terrace 105 B8
Temple Terrace Jct 105 B8
Tendil Crossing 21 A5
Tenile 15 C7
Tenmile Corner 149 B6
Tennille 73 A5
Tequesta 134 A3
Terra Mana 113 C5
Terra Ceia 113 C5
Terra Mar 141 D7
Terrell 98 A2
Terrytown 140 C2
Thames 74 B4
The Bamboos 144 B3
The Crossings 150 B4
The Hammocks 150 B3
The Jungle 112 A3
The Meadows 120 A3
The Moorings 142 A3
The Pocket 107 D7
The Rocks 89 A5
The Villages 91 A5
The Watson Place 148 A2
Theressa 64 D3
Thirteen Mile 69 A6
Thomas City 45 C5
Thompson 154 D3
Thonotosassa 106 B1
Three Lakes 150 B4
Three Oaks 136 B3
Tice 129 D7
Tidewater 82 C2
Tierra Verde 112 B4
Tiger Bay 115 A6
Tiger Point 35 C8
Tildenville 100 A1
Tilton 69 A7
Timber Pines 97 B5
Timberline Estates 89 B7
Tisonia 52 A1
Titusville 94 D2
Tocoi 66 D1
Tommytown 98 C2
Tomoka Estates 86 A3
Tooke Lake Junction 97 A8
Top of the World 83 D5
Torrey 115 B7
Town 'n' Country 105 B6
Town Park Estates 150 A4
Townsend 60 A4
Trail Center 145 D6
Trail City 149 A6
Trail Glade Tower 150 A3
Trailer Estates 113 D5
Trailtown 144 D4
Tranquility Park 107 B7
Trapnell 106 C3
Trappers Zoo 134 A3

Traxler 63 D6
Treasure Hill Park 34 C3
Treasure Island 112 A3
Trenton 74 B2
Trilby 98 B2
Trilcoochee 98 B2
Trinity 104 A4
Tristan Village 35 B5
Tropic 111 A5
Tropic Isle 141 B8
Tropical Gulf Acres 129 B5
Tropical Park 127 D5
Tropicana Lake 82 C3
Truck Corner 93 D6
Truckland 136 B1
Tryon 122 B1
Tuckers Corner 129 B7
Tulane 51 C5
Tully 57 A8
Turkey Creek 106 C2
Turkey Foot 144 B4
Turnbull 127 A5
Turquoise Beach 38 B1
Tuscannooga 91 D5
Twentymile 66 A3
Twentymile Bend 133 D8
Twin Lakes 147 A6
Twin Pole 56 A2
Two Egg 22 B4
Two Mile 69 A8
Tyler 74 B3

U

Uceta Yard 105 C8
Uleta 147 C6
Ulmerton 104 D3
Umatilla 92 A1
Underwood Crossing 21 A6
Union 19 B8
Union Park 101 A6
Union Station 51 C8
United 134 A1
University Park 101 A6; 141 C7; 150 A4
Up the Grove Beach 125 C8
Upper Grand Lagoon 53 A7
Usher 74 D3
Usinas Beach 67 C5
Utopia 120 B4

V

Valdez 93 B5
Valhalla 159 C5
Valkaria 111 C6
Valparaiso 37 A6
Valrico 106 C1
Valroy 113 B6
Vamo 77 D8
Vanderbilt Beach 136 D2
Vanderbilt Beach Estates 136 D2
Vanderbilt Park 150 A4
Vandolah 115 C5
Vaughn 132 D3
Vehlin 150 C3
Venetia 51 D8
Venetia Terrace 51 D8
Venice 120 D3
Venice East 120 D4
Venice Gardens 120 D4
Venice Groves 120 D4
Venus 123 D8
Vereen 44 D2
Vermont Heights 66 D4
Verna 121 A5
Vernon 20 D4
Vero Beach 119 B8
Vero Beach Highlands 119 C8
Vero Beach South 119 B7
Vero Lake Estates 119 A6
Vicksburg 40 C1
Victor 104 A3
Viera 102 D4
Viking 119 C8
Vilano Beach 67 C5
Vilas 42 D2
Villa City 91 D6
Villa Sabine 35 C6
Villa Tasso 37 B8
Villages of Oriole 141 B6
Vineland 100 C2
Vineyards 136 D4
Vista 80 A4
Vitis 98 D3
Volusia 85 C6

W

Wabasso 119 A7
Wabasso Beach 119 A8
Wacahoota 75 C8
Wacca 81 B8
Wacissa 45 C5

Waddells Mill 22 B1
Wade 75 A5
Wadesboro 44 A4
Wagner 93 C5
Wagon Wheel 144 A4
Wahneta 107 C8
Wahoo 90 D2
Waits Junction 99 A8
Wakulla 44 D2
Wakulla Beach 58 A1
Wakulla Gardens 58 A1
Wakulla Springs 44 D1
Walcan 19 C7
Waldo 76 A3
Walkill 66 C1
Wall Springs 104 A3
Wallace 16 D2
Walling 92 B3
Walnut Hill 15 B6
Walsingham 104 D3
Walter Hamilton Place 148 C2
Walton 127 A5
Wanamake 62 D2
Wannee 74 A1
Ward 42 C4
Ward Basin 36 A1
Ward Ridge 69 A5
Warm Mineral Springs 121 D5
Warrington 35 C5
Washington Gardens 105 A8
Washington Park 131 B7; 147 A6
Waterbury 114 D1
Watercolor 38 C3
Waters Lake 74 A4
Watertown 43 A5
Waterway Estates 129 D6
Watson 132 D2
Wauchula 115 C7
Wauchula Hills 115 C7
Waukeenah 45 B5
Wausau 21 D5
Waveland 127 B6
Waverly 108 C1
Weatherfield 92 D4
Weavers Station 143 C7
Webster 90 D4
Wedgefield 101 B8
Weeki Wachee 97 A6
Weeki Wachee Acres 97 B5
Weeki Wachee Gardens 97 A5
Weekiwachee Woodlands 97 B5
Weirsdale 91 A5
Wekiva 92 C3
Wekiwa Springs 92 C3
Welaka 77 D8
Welcome 106 D3
Welcome Junction 106 D3
Wellborn 48 D3
Wellington 134 D1
Wesconnett 51 D8
Wesley Chapel 98 D1
Wesley Chapel South 98 D1
West Bay 39 D6
West Bradenton 113 C5
West Deerfield Beach 141 C7
West DeLand 86 D1
West Delray Beach 141 B6
West Dixie Bend 141 C6
West Eau Gallie 110 A4
West Frostproof 116 A1
West Gate 134 D3
West Hills 75 B8
West Jacksonville 51 C8
West Jupiter 134 A3
West Lake 47 A7
West Lake Wales 108 D1
West Little River 147 D6
West Melbourne 111 B5
West Miami 151 A5
West Palm Beach 134 C3
West Panama City Beach 53 A7
West Park 105 B6
West Pensacola 35 B5
West Samoset 113 D6
West Scenic Park 108 C1
West Tampa 105 C6
West Tocoi 66 D1
West Vero Corridor 119 B7
Westchase 105 B5
Westchester 151 A5
Weston 146 A4
Westview 147 D6
Westville 20 C2
Westwood 51 D7
Westwood Acres 82 C4
Westwood Lakes 150 A4
Wetumpka 43 B5
Wewahitchka 55 A6
Whidden Corner 131 C8
Whiskey Creek 136 A2
Whisper Walk 141 C6
Whispering Hills 102 A2
Whispering Pines 125 B6
White Beach 120 B2
White City 55 D6; 127 A5
White Springs 42 B2; 48 C3
Whitehall Estates 82 D2

Whitehead Crossroads 20 C3
Whitehouse 51 C6
Whites Ford 66 B2
Whiteville 77 B5
Whitfield 113 D6
Whitfield Estates 113 D6
Whitney 91 B5
Whitney Beach 112 D4
Whittier 109 D8
Wilbur-by-the-Sea 87 C5
Wilburn 63 A6
Wilcox 74 B1
Wilcox Junction 74 B1
Wild Island 124 A2
Wildwood 90 B4
Wiley 94 D3
Williams Point 102 B3
Williamsburg 100 B3
Williford 74 A3
Willis 41 A6
Willis Landing 55 C8
Williston 82 B3
Williston Highlands 82 A2
Willoughby Acres 136 D3
Willow 113 B8
Willow Oak 106 C4
Willow Sink 97 B6
Wilma 56 A1
Wilson 94 D4
Wilson Corner 92 B4
Wilson Corners 98 A3
Wilton Manors 147 A7
Wimauma 114 A1
Wimberly Estates 75 B8
Windermere 100 B2
Windsor 76 B2
Winfield 48 D4
Winston 106 B4
Winter Beach 119 A7
Winter Garden 100 A1
Winter Haven 107 B8
Winter Park 92 D4
Winter Springs 93 D5
Wiscon 97 A7
Withla 99 C6
Wolfolk 108 D1
Wonderwood 52 C3
Woodlawn 66 C4
Woodlawn Beach 36 C1
Woodmere 120 D4
Woodruff Springs 92 B4
Woods 42 C1
Woods and Lakes 84 C2
Woodville 44 C1
Worthington Springs 63 C7
Wright 37 B5
Wulfert 135 B6
Wynnehaven Beach 36 B3
Wynnlum 21 A5

Y

Yalaha 91 C7
Yamato 141 B7
Yankeetown 81 D8
Yates Camp 60 D1
Ybel 135 B8
Ybor City 105 C7
Yeehaw 118 B2
Yeehaw Junction 118 B1
Yellow Bluff 85 B5
Yellow Jacket 73 D8
Yelvington 78 B2
Yent Place 56 D4
Yniestra 35 B7
Yonz Corner 97 A8
York 83 C5
Youmans 106 B4
Youngstown 40 C3
Yukon 51 D8
Yulee 33 D5
Yulee Heights 33 D5

Z

Zana 126 C1
Zellwood 92 C1
Zephyrhills 98 D2
Zephyrhills North 98 D3
Zephyrhills South 98 D2
Zephyrhills West 98 D2
Zolfo Springs 115 D7
Zuber 83 B6

Introduction

The thought of Florida conjures up exciting images: space exploration, theme parks, oranges, alligators, palm trees, beaches, golfing, the Keys. Explore the many botanical gardens, water sports, wildlife refuges, museums, historic sites, and recreation areas. The Sunshine State provides much to see and to do for both residents and visitors alike.

Locate your favorite activities—and discover some new favorites—with the help of the *Florida Atlas & Gazetteer*.

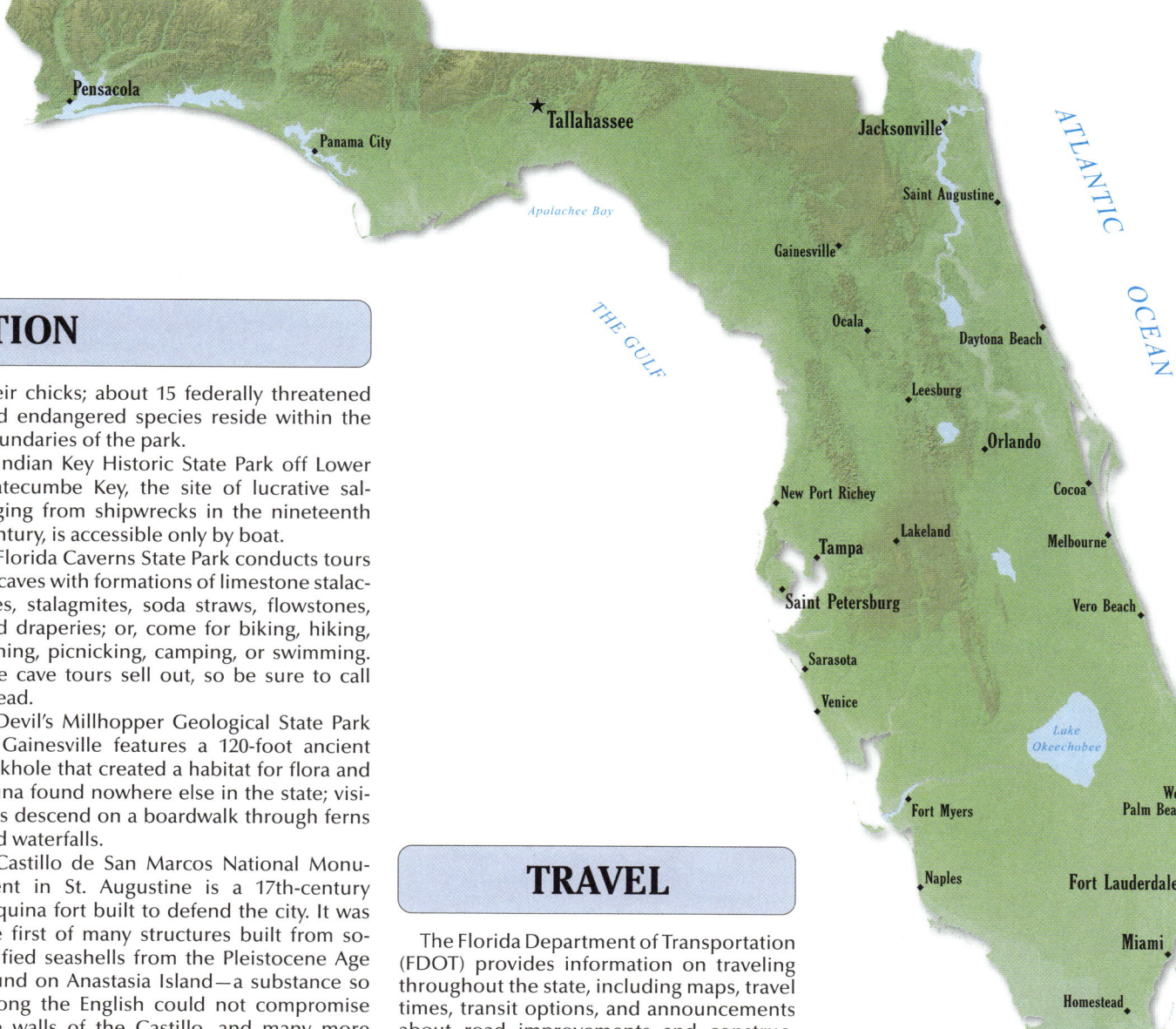

RECREATION

If you enjoy theme parks, Florida has what you're looking for: Disney World, Busch Gardens, SeaWorld, Gatorland, Jungle Island, Legoland, Gulf World Marine Park, Universal Studios, Lion Country Safari, Daytona International Speedway, Monkey Jungle, Weeki Wachi Springs, and Reptile World Serpentarium, to name a few. After enjoying the sights and food at these venues, Florida offers even more activities—from over 800 miles of beaches to over 400 golf courses with public access to a multitude of cultural events and museums, and recreational activities on local, state and national parks, forests and landmarks.

Bok Tower Gardens National Historic Landmark in central Florida's Lake Wales, with gardens designed by Frederick Law Olmsted, contains acres of ferns, palms, oaks, and pines, in addition to azaleas, camellias, and magnolia blossoms. The 205-foot neo-Gothic and art-deco Singing Tower houses a 60-bell carillon. The twelfth-century Monastery of St. Bernard in Miami is surrounded by six acres of formal gardens.

The Astronaut Hall of Fame in Titusville contains memorabilia as well as training simulators and interactive exhibits. Kennedy Space Center offers guided bus tours, exhibits, and demonstrations.

The Cape Florida Lighthouse in Key Biscayne was restored from 1825; guided tours of the lighthouse and keeper's home interpret early South Florida history and the Second Seminole War.

The John and Mable Ringling Museum of Art in Sarasota houses the collection of masterpieces this couple amassed, as well as the family's dazzling 56-room Venetian Gothic mansion, a circus museum, and stunning gardens and grounds. Potter's Wax Museum in St. Augustine contains 160 wax sculptures of famous personalities. The Morikami Museum and Japanese Gardens in Delray Beach feature the history of the Yamoto Colony of Japanese farmers, bonsai collection, Japanese folk art, garden, and a nature trail.

On Key West, find the Ernest Hemingway Home and Museum, pet a shark at the aquarium, visit the Museum of Art & History in the old Custom House, or stroll through the Butterfly & Nature Conservancy.

Florida is home to many Native American tribes, including the federally recognized Miccosukee and Seminole. The Ah-Tah-Thi-Ki Museum at Okalee Village showcases Seminole cultural and historical artifacts. The Miccosukee Indian Village in the Everglades demonstrates beading, doll-making, and woodworking, and explores the history of this ancient culture at the Miccosukee Museum.

Lake Wales Ridge in central Florida is a 100-mile-long ancient sand dune that was the area's only piece of dry land about two million years ago, resulting in plant and animal species evolving in isolation. Lake Wales Ridge State Forest offers hiking, canoeing, fishing, bird watching, and primitive camping.

Everglades National Park enchants with its seemingly endless marshes, dense mangroves, towering palms, alligator holes, and tropical fauna. The park serves as an important nursery ground for wood storks raising their chicks; about 15 federally threatened and endangered species reside within the boundaries of the park.

Indian Key Historic State Park off Lower Matecumbe Key, the site of lucrative salvaging from shipwrecks in the nineteenth century, is accessible only by boat.

Florida Caverns State Park conducts tours of caves with formations of limestone stalactites, stalagmites, soda straws, flowstones, and draperies; or, come for biking, hiking, fishing, picnicking, camping, or swimming. The cave tours sell out, so be sure to call ahead.

Devil's Millhopper Geological State Park in Gainesville features a 120-foot ancient sinkhole that created a habitat for flora and fauna found nowhere else in the state; visitors descend on a boardwalk through ferns and waterfalls.

Castillo de San Marcos National Monument in St. Augustine is a 17th-century coquina fort built to defend the city. It was the first of many structures built from solidified seashells from the Pleistocene Age found on Anastasia Island—a substance so strong the English could not compromise the walls of the Castillo, and many more buildings in St. Augustine were subsequently fashioned from it.

Dry Tortugas National Park on seven tiny islands made up of coral reefs, beaches, and tropical waters is home to historic Fort Jefferson and offers activities from snorkeling to bird watching and camping. A serious navigation hazard, waters surrounding the Dry Tortugas are home to hundreds of shipwrecks.

Waccasassa Bay Preserve State Park on the Gulf Coast—accessible only by boat—boasts freshwater and saltwater fishing; bald eagles, manatees, alligators, and black bears can be found in the preserve. Tarkiln Bayou Preserve State Park in Pensacola contains several endangered plant species, with a boardwalk for viewing the bayou.

For general information and more details on state and federal lands, contact the following agencies:

Florida Tourism
www.visitflorida.com
(888) 735-2872

Florida State Parks
www.floridastateparks.org
(850) 245-2157

National Park Service
www.nps.gov/state/FL

U.S. Forest Service
www.fs.usda.gov/r08/florida
(850) 523-8500

National Wildlife Refuges,
U.S. Fish & Wildlife Service
www.fws.gov/refuges
(800) 344-WILD (9453)

FISHING AND HUNTING

Freshwater fishing opportunities in Florida include bass, crappie, and catfish; saltwater catches may include shark, triggerfish, grouper, snapper, crab, lobster, shrimp, and scallops. Hunt for whitetail deer, turkey, bobcat, beaver, coyote, and quail.

Familiarize yourself with the local restrictions, regulations, and licensing requirements by contacting:

Florida Fish & Wildlife Conservation
www.myfwc.com
(850) 488-4676

TRAVEL

The Florida Department of Transportation (FDOT) provides information on traveling throughout the state, including maps, travel times, transit options, and announcements about road improvements and construction. Learn about travel into and around the state as well as updates on travel conditions by contacting:

Florida Department of Transportation
www.dot.state.fl.us
(850) 414-4100

STATE FACTS

Admitted to the Union: March 3, 1845; 27th state
Capital: Tallahassee
Size: 53,927 square miles
Population: 21,477,737 (2019 estimate)
Nickname: Sunshine State
Motto: In God We Trust
Bird: Mockingbird
Flower: Orange Blossom
Wildflower: Coreopsis (Tickseed)
Tree: Sabal Palm
Fruit: Orange
Animal: Florida Panther
Marine Mammal: Manatee
Saltwater Mammal: Porpoise or Dolphin
Reptile: Alligator
Saltwater Reptile: Loggerhead Turtle
Butterfly: Zebra Longwing
Saltwater Fish: Sailfish
Freshwater Fish: Largemouth Bass
Stone: Agatized Coral
Gem: Moonstone
Shell: Horse Conch
Soil: Myakka
Beverage: Orange Juice
Song: "The Swanee River"

Name for Residents: Floridians
Major Industries: International trade, tourism, space industry, agriculture (oranges, tomatoes, soybeans, tobacco, poultry), food processing, health care, real estate, mining, commercial fishing
Major Cities with populations:
Jacksonville 911,507
Miami 467,963
Tampa 399,700
Orlando 287,442
St. Petersburg 265,351
Hialeah 233,339
Tallahassee 194,500
Fort Lauderdale 182,437
Highest Point: Britton Hill 345 feet
Lowest Point: Atlantic and Gulf coasts (sea level)
Major Lakes:
Lake Okeechobee .... 730 square miles
Lake George .... 72 square miles
Major Rivers:
St. Johns .... 310 miles
Suwannee River .... 246 miles
St. Marys .... 126 miles

CAMPGROUNDS

Campgrounds with a variety of different facilities are located on state, federal and private lands. The public campground symbol, as shown in the Legend (see inside front cover), identifies campgrounds located within national forests and parks. For information on fees, services and reservations at public campgrounds, contact one of the state or federal agencies listed above.

The Gazetteer also lists information on a selection of privately owned and operated campgrounds. To locate campgrounds listed in the Gazetteer on the maps, look on the given page for the purple campground symbol and corresponding four-digit number.

Family Outings

A1A SCENIC & HISTORIC COASTAL BYWAY – Ponte Vedra Beach – 52 D4 Road traverses a narrow barrier island. 72-mile stretch offers views of sandy beaches and the blue waters of the Atlantic Ocean. Passes St. Augustine, the oldest European settlement in the country.

AIR FORCE ARMAMENT MUSEUM – Fort Walton Beach – 37 B6 Guns, missiles, rockets and historic aircraft from World War I to the present. Air Commando and Special Operations units exhibit.

ALFRED B. MACLAY GARDENS STATE PARK – Tallahassee – 44 A1 Ornamental gardens planted in 1923. Park features azaleas (bloom December-May), camellias and rare native species. Nature trails and secret garden. Maclay House Museum.

AMALIE ARENA – Tampa – 105 C7 – Indoor arena hosts home games for the Tampa Bay Lightning of the NHL. Opened in 1996 with a seating capacity of 21,500.

AMERANT BANK ARENA – Sunrise – 147 A5 1998 stadium built for the Florida Panthers, an NHL hockey team. Seating capacity of 19,250.

ANIMAL KINGDOM – Lake Buena Vista – 100 C1 The world of animals, real, prehistoric and legendary, is brought to life through rides, shows and live-animal exhibits at Disney's fourth theme park. Kilimanjaro Safari takes visitors on a narrated tour of free-roaming animals on a faithfully re-created, 110-acre African savannah. The ride Dinosaur brings travelers back to the final days of the dinosaur. Expedition Everest is a roller coaster that brings guests face-to-face with the mythical Yeti. Performers don colorful costumes and sing and dance to well-known Disney songs at Festival of the Lion King.

THE ASHLEY GIBSON BARNETT MUSEUM OF ART – Lakeland – 107 B5 15th-18th century European ceramics, pre-Columbian and contemporary art.

ASTRONAUT HALL OF FAME – Titusville – 102 A4 Museum focuses on lives and experiences of US astronauts as well as space program history. Features extensive collection of astronaut artifacts and memorabilia. Spacecraft displays. Interactive exhibits and astronaut training simulators.

AUDUBON HOUSE & GARDENS – Key West – 156 D3 Restored home of the naturalist/painter, John James Audubon, completely furnished with 18th- and 19th-century antiques. Many original Audubon pieces. Tropical gardens feature orchids and bromeliads.

THE BAILEY–MATTHEWS NATIONAL SHELL MUSEUM – Sanibel – 135 B7 Over 600,000 shells found locally and throughout the world. Exhibits focus on shell habitats, mollusks, scallops, fossil shells and shells in art and architecture.

THE BARNACLE HISTORIC STATE PARK – Coconut Grove – 151 A6 1891 home and sailing ketch of Commodore Ralph Monroe. Many original furnishings and historical photographs of Coral Gables. Guided tours.

BASS MUSEUM OF ART – Miami Beach – 151 A7 Collection of European master works from the 15th-20th centuries. Sculptures and textiles. Highlighted by Botticelli altarpiece.

BIG BEND SCENIC BYWAY – Apalachicola – 70 A1 Route traverses coastal flats along The Gulf before making a wide loop through the forests and swamps of Apalachicola National Forest. 220 miles.

BISHOP MUSEUM OF SCIENCE & NATURE – Bradenton – 113 D6 Natural and cultural history museum. Exhibits include Spanish exploration, early mammals and Florida ecology. Parker Manatee Aquarium. Bishop Planetarium.

BLIZZARD BEACH – Lake Buena Vista – 100 C2 Water park showcases what happens when a freak storm transplants a ski mountain to central Florida. Summit Plummet, a speed slide, drops guests 120 feet. Slides re-create winter sports, from bobsledding to slalom skiing. Wave pool, lazy river ride and family raft ride.

BREVARD ZOO – Melbourne – 102 D4 Zoo features animals from Africa, South America and Australia. Rainforest Revealed. Wild Florida exhibit.

BULOW PLANTATION RUINS HISTORIC STATE PARK – Bunnell – 79 D7 4,675 acre plantation was abandoned to the Seminoles in the 1830s. Thick stone ruins of the old house and sugar mill remain among reforested landscape.

BUSCH GARDENS – Tampa – 105 B7 Theme park and safari takes visitors to 19th-Century Africa. Monorail, skyride and tram pass over free-roaming animals of the Serengeti Plain. Immense steel coasters continue the animal theme. Variety of rides, shows and animal attractions.

BUTTERFLY WORLD – Coconut Creek – 141 D6 Screened walk-through aviaries with gardens and simulated tropical rain forest are home to 150 species of butterflies, as well as hummingbirds and lorikeets.

CAPE FLORIDA LIGHTHOUSE – Key Biscayne – 151 B7 Restored 1825 lighthouse and keeper's home. Guided tours interpret early South Florida history and the Second Seminole War.

CASTILLO DE SAN MARCOS NATIONAL MONUMENT – St. Augustine – 67 D5 Spaniards constructed the coquina fort in 1672-1695 to defend the city. Fort withstood two English sieges and was never captured by an enemy. Museum contains Indian, Spanish, and English artifacts and artillery. Tours.

CEDAR KEY MUSEUM STATE PARK – Cedar Key – 80 C4 Features local and natural history exhibits. Shell collection.

CENTRAL FLORIDA ZOO & BOTANNICAL GARDENS – Lake Monroe – 93 B5 Florida panther and endangered red-ruffed lemur among tropical animals from all over the world. Extensive reptile collection. Aviary.

CHARLES HOSMER MORSE MUSEUM OF AMERICAN ART – Winter Park – 92 D4 Windows, lamps, blown glass, pottery and paintings by Louis Comfort Tiffany and other masters.

CLEARWATER MARINE AQUARIUM – Clearwater – 104 C3 Working aquarium devoted to rescue, rehabilitation and release of injured and sick marine animals. Holding tanks display dolphins, otters, sea turtles, sharks and stingrays. Animal care and training presentations. Touch tanks.

COLONIAL QUARTER – St. Augustine – 67 D5 Living history museum with nine restored or reconstructed buildings. Costumed interpreters depict life in mid-18th century St. Augustine.

CONSTITUTION CONVENTION MUSEUM STATE PARK – Port St. Joe – 69 A5 Commemorates the signing of Florida's first constitution. Exhibits on life in the 19th century.

COX SCIENCE CENTER & AQUARIUM – West Palm Beach – 134 D4 Hands-on exhibits explore light, color, sound, electricity, weather and paleontology. Also features aquarium displays, Marvin Dekelboum Planetarium and Marmot Observatory.

CRYSTAL RIVER ARCHAEOLOGICAL STATE PARK – Crystal River – 89 A5 Temple mounds, burial mounds and middens mark the site of 1,600 years of Native American occupation. Visitor center. Nature trails.

CUMMER MUSEUM OF ART & GARDENS – Jacksonville – 51 C8 Paintings by American and European masters, sculpture, prints and tapestries. Asian art and early Meissen porcelain. Historic formal gardens.

DADE BATTLEFIELD HISTORIC STATE PARK – Bushnell – 90 D3 Second Seminole War began here in 1835 when Osceola's allies, Alligator and Micanopy, slaughtered a U.S. Army detachment led by Major Francis Dade. Exhibits and video presentation.

DAYTONA INTERNATIONAL SPEEDWAY – Daytona Beach – 86 C4 Hosts the Daytona 500, the most prestigious race of the NASCAR circuit. Opened in 1959, the Tri-oval (2.5 miles) seats 101,500 spectators. Museum hosts historical exhibits on the people and autos of Daytona. Nascar Racing Experience allows visitors to get behind the wheel. IMAX Theater.

DE SOTO NATIONAL MEMORIAL – Bradenton – 113 C5 Commemorates Hernando DeSoto's 1539 landing and four-year journey through the New World. Living history camp with park rangers in period dress provides insight into 16th- century life. Visitor center offers exhibits on period armor and weapons. Nature trail.

DEVIL'S MILLHOPPER GEOLOGICAL STATE PARK – Gainesville – 75 A8 Ancient sinkhole (120 feet deep) has created a favorable habitat for plants and animals found nowhere else in Florida. A boardwalk descends through ferns and small waterfalls to the bottom.

DISNEY'S HOLLYWOOD STUDIOS – Lake Buena Vista – 100 C2 Theme park re-creates the world of film, situating guests in old Hollywood or a New York City set. Enter the Twilight Zone at the Tower of Terror, a free-fall journey through time and space. Toy Story Mania! is a frantic, moving, rotating, 4D carnival game.

DISNEY SPRINGS – Lake Buena Vista – 100 C2 Complex of shops and restaurants includes Rainforest Cafe and Paddlefish. Live entertainment at House of Blues. Attractions include Cirque du Soleil: Drawn to Life, an avant-garde circus that is truly unique. The NBA experience.

DON GARLITS MUSEUM OF DRAG RACING – Ocala – 83 D7 Exhibits cars from the beginning of drag racing to the present. Memorabilia and photographs. Early Ford exhibit.

EDEN GARDENS STATE PARK – Point Washington – 38 C3 Restored 1897 house in Greek Revival style. Period furniture including Louis XV, Louis XVI and American Empire. Gardens feature large live oaks covered with Spanish moss, azaleas and camellias. Guided tours.

EDISON & FORD WINTER ESTATES – Fort Myers – 129 D6 Winter homes of inventor Thomas Edison and automaker Henry Ford. Also includes Edison's laboratory, guest house and botanical garden. Museum features inventions and research of Edison and Ford. Guided tours.

EDWARD BALL WAKULLA SPRINGS STATE PARK – Wakulla – 44 D1 Glass bottom boat rides over the world's deepest spring. Jungle boat cruises down the Wakulla River pass abundant area wildlife.

ELLIE SCHILLER HOMOSASSA SPRINGS WILDLIFE STATE PARK – Homosassa Springs – 89 B5 Jungle cruise to the springs. Petting park, narrated alligator feedings, manatees, waterfowl and over thirty species of fish at underwater spring observatory. Elevated boardwalk offers views of panthers and other Florida wildlife.

ELLIOTT MUSEUM – Stuart – 127 B6 Diverse museum features the last remaining house of refuge, a station for saving shipwreck victims. Antique car collection. Inventions of Sterling Elliott. Baseball memorabilia. Contemporary art gallery.

EPCOT – Lake Buena Vista – 100 C2 Two distinct lands come together at Walt Disney's Experimental Prototype Community of Tomorrow. Future World exhibits the technologies of today and tomorrow in a permanent World's Fair. Guests subject automobiles to a thorough examination on Test Track or launch a shuttle to Mars at Mission Space. Soarin' takes flight over the landscapes and landmarks of California. World Showcase provides a place for eleven countries to exhibit their culture, history and cuisine.

ERNEST HEMINGWAY HOME & MUSEUM – Key West – 156 D3 Spanish Colonial-style home of the famous writer is filled with items collected on his worldwide adventures. Original furnishings of the time Papa Hemingway was in residence. Numerous cats, descendants of those belonging to Hemingway, are in residence.

ESPN WIDE WORLD OF SPORTS COMPLEX – Lake Buena Vista – 100 C2 Sports complex provides a preseason camp for the Tampa Bay Buccaneers, an NFL football team. Used extensively for amateur athletics.

EVERBANK STADIUM – Jacksonville – 52 C1 Home field for the Jacksonville Jaguars of the NFL. Built in 1995 on the site of the original Gator Bowl. Seating capacity of 82,000.

FAIRCHILD TROPICAL BOTANIC GARDEN – Coral Gables – 151 B5 Narrated tram, walking or guided tours through 83-acre tropical garden, largest in continental US. Extensive rare tropical plant collections include palms, cycads, flowering trees and vines. Conservatory, rainforest exhibit and Montgomery Palmetum.

FLAMINGO GARDENS – Fort Lauderdale – 147 B5 Free-flight aviary and collection of rare, exotic and indigenous plant life. Narrated tram tours of citrus groves and rain forest exhibit. Wildlife encounter shows.

THE FLORIDA AQUARIUM – Tampa – 105 C7 Four Florida marine habitat galleries trace journey of a drop of water from freshwater spring to open sea. Wetlands, Bays and Beaches, Coral Reefs Waves of Wonder and Heart of the Seas galleries feature over 18,000 aquatic plants and animals.

FLORIDA BLACK BEAR SCENIC BYWAY – Silver Springs – 83 B8 60-mile route from Silver Springs to Ormond Beach traverses Ocala National Forest. Rare plant life and natural springs.

FLORIDA HOLOCAUST MUSEUM – St. Petersburg – 113 A5 Rotating and permanent exhibits honor the memory of millions of holocaust victims. Includes prisoner transport boxcar exhibit and extensive collection of photographs and artifacts.

FLORIDA KEYS SCENIC HIGHWAY – Key Largo – 154 D3 Highway runs the 106-mile length of the Keys, hopping from key to key along two-lane bridges. Outstanding views of the shallow water at the boundary of the Atlantic Ocean and The Gulf. Small historic towns and untouched islands.

FLORIDA MUSEUM OF NATURAL HISTORY – Gainesville – 75 B8 Archaeological, anthropological and ecological exhibits feature over 25 million specimens.

FOREST CAPITAL MUSEUM STATE PARK – Perry – 60 B2 Museum displays exhibits on the logging industry, especially of longleaf pines. 19th-century homestead.

FORT CAROLINE NATIONAL MEMORIAL – Jacksonville – 52 C3 Reconstructed walls of a 16th-century French fort on the banks of the St. Johns River. Site of several French/Spanish confrontations. Interpretive programs.

FORT CHRISTMAS MUSEUM – Christmas – 101 A8 Replica of an 1837 fort featuring exhibits on the Seminole Wars and the Florida pioneers. Seven restored homes exhibit local architecture.

FORT CLINCH STATE PARK – Fernandina Beach – 33 C7 Excellently preserved fort from the Civil War. Park rangers in Union uniforms act out the daily life of a garrison soldier in 1864. Interpretive center. Nature trail.

FORT EAST MARTELLO MUSEUM – Key West – 156 D3 Civil War Martello tower houses exhibits including local historical and military items, clocks and watches and local paintings. Martello forts were invulnerable to the artillery of their time.

FORT FOSTER STATE HISTORIC SITE – Thonotassa – 106 A2 Authentic replica of 1837 fort built during the Second Seminole War to protect the bridge across the Hillsborough River. Park rangers in period uniforms portray life at a wilderness post.

FORT JEFFERSON – Dry Tortugas – 156 A1 Largest brick fort in the Western Hemisphere, once used as a federal prison. Construction began in 1846 and took more than thirty years to complete. Accessible by seaplane or boat.

FORT LAUDERDALE HISTORY CENTER – Fort Lauderdale – 147 A7 Historic village features 1905 New River Inn, 1905 Philemon Bryan House, 1907 King-Cromartie House and replica 1899 schoolhouse. Archives and extensive collection of artifacts highlight state and local history.

FORT MATANZAS NATIONAL MONUMENT – Crescent Beach – 79 A6 Accessible only by ferry, this small coquina fort was constructed by the Spaniards in 1740 to monitor the entrance to Matanzas inlet. Area has been known as Matanzas (Spanish for slaughter) since 1565 when 245 Frenchmen were put to death. Interpretive guides.

GAMBLE PLANTATION HISTORIC STATE PARK – Ellenton – 113 C6 Restored, 1840s mansion furnished with period antiques. Guided tours interpret the life of a wealthy planter of the era.

GATORAMA – Palmdale – 131 A5 1,000-foot covered walkway through habitat for approximately 2,000 alligators and 200 crocodiles. Live shows. Panthers, bobcats and native animals.

GATORLAND – Kissimmee – 100 C4 2,000alligators from tiny to huge. Periodic feedings, tram ride, poisonous snake pit, flamingo lagoon and other animals. 2,000 foot boardwalk through swamp.

GEORGE M STEINBRENNER FIELD – Tampa – 105 C6 Baseball stadium is the home of the Class A Advanced Florida State League Tampa Tarpons. Built in 1996 with a seating capacity of 11,026, it is spring training home for the New York Yankees.

GULF BREEZE ZOO – Gulf Breeze – 36 B1 Over 1,000 mammals, reptiles and birds reside in enclosures simulating their natural habitats. Home of the Florida Wildlife Rescue Center.

HARD ROCK STADIUM – Miami – 147 C6 Football stadium originally named Joe Robbie Stadium for the founder of the Miami Dolphins. In addition to Dolphin home games, the stadium is home to the Miami Hurricanes. Annually hosts the Orange Bowl. Seating capacity of 64,767.

HARRY P. LEU GARDENS – Orlando – 100 A4 Gardens on Lake Rowena feature tropical plants and trees. Orchid house. Butterfly garden. Guided tours of preserved 19th-century home.

HENRY B. PLANT MUSEUM – Tampa – 105 C7 Former Tampa Bay Hotel, built in 1891 by railroad magnate Henry B. Plant. Wedgewood collection, other decorative arts, Victorian furniture and Japanese earthenware.

HENRY MORRISON FLAGLER MUSEUM – Palm Beach – 134 C4 1902 Whitehall Mansion of industrialist Henry Flagler. Collections include paintings, sculpture, porcelains, linen, silver, family memorabilia and period rooms.

Family Outings, *continued*

HERITAGE MUSEUM OF NORTHWEST FLORIDA – Valparaiso – 37 A7 Artifacts covering the history and development of the area from prehistoric times. Focus on the area as a fishing and shipbuilding center. Emphasis is on the pioneer period of 1800-1940.

HERITAGE VILLAGE – Largo – 104 D3 Living history museum features over 28 structures, some from the mid- to late-19th century. Homes include 1852 McMullen Log Cabin and 1907 House of Seven Gables. Pinellas County Historical Museum.

HISTORY MIAMI MUSEUM – Miami – 151 A6 Maps, photos, historical and archaeological artifacts from the time of the Tequesta to the present. Changing and permanent exhibits.

HOMESTEAD–MIAMI SPEEDWAY – Homestead – 150 D4 1.5 mile oval track provides the site for the final Sprint Cup and IRL events annually. Opened in 1995 with a seating capacity of 55,000.

INDIAN KEY HISTORIC STATE PARK – 3/4 mi SE off N shore Matecumbe – 159 B8 11-acre island was the hometown of the ship salvage business of Jacob Houseman. Burned during the Second Seminole War in 1840. Streets and foundations remain. Observation tower, boat dock, shelter and trails.

INDIAN RIVER LAGOON NATIONAL SCENIC HIGHWAY – Titusville – 94 D3 Scenic route runs along a natural estuary, looping back on the other side through beach towns. 233 miles.

INDIAN TEMPLE MOUND MUSEUM – Fort Walton Beach – 37 B5 Large restored ceremonial mound. Museum exhibits regional artifacts from the past 12,000 years. Weeden Island and Fort Walton culture pottery. Early European trade items.

INTERNATIONAL SWIMMING HALL OF FAME FORT LAUDERDALE – 147 A7 Exhibits, photos, dioramas, medals, films, books, murals, art and sculpture—all with an aquatic theme.

ISLANDS OF ADVENTURE – Orlando – 100 B3 Theme park features thrill rides on a series of themed "Islands" around a central lake. Marvel Island features Spiderman: The Ride, an innovative 3D coaster. Toon Lagoon is a water-based theme park, in a three-dimensional colorful fantasy. Jurassic Park River adventure. Wizarding World of Harry Potter. Seuss Landing offers kiddie rides.

JACKSONVILLE ZOO – Jacksonville – 52 B1 Over 2,000 animals and 1,000 plant varieties in expansive natural settings. Raised boardwalk traverses Plains of East Africa exhibit. Range of the Jaguar features giant otters. Themed garden areas. Aviary.

THE JOHN & MABLE RINGLING MUSEUM OF ART – Sarasota – 120 A2 Venetian Gothic mansion of circus entrepreneur John Ringling on 66-acre museum complex. House contains artwork and original furnishings. Art museum specializes in Baroque art with old master works and a sculpture garden. Circus museum features a scale model of a Ringling Brothers circus and John Ringling's private rail car. Historic Asolo Theater, transported from Italy, holds regular performances.

JOHN GORRIE MUSEUM STATE PARK – Apalachicola – 70 A1 Replica of the first ice-making machine, a John Gorrie invention. Historical exhibits dealing with the Apalachicola River and town.

JUNGLE ADVENTURES – Christmas – 102 A1 2000-foot boardwalk. Guided tours include encounters with panthers, bears and tropical birds. Cruise through swamp populated by 200 alligators. Live shows. Replica Spanish fort and Native American village.

JUNGLE ISLAND – Miami – 151 A6 Habitat for free-flying parrots. Birds fly freely among paths and exhibits. Trained birds in live show. Kangaroos and tigers.

KANAPAHA BOTANICAL GARDENS – Gainesville – 75 B8 1.5-mile paved walkway winds through 68 acres of gardens amongst meadows and woodlands. Features butterfly, vinery, herb, bamboo, hummingbird, rock, water, bog and sunken gardens.

KASEYA CENTER – Miami – 151 A6 Home court for the Miami Heat of the NBA. Opened in 1999. Seating capacity of 19,600. Housed within the arena is Florida's largest theater, the Waterfront Theater.

KENNEDY SPACE CENTER VISITOR COMPLEX – Merritt Island – 102 A4 Exhibits, movies, demonstrations and lectures. Guided bus tour around facility. Shuttle Launch Experience. Astronaut Training Experience. IMAX Theater.

KEY WEST LIGHTHOUSE & KEEPER'S QUARTERS MUSEUM – Key West – 156 D3 Restored 1848 lighthouse keeper's quarters houses lighthouse artifacts as well as maritime and military collections. 1848 lighthouse affords panoramic views of Key West.

KIA CENTER – Orlando – 100 A4 Home court for the Orlando Magic of the NBA. Opened in 2010. Seating capacity of 20,000.

KINGSLEY PLANTATION – Fort George Island – 52 B3 Well-preserved big house, slave quarters and stable of a circa 1817 plantation. Museum and guided tours interpret the hard life of early Floridians.

KORESHAN STATE HISTORIC SITE – Estero – 136 B3 Cyrus Reed Teed founded the religion of Koreshanity and this settlement in the mid-1800s. Rangers lead tours of the original buildings. Campground and nature trail.

LEGOLAND FLORIDA RESORT – Winter Haven – 107 C8 150-acre interactive family theme park. 50 rides, shows and other attractions. Includes a water park and Cypress Gardens botannical garden.

LIGHTNER MUSEUM – St. Augustine – 67 D5 Former Alcazar Hotel houses collection of Victorian era items. Featured are Tiffany glass, period furnishings and mechanical musical instruments.

LIGNUMVITAE KEY BOTANICAL STATE PARK – near Islamorada – 159 A8 Only undisturbed natural community left in the Keys. Seventy species of rare trees. Ranger-led tours. Accessible by boat only.

LION COUNTRY SAFARI – West Palm Beach – 134 C1 Drive-through safari where wild animals roam 340 acres. Divided into seven sections with five African areas, one Asian and one South American. Safari Camp Complex includes walk through area with animals, shops and rides.

LOANDEPOT PARK – Miami – 151 A6 Home to the MLB Miami Marlins, the stadium is the fifth to have a retractable roof. Constructed on the site of the former Miami Orange Bowl, the new ballpark is located in the Little Havana section of Miami. Seating capacity of 37,440.

LOWE ART MUSEUM – Coral Gables – 151 A5 Diverse collection of art, artifacts and textiles. Focus on European Renaissance and Baroque works. Modern and ancient American collections. Asian ceramics and sculpture.

MAGIC KINGDOM – Lake Buena Vista – 100 B2 Seven immaculately themed lands surround Cinderella's Castle in the "Happiest Place on Earth." Guests enter through Main Street USA, an image of early-20th century America inspired by Walt Disney's boyhood home in Marceline, Missouri. Adventureland recalls Disney's live films of the 1950s where guests set sail with the Pirates of the Caribbean or explore the world's great rivers on a Jungle Cruise. Frontierland re-creates the old west replete with a runaway train on Big Thunder Mountain. Tiana's Bayou Adventure attraction is based on Disney's animated movie The Princess and the Frog. Liberty Square takes guests back to the days of the American Revolution while Tomorrowland offers a vision of the future. Space Mountain completes Disney's mountain range with an indoor roller coaster that launches guests into the future. Younger guests can meet Mickey and friends at Town Square Theatre on Main St. Classic animated films are brought to life in the New Fantasyland with themed zones, like the Enchanted Forest and Storybook Circus, incorporating more princess stories.

MAITLAND ART CENTER – Maitland – 92 D4 Mayan revival building hosts the works of artists in residence from 1937 on. Collected works of founder Andre Smith. Stone lithography prints by Jerry Raidiger.

MARIE SELBY BOTANICAL GARDENS – Sarasota – 120 A2 Specializes in epiphytes (air plants). Blooming orchids and bromeliads in the Tropical Display House, hibiscus, succulent gardens, bamboo and banyan groves.

MARINELAND – St. Augustine – 79 B6 Performing porpoises, sharks fed by divers and windowed walkways surrounding two large aquariums packed with marine life. More exhibits and 3D underwater film at the Aquarius Theater.

MARJORIE KINNAN RAWLINGS HISTORIC STATE PARK – Cross Creek – 76 D3 Presence of *The Yearling* author is reenacted by a ranger dressed as Marjorie. She gives tours of "her" house, does chores and tends the garden.

MCLARTY TREASURE MUSEUM – Vero Beach – 111 D7 Display of recovered treasure and artifacts from a Spanish fleet. Built at the site of the 1715 shipwreck within Sebastian Inlet State Recreation Area.

MEL FISHER MARITIME MUSEUM – Key West – 156 D3 Display of treasure from the Spanish wrecks *Nuestra Señora de Atocha* and *Santa Margarita* discovered by Mel Fisher. Also includes artifacts from English merchant slave ship *Henrietta Marie*.

MIAMI SEAQUARIUM – Miami – 151 A7 Underwater walkways surrounding two large marine life aquariums. Sharks may be observed from bridges over the shallow shark channel. Shows include dolphins, sea lions and seals.

MISSION OF NOMBRE DE DIOS – St. Augustine – 67 C5 First mission in the US and site of the first Christian Mass in 1565. 208-foot stainless steel cross marks the spot where the crucifix was first planted. Walking tour of grounds.

MONKEY JUNGLE – Miami – 150 C3 Wildlife preserve where monkeys romp in a tropical rain forest while people observe from wire covered walkways. Thirty species including endangered golden lion tamarin.

MORIKAMI MUSEUM & JAPANESE GARDENS – Delray Beach – 141 B7 Japanese villa houses an extensive collection of Japanese art and artifacts.

NSU ART MUSEUM FORT LAUDERDALE – Ft. Lauderdale – 147 A7 American and European art from the late 19th century to the present. Pre-Columbian, American Indian, Oceanic stone and wood carvings, ceramics, basketry and textiles. African tribal sculpture.

MUSEUM OF ARTS & SCIENCES – Daytona Beach – 86 C4 Art, history and science museum holds over 30,000 objects. Cuban art. Chapman root collection of Americana. Tumucuan Indian artifacts, Pleistocene fossils and sculpture garden. Children's museum. Planetarium.

MUSEUM OF CONTEMPORARY ART – Jacksonville – 52 C1 Collection of 1,000 pieces from the second half of the 20th century. Paintings, photography and sculpture. Various temporary and travelling exhibits.

MUSEUM OF DISCOVERY & SCIENCE – Fort Lauderdale – 147 A7 30 exhibits offer a hands-on approach to science. Exhibits on sound and light, as well as Florida ecosystems and minerals. IMAX Theater.

MUSEUM OF FINE ARTS – St. Petersburg – 113 A5 American and European paintings, drawings, prints, photographs and sculpture. Far Eastern sculpture and pre-Columbian art.

MUSEUM OF FLORIDA HISTORY – Tallahassee – 44 B1 Collections present evidence of humans in Florida from prehistoric times to the present. Extensive Spanish treasure exhibit. New permanent exibit: Forever Changed La Florida 1513-1821.

MUSEUM OF SCIENCE & HISTORY – Jacksonville – 52 C1 Natural and physical science and regional history exhibits include an Allosaurus skeleton, marsh room with live animals, sunken Civil War steamship artifacts and science theater. Alexander Brest Planetarium.

MUSEUM OF SCIENCE & INDUSTRY – Tampa – 105 B8 Features over 100 interactive exhibits focusing on science, industry and technology. Massive Diplodocus skeletons. Saunders Planetarium.

NAPLES ZOO – Naples – 142 A3 Many African and Asian animals situated throughout 43 acres of exotic gardens. Only zoo in America with fosas, a Madagascar carnivore. Tram rides, animal performance amphitheater, petting zoo and orchid cathedral.

NATIONAL NAVAL AVIATION MUSEUM – Pensacola – 35 C5 Over 150 aircraft in rotating display schedule. Aircraft engine, aircraft carrier, and Fighter Aces displays.

NATURAL BRIDGE BATTLEFIELD HISTORIC STATE PARK – Woodville – 44 D3 Monument marks the site where Confederate troops successfully defended Tallahassee against Union forces late in the Civil War. The St. Marks River goes underground for several yards and then reappears, creating a natural bridge. Reenactments.

NEW SMYRNA SUGAR MILL RUINS HISTORIC STATE SITE – New Smyrna Beach – 87 D5 Coquina stone walls of the sugar mill are all that remain of a large plantation burned by the Seminole in 1835. Explanatory plaques and nature trail.

NORTON MUSEUM OF ART – West Palm Beach – 134 C4 8,200 piece collection includes 19th- and 20th-century French and American paintings and sculpture, Chinese bronzes, jades and Buddhist sculpture.

OLDEST HOUSE – St. Augustine – 67 D5 Gonzalez-Alvarez House is the oldest surviving Spanish dwelling in the US. Current house built in the early 1700s on a site that has been occupied by settlers since the early 1600s. Guided tours. Garden. Adjacent museum features exhibits on the history of the house and town, from settlement to the railroads.

OLUSTEE BATTLEFIELD HISTORIC STATE PARK – Olustee – 49 D8 Annual reenactment of Confederate victory in Florida's major Civil War battle takes place here in late February. Small museum and trail through battlefield.

ORLANDO MUSEUM OF ART – Orlando – 100 A4 Museum boasts a fine collection of pre-Columbian art. 20th-century American and African art.

ORLANDO SCIENCE CENTER – Orlando – 100 A4 Many participatory exhibits deal with both physical and life sciences. Dinosaurs, medical practice and simulation Earth. Touring exhibits. Planetarium and observatory.

ORMOND SCENIC LOOP & TRAIL – Ormond Beach – 86 B4 Short, 36-mile loop through natural settings of estuary and shoreline.

PALM BEACH ZOO – West Palm Beach – 134 D4 Over 500 tropical animals and birds. Giant anteaters, Malayan tigers and Florida panthers.

PAYNES CREEK HISTORIC STATE PARK – Bowling Green – 115 B7 US Army built trading post, fort and blockhouse here in 1849-1858 in an effort to rid Florida of the Seminoles. Visitor center with historical exhibits and artifacts. Nature trails.

PENSACOLA MUSEUM OF ART – Pensacola – 35 B6 Paintings and graphics with an emphasis on American contemporary art. Travelling exhibits.

PÉREZ ART MUSEUM MIAMI – Miami – 151 A6 Indoor-outdoor museum integrated into gardens focuses on modern & contemporary international art from the past two centuries. Changing and permanent exhibits.

PHILIP & PATRICIA FROST MUSEUM OF SCIENCE – Miami – 151 A6 Extensive natural science collections, many hands-on exhibits and observatory/planetarium. Live animal exploratorium with native and tropical animals.

PIONEER FLORIDA MUSEUM – Dade City – 98 C2 Restored one-room schoolhouse, church, depot and 1864 John Overstreet House contain articles from pioneer family life and other historical items.

POTTER'S WAX MUSEUM – St. Augustine – 67 D5 Over 160 wax sculptures of famous personalities from history and legend in period settings of authentic antiques.

PRESIDENTS HALL OF FAME – Clermont – 99 A8 Life-size wax figures of America's presidents from George Washington to Donald Trump. White House memorabilia and video presentations.

PROSPECT BLUFF HISTORIC SITES – Apalachicola National Forest – 55 C8 Fort built by Andrew Jackson on the banks of the Apalachicola River in 1818. Visible ruins of two forts.

RAVINE GARDENS STATE PARK – Palatka – 78 B1 Nature trails follow three ravines that drop to depths of 70-120 feet. thousands of azaleas bloom in spring.

RAYMOND JAMES STADIUM – Tampa – 105 C6 Locally called the "Ray Jay" the football stadium is the home of the NFL's Tampa Bay Buccaneers. The 1998 stadium features a 103-foot replica pirate ship, in keeping with the team's nickname. Seating capacity of 75,000.

ROOKERY BAY NATIONAL ESTUARINE RESEARCH RESERVE – Shell Island – 142 B4 Mangrove estuary and pine forest. Many wading birds. Briggs Nature Center offers exhibits, scheduled boat trips, 2,500 foot boardwalk and observation platform.

SALVADOR DALI MUSEUM – St. Petersburg – 113 A5 Showcases 99 paintings and over 2,100 other works of art by the famous surrealist.

SAN MARCOS DE APALACHE HISTORIC STATE PARK – St. Marks – 58 A2 Spanish, Native Americans, English, Americans and pirates vied for control of this strategic site early in Florida's history. Museum, nature trail and boardwalk.

SARASOTA JUNGLE GARDENS – Sarasota – 120 A2 Winding paths through twelve acres of landscaped gardens filled with spectacularly plumed birds and animals. Free-roaming flamingos.

Family Outings, *continued*

SCIENCE & DISCOVERY CENTER – Panama City – 54 A1 Children's museum features hands-on exhibits and programs focusing on science, history, cultural studies and the environment. Florida pioneer log structures and grist mill, farming instruments and local historical items. Nature trail and art gallery.

SEAWORLD – Orlando – 100 B3 Marine park features animal attractions, aquarium exhibits, thrill rides and live shows. Manta roller coaster hangs guests upside down over a tropical fish tank. Acrylic tunnel through a shark tank. Dolphins, penguins, manatees and sea turtles.

SILVER SPRINGS STATE PARK – Silver Springs – 83 B8 Glass bottom boat rides and jungle cruises up the Silver River. Variety of cruises emphasize history and ecology of the region. Wildlife exhibits.

ST. AUGUSTINE ALLIGATOR FARM ZOOLOGICAL PARK – St. Augustine – 67 D5 Elevated nature walk around alligator lagoon. Alligator wrestling and reptile show, ziplines and aerial park. Many other animals from wading birds to bobcats.

STEPHEN FOSTER FOLK CULTURE CENTER STATE PARK – White Springs – 48 C3 Visitor center and carillon tower honor the famous composer with dioramas depicting scenes from his songs. Camping, hiking paddling.

TAMPA MUSEUM OF ART – Tampa – 105 C7 15th-20th century paintings and prints, Greek and Roman artifacts, and pre-Columbian sculpture.

TROPICANA FIELD – St. Petersburg – 113 A5 Domed baseball field provides a home field for the Tampa Bay Rays of baseball's American League. Built in 1986 to attract a team, the Rays moved here in 1998. Seating capacity of 42,735.

TYPHOON LAGOON – Lake Buena Vista – 100 C2 Water park themed around a surf resort wrecked by a tropical storm. Wave pool features 6-foot waves. Lazy river ride encircles the entire park. Humunga Cowabunga, a 5-story speed slide among tube, family and body slides. Water coaster.

UNIVERSAL STUDIOS FLORIDA – Orlando – 100 B3 Theme park and working studio offers attractions based around television and the movies. Guests enter through old Hollywood-style gates and find coasters, family rides and shows in areas themed to familiar film locations. Revenge of the Mummy takes guests on an indoor coaster, periodically interrupted by the undead. Wizarding World of Harry Potter™ theme park.

UNIVERSITY GALLERY – Gainesville – 75 B8 Florida archives of photography, Indian sculpture and paintings, African sculpture, pre-Columbian artifacts, graphics and decorative arts.

VILLA ZORAYDA MUSEUM – St. Augustine – 67 D5 Moorish castle built in 1893 by Franklin Smith. Oriental art collection. Guided tours.

VIZCAYA MUSEUM & GARDENS – Miami – 151 A6 1916 Italian Renaissance Palace built by James Deering. Interiors are original materials from 16th-19th century European palaces. Art objects in all media from the same period.

WASHINGTON OAKS GARDENS STATE PARK – Palm Coast – 79 B6 Many varieties of exotic plants grow on old plantation site. Nature trails. Rock formations along shoreline.

WEEKI WACHEE SPRING STATE PARK – Weeki Wachee – 97 A6 Mermaids perform in the Underwater Theatre. Native Florida wildlife shows. Wilderness River Cruises. Buccaneer Bay water park.

YBOR CITY MUSEUM – Tampa – 105 C7 Museum complex features historical exhibits of Tampa's Latin section, cigar memorabilia from the 1930s, and three restored cigar worker's houses.

YULEE SUGAR MILL RUINS HISTORIC STATE PARK – Homossassa – 89 C5 Partially restored limestone sugar mill from the 1850s, consisting of the chimney, boiler and grinding machinery. Interpretive signs serve as a guide.

ZOO MIAMI – Miami – 150 B4 Vast, natural environments for over 2,000 animals on 750 acres. Monorail trips over the habitats of Africa, Asia and the Amazon. Over 375 species include forty endangered species. Aviary. Live shows include up-close encounters.

ZOOTAMPA AT LOWRY PARK – Tampa – 105 B7 Over 1,300 animals on 56 acres of natural habitats. Asian forest, African safari and free-flight aviary. Florida boardwalk features panthers and stingrays. Aquatic center with manatees.

Outdoor Adventures

BIKING

BLACKWATER HERITAGE STATE TRAIL – Milton – 16 D4 Rural rail trail traverses 8 miles of coastal plains. Mostly secluded in wooded terrain, but access points at several crossroads. Connects to Military Trail, a further three miles of former railroad bed. Multi-use.

GAINESVILLE–HAWTHORNE STATE TRAIL – Hawthorne – 76 C3 Multi-use rail trail traverses 16 miles of forests and prairies. Isolated setting through preservation areas provides seclusion just outside of Gainesville. Three trailheads provide access points for trips of various lengths.

GENERAL JAMES A. VAN FLEET STATE TRAIL – Mabel – 99 A5 Former railroad line provides 29-mile trip through central Florida's Green Swamp. Abundant wildlife can be seen as the multi-use path traverses citrus lands and old cattle farms. Four access points offer various length trips.

JACKSONVILLE–Baldwin Trail – MacClenny – 50 C4 Paved, multi-use trail extends 14.5 miles from the edges of Jacksonville to the town of Baldwin. Flat route traverses forest and wetlands with abundant wildlife. Termini at Imeson Road and Brandy Beach Road.

LAKE OKEECHOBEE SCENIC TRAIL – Pahokee – 133 B5 Gravel, doubletrack trail encircles Lake Okeechobee. 110-mile length offers outstanding wildlife viewing opportunities, including egrets and migratory birds. Various access points to trail, which sits atop flood protection dikes.

TALLAHASSEE–ST. MARKS HISTORIC RAILROAD STATE TRAIL – Tallahassee – 44 C1 Multi-use rail-trail carves 16-mile path from Tallahassee to a small town on The Gulf. Partially adjacent to Apalachicola National Forest. Three access points include entrance to off-road trails in the national forest.

WEST ORANGE TRAIL – Oakland – 100 A1 22-mile rail trail offers varied scenery as it passes through small towns, skirts Lake Apopka and encounters a butterfly garden. Six access points offer various possible trips. Multi-use.

WITHLACOOCHEE STATE TRAIL – Dunnello – 82 D3 46-mile trail on former railroad bed offers an extremely flat route with varied scenery. Passes through natural areas, including two state parks, as well as cattle ranches and several small towns. Eight access points. Multi-use.

PADDLING

ALAFIA RIVER – Lithia – 106 D3 Relatively easy float for beginners and intermediate paddlers features a plentitude of Class I rapids. Put-in at Alderman's Ford Park. Takeout 10 miles downstream at Lithia Springs Park.

AUCILLA RIVER – Lamont – 45 C7 One of Florida's wilder rivers features moderate rapids and tight turns amidst crowding forests and limestone banks. Put-in at US 27 bridge near Lamont. Takeout 19 miles downstream at Public River Access on Powell Hammock Road. Several access points.

BLACKWATER RIVER – Munson – 17 A8 Relatively easy 31-mile paddle through flat, coffee-coloredwaterinsecludedforests,wheretreesedge right up to the river. Put-in at Kennedy Bridge near Munson. Takeout 31 miles downstream at Blackwater River State Park. Several access points offer shorter trips.

BULOW CREEK – Bunnell – 79 D7 Relatively easy, partially tidal paddle through coastal marsh. Put-in at Bulow Plantation Ruins Historic State Park. Paddle upstream, then return and continue downstream to takeout at Intercoastal Waterway for a 13 mile trip.

CHIPOLA RIVER – Marianna – 22 C2 Lengthy paddle of moderate difficulty with a few shoals and rapids that can be traversed or portaged. Views of caverns and bluffs on 51-mile route through forests and swamps. Put-in at SR 166 bridge near Marianna. Takeout at SR 71 bridge or at various points in between.

COLDWATER CREEK – Munson – 17 B5 Paddle of relative ease through swiftly flowing water. Put-in at SR 4 bridge near Munson. Takeout 19 miles downstream at CR 191 bridge.

ECONFINA CREEK – Betts – 40 A3 Remote stretch of river is one of the most difficult whitewater runs in the state. Tight turns and swift-moving chutes amidst steeply sloped banks. Lower section of river is calm and acceptable for beginners. Put-in at Scotts Road Bridge off of US 231. Takeout 24 miles downstream at SR 388 bridge south of Econfina. Alternative put-in at Walsingham Park to bypass difficult stretch.

ECONLOCKHATCHEE RIVER – Oviedo – 93 D6 Relatively easy paddle that is suitable for beginners during most water conditions. Put-in at CR 419 bridge near Chulota. Takeout 19 miles downstream at SR 46 bridge.

HICKEY CREEK – Alva – 130 C1 Short, easy trip upstream and back through area frequented by migrating birds. Put-in and takeout at Alva Boat Ramp. 8 miles.

LITTLE MANATEE RIVER – Sun City Center – 113 B8 Beginner level paddle through marshes and forests. Abundant wildlife. Put-in at Leonard Reed Road. Takeout 7 miles downstream at Manatee River State Park or continue through 9 miles of open tidal waters and marsh to Sun City Heritage Park.

LOXAHATCHEE RIVER – Jupiter – 134 A2 Wild river features tight turns and shallow bottoms, suitable for moderately experienced paddlers. Lower stretches are more open and tidally influenced. Put-in at Riverbend Park. Takeout 8.5 miles downstream at Jonathan Dickson State Park.

OCHLOCKONEE RIVER – Jackson Bluff – 43 C5 Moderately difficult paddle with mostly mild current and rare obstructions. Put-in at SR 20 bridge. Takeout 62 miles downstream at Ochlockonee State Park or at numerous access points in between.

PEACE RIVER – Fort Meade – 115 A7 Slow-moving river meanders through forested banks and small ponds on a 67-mile journey. Few difficult stretches on beginner-level river. Put-in at Fort Meade Recreation Area. Takeout at DeSoto County Park in Arcadia or at various points along the way.

PELLICER CREEK – Palm Coast – 79 B5 Beginner-level paddle is a 7-mile up-and-back trip on tidal flatwater. Put-in and takeout at Faver-Dykes State Park.

PITHLACHASCOTEE RIVER – New Port Richey – 96 D4 Open water paddling on tidally-influenced river. Put-in at James E. Grey Preserve. Takeout 6 miles downstream at Sims City Park. Tidal bays offer further exploration.

SANTA FE RIVER – High Springs – 63 D5 Calm, slow-moving river features wide arching curves and swampy terrain. A few rocks and shoals but suitable for beginners. Put-in at US 441 bridge near River Rise State Park. Takeout 26 miles downstream at US 129 bridge.

SOPCHOPPY RIVER – Crawfordville – 57 A7 Slow-moving river winds through the swampy ponds and cypress groves of Apalachicola National Forest. Put-in at Oak Park Cemetery Bridge on Revell Road. Takeout 15 miles downstream at US 319 bridge. One additional access point.

SPRUCE CREEK – Daytona Beach – 86 D4 Easy paddle on freshwater swamp, tidal river, and saltwater estuary. Put-in at Spruce Creek Park, paddle upstream for 8 miles and return to start.

ST. MARYS RIVER – MacClenny – 50 C3 Easy, beginner-level paddle along Florida-Georgia border features the cypress trees common south of Okeefenokee Swamp. Put-in at SR 121 bridge. Takeout 60 miles downstream at Scotts Landing, near Boulogne. Several access points. Abundant wildlife.

SUWANNEE RIVER – Belmont – 48 A4 163-mile stretch of navigable river features a variety of access points to allow trips of all lengths and difficulties. Portions are swift-moving while others are extremely flat. Campsites and access to all types of recreation. Put-in CR 6. Take-out at Anderson's Landing in Suwannee or at many points in between.

TOMOKA RIVER – Ormond Beach – 86 A3 Calm, tranquil river can be paddled by all skill levels. Swampy coastal plains with abundant wildlife. Put-in at Tomoka State Park. Paddle 13 miles upstream and return.

UPPER MANATEE RIVER – Rye – 113 C8 Slow-moving stretch of river between two reservoirs can be paddled in either direction. Put-in at Rye Road Bridge. Takeout 6 miles downstream at Fort Hammer Boat Ramp or paddle 3 miles upstream to the Lake Manatee dam.

WACISSA RIVER – Wacissa – 45 C5 Moderately difficult paddle is usually free of rapids but has some obstructions. Put-in 1 mile south of Wacissa off of SR 59. Takeout 14 miles downstream at Nutall Rise Landing.

WAKULLA RIVER – Wakulla – 44 D1 Wide, slow-moving river can be paddled in either direction. Put-in at CR 365 bridge. Takeout 4 miles downstream at US 98 bridge or return upstream. St. Marks City Park is an additional 4 miles downstream.

WEKIVA RIVER – Apopka – 92 C2 Swift-moving, moderately challenging river through swamps and forests. Put-in at King's Landing, off of Mount Plymouth Road. Takeout 27 miles downstream at High Banks Landing or at several points in between. Primitive camping.

WITHLACOOCHEE RIVER – Pinetta – 28 D1 Gentle, slow-moving river for beginning paddlers traverses hardwood forests. Put-in at SR 145 bridge on the Georgia border. Takeout 28 miles downstream at Suwannee River State Park. Several access points.

WITHLACOOCHEE RIVER (SOUTH) – Lacoochee – 98 B3 Long, slow-moving river features 76-mile stretch of meandering, navigable river. Easy water is suitable for beginners. Put-in at Lacoochee Park or at one of many access points. Final takeout at Dunnellon Wayside Park. Trips of various lengths possible.

YELLOW RIVER – Laurel Hill – 18 A2 Moderately difficult paddle is often swift with many partially submerged logs. Put-in at CR 2 bridge. Takeout 18 miles downstream at Milligan Boat Ramp or continue on to slower part of the river.

FLORIDA NATIONAL SCENIC TRAIL

Designated a National Scenic Trail in 1983, the Florida Trail continues to be developed by volunteers and members of the Florida Trail Association. Once complete, the trail will stretch across the entire state starting at the Blackwater State Forest in the north, down to the Cypress National Preserve in the south. Completed trail sections total over 1,300 miles with enough continuous miles of trail to provide extended hiking trips and many overnight camping opportunities. The trail is primarily a footpath with sections of limited biking and horseback riding. The best hiking is during the dry season starting in late fall through to early spring.

The trail passes through most of Florida's natural habitats:

Southern Florida – including Big Cypress National Preserve, is low-lying, semitropical ecosystem featuring cypress trees, orchids, Spanish moss and ornamentals.

Central Florida – rolling pinelands, palm hammocks, oak forests, limestone caves, and numerous bass fishing lakes. Some of the longer trail sections are found around the shore of Lake Okeechobee and Ocala National Forest.

Western Corridor – pine flatwoods, rolling sandhills, and floodplain forests of the Withlacoochee River continuing along the Cross Florida Greenway through jungle-like forests of Silver River to meet up with the eastern section in the Ocala National Forest.

Northern Florida – known for its rivers, ravines, salt marshes and dense forests. Trail sections cross the Suwannee River and the Apalachicola and Osceola National Forests.

Florida Panhandle – mostly undeveloped small sections include gum swamp forests, steep sandhill ravines near Eglin AFB and the dunes of Gulf Islands National Seashore.

Recreation Areas

Swimming/Fishing abbreviations
S=saltwater; F=freshwater

NAME, LOCATION	PAGE & GRID	CAMPSITES	BOATING	FISHING	HIKING	SWIMMING	COMMENTS
Amelia Island State Park, Amelia City	52 A3			S	•	S	Pristine beaches, salt marshes, coastal marine forest.
Anastasia State Park, St. Augustine Beach	67 D5	139	•	S	•	S	4 miles of beach and dunes, camping, surfing and wildlife viewing.
Apalachicola National Forest, Tallahassee	43 C8	133	•	F	•	F	500,000 acres of longleaf and slash pine (Florida's largest), historic Fort Gadsden.
Bahia Honda State Park, Big Pine Key	158 D1	80	•	S	•	S	Tropical setting, dive shop.
Big Cypress National Preserve, Ochopee	144 D4	72	•	•	•		Primitive backpacking and camping throughout.
Big Lagoon State Park, Gulf Beach	34 C4	•	•	•	•	S	Good picnic spot, sandy beach.
Big Talbot Island State Park, Jacksonville	52 B3		•	S	•		Premier spot for nature study, birding and photography.
Bill Baggs Cape Florida State Park, Key Biscayne	151 B7	•	•	•	•		Popular beach, restored lighthouse.
Biscayne National Park, Homestead	150 D4	•	•	S	•	S	Boat tours, snorkeling, scuba diving, picnicking, within sight of downtown Miami.
Blackwater River State Forest, Munson	17 A7	166	•	F	•	F	Hilly pine forest, sandy bottomed rivers, good canoeing.
Blackwater River State Park, Harold	17 C6	30	•	F	•	F	Located in Blackwater River State Forest.
Blue Spring State Park, Orange City	92 A4	51	•	F	•	F	Manatee's winter refuge, good canoeing and fishing.
Bulow Creek State Park, Ormond Beach	79 D7	100					800-year-old Fairchild live oak.
Caladesi Island State Park, Dunedin	104 B3		•	S	•	S	Natural barrier island accessible only by boat or ferry.
Canaveral National Seashore, Edgewater	94 A3	•	•	S	•	S	20 miles of wilderness beach, sea turtle nesting site.
Cary State Forest, Bryceville	51 C6	•			•		Open air teaching pavilion and nature trail environmental education.
Collier-Seminole State Park, Naples	143 C5	130	•	S	•		Mangrove swamp and marsh, buggy in summer.
De Leon Springs State Park, De Leon Springs	85 C8		•	F	•	F	Canoe access to Lake Woodruff National Wildlife Refuge, popular on weekends.
Delnor-Wiggins Pass State Park, Naples Park	136 D3		•	S		S	Picnic area, popular beach, turtle nesting site.
Don Pedro Island State Park, Boca Grande	128 B1		•	F	•	F	Accessible by boat or ferry only, picnicking, nature study.
Dr. Julian G. Bruce St. George Island State Park, St. George Island	70 A4	60	•	S	•	S	9 miles of undeveloped beach and dunes, primitive camping.
Dry Tortugas National Park, Key West	156 A1	•	•			S	Picnicking, primitive camping, Fort Jefferson.
Econfina River State Park, Lamont	59 B6	•	•	S	•		Nearly 4,400 acres of greatly varied landscapes, spectacular vistas, scenic beauty.
Edward Ball Wakulla Springs State Park, Wakulla	44 D1	•			•	F	One of the largest and deepest freshwater springs in the world, glass bottom boat tours. Nature trails and picnicking.
Etoniah Creek State Forest, Florahome	77 A6	•		F	•		Pine flatwoods, xeric pines, longleaf pine, sandhills.
Everglades National Park, Homestead	154 A1	393	•	F/S	•		Vast sawgrass marsh, scarce services, busy in summer, tours, canoe rentals.
Falling Waters State Park, Chipley	21 C6	24		F	•	F	Florida's highest waterfall.
Faver-Dykes State Park, Palm Coast	79 B5	30	•	F/S	•		Heavily forested, canoeing.
Florida Caverns State Park, Marianna	22 B2	35	•	F	•	F	Cave tours, picnicking, natural bridge over Chipola River.
Fort Clinch State Park, Fernandina Beach	33 D7	61	•	S	•	S	Forested dunes, sandy beach, living history program.
Fort Cooper State Park, Inverness	90 B1	•		F	•	F	Hardwood forest surrounding lake, day-use only.
Fort Pierce Inlet State Park, Fort Pierce	127 B8			S	•	S	Picnicking, surfing, birding on Jack Island, fishing jetty, great fishing from land.
Fred Gannon Rocky Bayou State Park, Seminole	37 B7	42	•	F/S	•	S	Sand pine, magnolia and oak. Picnic area.
Gamble Rogers Memorial State Recreation Area at Flagler Beach, Flagler Beach	79 D7	34	•	S	•	S	Campsites overlook Atlantic, kayaks, canoes and bicycles available for rent.
Gasparilla Island State Park, Boca Grande	128 C1			S		S	Picnicking, nature study, Boca Grande Lighthouse Museum.
Goethe State Forest, Dunnellon	82 C2	•			•		Horse trails, hunting, 15+ different natural communities, rare plants and animals.
Grayton Beach State Park, Grayton Beach	38 C3	34	•	F/S	•	S	White sand beach, dunes and scrub forest.
Guana Tolomato Matanzas National Estuarine Research Reserve, Ponte Vedra Beach	67 B5	•	•	F/S	•	F	Dedicated conservationists, protectors of over 73,000 acres, environmental education center.
Gulf Islands National Seashore, Gulf Breeze	35 C5	•		S		S	Historic Fort Pickens, many different camping options.
Henderson Beach State Park, Destin	37 C7	60		S	•	S	Over 6,000 feet of natural scenic shoreline bordering The Gulf.
Highlands Hammock State Park, Sebring	116 D2	•			•		3,800 acres of virgin forest, abundant wildlife.
Hillsborough River State Park, Thonotosassa	106 A2	118	•	F	•	F	Picnicking, canoeing, swimming in river and man-made lake.
Honeymoon Island State Park, Dunedin	104 B3		•	S	•	S	About 4 miles of white sand beach, dogs allowed on south end, picnic area.
Hontoon Island State Park, De Land	92 A4	•	•	F	•		Accessible by boat or ferry only, primarily wilderness.
Hugh Taylor Birch State Park, Fort Lauderdale	147 A7	•	•	S	•	S	180 acres of Australian pine and beach in downtown Fort Lauderdale.
Ichetucknee Springs State Park, Fort White	62 C3				•	F	Very popular tubing and snorkeling spot, limited parking.
Jennings State Forest, Middleburg	65 A6			•	•		Canoeing, hunting, abundant wildlife.
John D. MacArthur Beach State Park, North Palm Beach	134 B4			S	•	S	Undeveloped barrier island, 2 miles of beachfront.
John Pennekamp Coral Reef State Park, Key Largo	154 C4	47	•	S	•	S	North America's only living coral reef, glass bottom boat rides, scuba diving and snorkeling.
John U. Lloyd Beach State Park, Dania	147 B7		•	S	•	S	Popular beach, picnic area, scuba diving, fishing jetty.
Jonathan Dickinson State Park, Hobe Sound	127 D7	135	•	F/S	•	F/S	11,000 acres of forest, unspoiled Loxahatchee River.
Lake George State Forest, Barberville	85 C7	•			•	F	Hunting, pets on leash.
Lake Griffin State Park, Fruitland Park	91 B6	40	•	F	•		Picnicking, oak, pine, sandhills, marsh setting.
Lake Kissimmee State Park, Lake Wales	108 C4	60	•	F	•		Pine flatwoods and floodplain prairies, abundant wildlife, over 13 miles of trails.
Lake Louisa State Park, Clermont	99 B8	60	•	F	•	F	6 different lakes, rolling hills, scenic landscapes.
Lake Manatee State Park, Bradenton	113 D8	60	•	F	•	F	Pine flatwoods and sand pine scrub, river dam blocks view of manatees despite name of park.
Lake Talquin State Forest, Tallahassee	43 B8	•	•	F	•		Horse trail, picnicking, birding and nature study.
Lake Talquin State Park, Tallahassee	43 B6		•	F	•		Rolling hills, deep ravines, pine and hardwood forests, picnicking at River Bluff.
Lake Wales Ridge State Forest, Frostproof	108 A2	•			•		Large concentration of endangered plants, bring own water.
Little Big Econ State Forest, Geneva	93 D7	•	•		•		Canoeing popular at this location.
Little Manatee River State Park, Sun City Center	113 B8	•		F	•		Scenic picnic area, 12 miles of equestrian trails, many camping options.
Little Talbot Island State Park, Jacksonville	52 B4	40	•	S	•	S	Unspoiled barrier island, 5 miles of beach.
Long Key State Park, Long Key	159 B7	60	•	S	•	S	Narrow beach, shaded campsites, reservations advised.
Lovers Key State Park, Fort Myers Beach	136 C2			S	•	S	Habitat for wildlife, many recreational opportunities.
Manatee Springs State Park, Chiefland	74 D1	100	•	F	•	F	Hardwood and pine forest, canoeing, snorkeling and scuba diving.
Marjorie Harris Carr Cross Florida Greenway, Ocala	83 C8		•	•	•		110-mile corridor with diverse natural habitats and recreational possibilities.
Mike Roess Gold Head Branch State Park, Keystone Heights	65 D5	74	•	F	•	F	Sandhill forest, deep ravine, lake popular in summer.
Myakka River State Park, Sarasota	121 B5	76	•	F	•		Abundant wildlife, boat and tram tours, borders on preserve.
Myakka State Forest, Englewood	128 A1	•		F	•		Open south Florida flatwood and pine forests.
Ocala National Forest, Lynn	84 C2	772		F	•	F	World's largest contiguous sand pine scrub forest, over 600 lakes, rivers, and springs.
Ochlockonee River State Park, Sopchoppy	57 B7	30	•	F/S	•	F	Lightly forested pine flatwoods.
O'Leno State Park, High Springs	63 C5	61		F	•	F	Hardwood forest, natural bridge over Santa Fe River.
Oleta River State Park, North Miami	147 C7		•	F/S	•		River, lagoon, and beach frontage, day-use only.
Oscar Scherer State Park, Osprey	120 C3	104	•	F/S	•	F	Canoeing, picnicking, occasional bald eagles.
Osceola National Forest, Olustee	49 C6	98	•	F	•	F	Pine flatwoods, Battle of Olustee reenactment.
Perdido Key State Park, Gulf Beach	34 D3			S		S	247-acre barrier island, swimming/sunbathing popular, habitat for shore birds and other coastal wildlife.
Picayune Strand State Forest, Naples	143 A6			•	•		22-mile horse trail, equestrian camping, pets on leash, picnicking.
Pine Log State Forest, Ebro	39 B6	20	•	F	•	F	Two lakes, picnic area, abundance of outdoor recreational opportunities.

11

Recreation Areas, continued

Swimming/Fishing abbreviations
S=saltwater; F=freshwater

NAME, LOCATION	PAGE & GRID	CAMPSITES	BOATING	FISHING	HIKING	SWIMMING	COMMENTS
Point Washington State Forest, Santa Rosa Beach	38 C3				●		Sandhills, off-road bicycling, hiking.
Ponce de Leon Springs State Park, Ponce de Leon	20 C1			F	●	F	Picnic area, day-use only, water remains a constant 68 degrees Fahrenheit.
Rainbow Springs State Park, Dunnellon	82 C3		●	F	●	F	Picnicking, canoe and inner tube rentals, fishing popular from campsites.
Sebastian Inlet State Park, Melbourne Beach	111 D7	51	●	S		S	Great surfing, fishing jetty, turtle nesting site.
Seminole State Forest, Leesburg	92 B3	●		●	●	●	Ecologically diverse, horse trail, off-road biking, picnicking.
St. Andrews State Park, Panama City	53 A8	176	●	S		S	Two miles of beachfront and tall dunes.
Suwannee River State Park, Ellaville	47 B7	31		F	●		Dark waters, high limestone banks.
T.H. Stone Memorial St. Joseph Peninsula State Park, Port St. Joe	68 A4	119	●	S		S	Ocean and bay frontage, borders on wilderness preserve.
Tate's Hell State Forest, Carrabelle	56 C3	●	●	●	●	F	Horse trail, hunting.
Three Rivers State Park, Sneads	23 C5	65	●	F	●		Picnic area, hardwood forest.
Tiger Bay State Forest, Daytona Beach	86 C2	●		F	●		Hunting, bicycling, primitive camping with permit, pets on leash.
Tomoka State Park, Ormond Beach	86 A3	100	●	S	●		Canopied forest, picnic areas, canoeing.
Torreya State Park, Bristol	42 A1	30			●		Hilly forests and ravines, several rare plant species.
Twin Rivers State Forest, Ellaville	47 C6	●		●	●	●	Picnicking, horse trail, biking, 14 noncontiguous tracts of land.
Wekiwa Springs State Park, Apopka	92 C3	60	●	F	●	F	Varied forest with abundant wildlife, popular swimming spot.
Welaka State Forest, Welaka	78 D1	●		●	●		Horse trail, pets on leash, east bank of historic St. Johns River.
Wes Skiles Peacock Springs State Park, Luraville	61 A7			●	●	F	Scuba diving, picnicking, two springs, spring run, and six sinkholes.
Withlacoochee State Forest, Lacoochee	98 B4	255	●	F	●	F	Rated one of "10 Coolest Places You've Never Been in North America" by the World Wildlife Fund, abundance of outdoor activities.

Fishing

Lakes

		BASS	BASS	OTHER	OTHER	OTHER
NUMBER, BODY OF WATER	PAGE & GRID	LARGEMOUTH BASS	SUNSHINE BASS	BLACK CRAPPIE	BREAM	CATFISH
1000 Alligator Lake	63 A5	●		●	●	
1024 Bear Lake	17 B7	●		●	●	●
1033 Blue Cypress Lake	118 A3	●	●	●	●	
1039 Boones Lake	16 D2	●		●	●	
1069 Crescent Lake	85 A7	●		●	●	
1078 Dead Lakes	55 A6	●		●	●	
1081 Deer Point Lake	40 C2	●		●	●	
1090 Edward Medard Reservoir	106 C3	●	●	●	●	●
1117 Hurricane Lake	17 A7	●		●	●	
1123 Jensen Savannas Lake	127 A5	●		●		
1126 Juniper Lake	19 C7	●		●	●	
1129 Karick Lake	18 B1	●		●	●	●
1132 Lake Bryant	84 C2	●		●	●	
1135 Lake Butler	100 B2	●		●	●	
1138 Lake Conway	100 B4	●		●	●	
1141 Lake Dexter	85 C7	●		●	●	●
1144 Lake Dorr	92 A1	●		●	●	
1147 Lake George	85 B5	●	●	●	●	
1150 Lake Griffin	91 B6	●		●	●	
1153 Lake Hancock	107 C6	●		●	●	
1156 Lake Harney	93 C8	●		●	●	●
1159 Lake Harris	91 C7	●	●	●	●	
1162 Lake Hart	101 C6	●		●	●	
1165 Lake Hatchineha	108 B3	●		●	●	
1168 Lake Iamonia	25 D6	●		●	●	
1171 Lake Istokpoga	124 A1	●		●	●	
1174 Lake Jackson	43 A8	●		●	●	
1177 Lake Jessup	93 C6	●		●	●	
1180 Lake June in Winter	123 A8	●		●	●	
1183 Lake Kerr	84 A3	●		●	●	
1186 Lake Kissimmee	109 C5	●		●	●	
1189 Lake Louisa	99 B8	●		●	●	●
1192 Lake Marion	108 B2	●		●	●	
1195 Lake Miccosukee	45 A5	●		●	●	
1198 Lake Monroe	93 B5	●	●	●	●	
1201 Lake Okahumpka	90 B4	●		●	●	
1204 Lake Okeechobee	132 B2	●		●	●	
1207 Lake Osborne	134 D4	●		●	●	
1210 Lake Panasoffkee	90 C3	●		●	●	
1213 Lake Parker	107 B5	●		●	●	●
1216 Lake Poinsett	102 C2	●		●	●	
1219 Lake Rousseau	82 D2	●		●	●	
1222 Lake Rowell	64 C3	●	●	●	●	
1225 Lake Sampson	64 C2	●		●	●	
1228 Lake Seminole	23 C6	●		●	●	
1231 Lake Stella	78 D2	●		●	●	
1234 Lake Stone	16 A1	●		●	●	●
1237 Lake Tarpon	104 A4	●		●	●	
1240 Lake Thonotassa	106 B1	●		●	●	
1243 Lake Tohopekaliga, East	101 D5	●		●	●	

Lakes, continued

		BASS	BASS	OTHER	OTHER	OTHER
NUMBER, BODY OF WATER	PAGE & GRID	LARGEMOUTH BASS	SUNSHINE BASS	BLACK CRAPPIE	BREAM	CATFISH
1246 Lake Tohopekaliga, West	100 D4	●		●	●	
1249 Lake Trafford	137 B7	●		●	●	
1252 Lake Victor	20 A2	●		●	●	●
1255 Lake Washington	110 A4	●		●	●	
1258 Lake Weir	84 D1	●		●	●	
1261 Lake Weohyakapka	108 D3	●		●	●	
1264 Lake Winder	102 D2	●		●	●	
1267 Lake Woodruff	85 D7	●		●	●	
1273 Lake Yale	91 A8	●	●	●	●	
1282 Lochloosa Lake	76 C3	●		●	●	
1288 Meritts Mill Pond	22 C3	●		●	●	
1309 Newnans Lake	76 B2	●		●	●	
1315 Ocean Pond	49 D7	●		●	●	
1318 Ocheesee Pond	23 D5	●		●	●	
1327 Ocklawaha Lake	77 C6	●		●	●	
1336 Orange Lake	76 D2	●		●	●	
1339 Palestine Lake	63 A8	●		●	●	
1381 Santa Fe Lake	76 A4	●		●	●	
1396 Talquin Lake	43 B5	●		●	●	
1405 Tsala Apopka Lake	90 C1	●	●	●	●	
1411 Wauberg Lake	76 C1	●		●	●	
1417 Winter Haven Chain of Lakes	107 B8	●		●	●	

Rivers

		BASS	BASS	BASS	OTHER	OTHER	OTHER	OTHER
NUMBER, BODY OF WATER	PAGE & GRID	LARGEMOUTH BASS	SHOAL BASS	SUNSHINE BASS	SUWANNEE BASS	BLACK CRAPPIE	BREAM	CATFISH	SALTWATER SPECIES

NUMBER, BODY OF WATER	PAGE & GRID	LARGEMOUTH	SHOAL	SUNSHINE	SUWANNEE	BLACK CRAPPIE	BREAM	CATFISH	SALTWATER
1015 Apalachicola River, Lower	55 B7	●				●	●		
1018 Apalachicola River, Upper	42 A1	●				●	●		
1030 Blackwater River	17 B7	●					●		●
1057 Chassahowitzka River	89 C5	●					●		
1060 Chipola River	22 C2	●	●				●		
1063 Choctawhatchee River	20 C3	●				●	●		●
1072 Crystal River	88 A4	●					●		
1093 Escambia River	16 B1	●					●		
1114 Homosassa River	88 C4	●					●		
1321 Ochlockonee River	42 C4	●					●		
1324 Ochlockonee River, Upper	25 D5	●				●	●		
1330 Oklawaha River	84 B1	●					●		
1342 Peace River	115 A7	●					●		
1372 Saddle Creek	107 B6	●				●	●	●	
1384 St. Johns River	66 D1	●					●		
1393 Suwannee River	47 B7	●			●		●		
1420 Withlacoochee River	90 B1	●					●		
1423 Yellow River	18 B1	●					●		●

Campgrounds

To locate campgrounds in this atlas, look on the appropriate map for the campground symbol and corresponding four-digit number. Listed are members of the Florida Association of RV Parks & Campgrounds. Public campgrounds, located on state and federal lands, can be identified by the symbol indicated in the Legend. For information on camping in these lands, see Recreation Areas.

NUMBER, NAME, LOCATION	PAGE & GRID	SITES	BEACH	BOAT RAMP	CAMPFIRES PERMITTED	FISHING	FULL HOOK-UPS	GROCERIES	LAUNDRY	ON-SITE RENTALS	PETS ON LEASH	PLAYGROUND	POOL	PROPANE	REC HALL	TENTERS WELCOME
4000 A Camper's World RV Park, Monticello	45 B6	29			•		•		•		•		•	•		•	•
4003 Adventures Unlimited, Milton	17 C5	14	•		•	•				•	•	•				•
4005 Barlow's Fish & RV Camp, Okeechobee	125 C8	47		•		•	•		•		•			•	•	
4006 Bay Aire RV Park, Palm Harbor	104 B3	170					•		•		•		•		•	•
4009 Bay Bayou RV Resort, Tampa	105 B5	300			•	•	•		•		•		•		•	•
4010 Big Oak RV Park, Tallahassee	43 A8	156					•		•		•					
4012 Big Pine Key Fishing Lodge, Big Pine Key	158 D1	179	•	•		•	•	•	•		•		•		•	•
4015 Bluewater Key RV Resort, Sugarloaf Key	157 C5	81		•		•	•		•		•				•	
4017 Blueway RV Village, Fort Myers	136 B3	291					•	•	•		•		•		•	
4018 Bonita Beach Trailer Park Co-Op, Bonita Springs	136 C3	26					•		•		•					
4021 Boyd's Key West Campgrounds, Stock Island	156 D4	220	•	•		•	•	•	•		•	•	•		•	•
4024 Bryn Mawr Ocean Resort, Butler Beach	67 D5	250	•				•		•		•	•	•		•	
4027 Bulow RV Resort, Flagler Beach	79 D7	385			•	•	•		•		•	•	•		•	
4033 Buttonwood Bay RV Resort, Sebring	116 D3	165		•		•	•		•		•		•		•	
4036 Caladesi RV Park, Palm Harbor	104 B3	102					•		•		•					
4039 Calusa Campground Resort & Marina, Key Largo	154 C3	367		•		•	•		•		•				•	
4040 Calypso Cove RV Park, Freeport	38 B3	59	•				•		•		•			•		•
4042 Camp Florida Resort, Lake Placid	123 B8	396		•	•	•	•		•		•	•	•		•	
4045 Camp Gulf, Destin	37 C8	194	•			•	•	•	•		•	•	•	•	•	•
4048 Camp 'N' Water Outdoor Resort, Homosassa	89 C5	89		•		•	•		•		•		•		•	
4049 Camp Venice Retreat, Venice	120 D4	104		•		•	•		•		•	•			•	•
4051 Campers Inn, Panama City Beach	53 A7	114	•				•		•		•		•		•	•
4053 Cape Kennedy RV Resort, Mims	94 D2	147			•		•		•		•	•	•		•	
4054 Carrabelle Beach RV Resort, Carrabelle	56 D4	90	•				•		•		•		•		•	
4056 Cedar Blessing RV Park, Cedar Key	81 B5	77				•	•		•		•		•		•	
4057 Cedar Key RV Resort, Cedar Key	81 B5	99					•		•		•					
4063 Chassahowitzka River Campground, Homosassa	89 C6	53		•	•	•		•	•		•			•		•
4070 Citrus Hills RV Park, Dover	106 C2	283					•		•		•					
4075 Clearwater RV Resort, Clearwater	104 C4	150					•		•		•					
4078 Clewiston RV Resort & Campground, Clewiston	132 C1	124					•		•		•		•			
4084 Coral Sands Oceanfront RV Resort, Ormond Beach	86 A4	37	•			•	•		•		•		•		•	
4087 Crescent City Cherry Blossom Campground, Crescent City	78 D2	80					•		•		•					
4090 Crooked Hook RV Park, Clewiston	132 C2	186					•		•		•		•		•	
4093 Crystal Isles RV Resort, Crystal River	89 B5	254		•		•	•		•		•	•	•		•	
4096 Crystal Lake RV Resort, Naples	136 D4	490				•	•		•		•		•		•	
4102 Crystal Lake Village, Wauchula	115 C7	404					•		•		•		•			
4105 Cypress Campground & RV Park, Winter Haven	108 C1	200					•		•		•					
4114 Daytona RV Oasis, Daytona Beach	86 C3	102			•		•		•		•		•		•	
4115 Daytona's Endless Summer Campground, Port Orange	86 C4	360			•		•		•		•		•			
4120 Deerhaven RV Park, Southport	40 D1	34				•			•		•					
4123 Del-Raton RV Park, Delray Beach	141 B8	60					•		•		•		•	•		
4126 Destin RV Beach Resort, Destin	37 C8	36	•				•		•		•		•		•	
4135 East Toho RV Resort & Marina, Kissimmee	101 C5	300		•		•	•		•		•		•		•	•
4138 Ebb Tide RV Park, Fort Myers Beach	136 B1	148		•			•		•		•		•	•	•	
4141 Embassy RV Park, Pembroke Park	147 C6	67					•		•		•					
4144 Emerald Beach RV Park, Navarre	36 B2	76	•			•	•		•		•		•		•	
4147 Endless Summer RV Park, Naples	142 A4	120					•		•		•		•		•	
4148 Fawn Ridge at Deer Creek, Davenport	100 D1	96					•		•		•		•			
4150 Fiesta Grove RV Resort, Palmetto	113 C6	220					•		•		•		•		•	
4153 Fiesta Key RV Resort & Marina, Fiesta Key	159 B7	324	•	•		•	•	•	•		•	•	•		•	
4159 Fisherman's Cove RV Resort, Palmetto	113 C6	82		•		•	•		•		•					
4162 Flamingo Lake RV Resort, Jacksonville	51 B8	285	•			•	•		•		•		•		•	
4164 Flat Creek Family Campground, Chattahoochee	23 D7	61			•		•		•		•					•
4168 Fort Myers Beach RV Resort, Fort Myers	136 A1	285					•		•		•				•	
4171 Fort Myers/Pine Island KOA, St. James City	135 A7	368				•	•		•		•	•	•		•	
4174 Fox Mobile Home & RV Park, North Fort Myers	129 D6	27					•		•		•					
4176 Frog Creek RV Resort & Campground, Palmetto	113 C6	174				•	•		•		•		•	•	•	
4177 Gator Park, Miami	150 A2	34		•		•					•					
4179 Ginnie Springs, High Springs	62 D4	129			•	•		•	•		•		•			•
4180 Gracious Tiny House Park, Okeechobee	125 C7	21				•			•		•				•	
4183 Great Oak RV Resort, Kissimmee	100 D3	196					•		•		•		•			
4186 Great Outdoors RV/Nature & Golf Resort, Titusville	102 A2	626				•	•		•		•		•		•	
4189 Gulf Air RV Resort, Fort Myers Beach	136 B1	209					•		•		•					
4192 Gulf View RV Resort, Punta Gorda	128 B4	204		•		•	•		•		•		•		•	
4195 Harbor Belle RV Resort, Punta Gorda	128 A4	223		•		•	•		•		•		•		•	

Campgrounds, continued

To locate campgrounds in this atlas, look on the appropriate map for the campground symbol and corresponding four-digit number. Listed are members of the Florida Association of RV Parks & Campgrounds. Public campgrounds, located on state and federal lands, can be identified by the symbol indicated in the Legend. For information on camping in these lands, see Recreation Areas.

NUMBER	NAME, LOCATION	PAGE & GRID	SITES	BEACH	BOAT RAMP	CAMPFIRES PERMITTED	FISHING	FULL HOOK-UPS	GROCERIES	LAUNDRY	ON-SITE RENTALS	PETS ON LEASH	PLAYGROUND	POOL	PROPANE	REC HALL	TENTERS WELCOME
4198	High Springs Campground, High Springs	63 D6	45			•		•		•	•	•	•	•		•	•
4201	Hillcrest RV Resort, Zephyrhills	98 D2	502					•		•		•		•	•	•	
4204	Holiday Campground, Panacea	57 C8	75				•			•		•					
4210	Holiday RV Park, Leesburg	91 C6	935		•	•	•	•		•		•		•		•	
4212	Homebound RV Parks-Bushnell, Bushnell	90 D2	125					•		•		•		•		•	
4213	Horseshoe Cove RV Resort, Bradenton	113 D7	470				•			•		•		•		•	
4228	Jennings KOA, Jennings	47 A7	102			•		•		•		•	•	•		•	•
4231	Jolly Roger RV Resort, Marathon	159 C5	160		•		•	•		•		•		•		•	
4234	Juno Ocean Walk RV Resort, Juno Beach	134 B4	246					•		•		•		•		•	
4237	Kelly's RV Park, White Springs	48 C4	72					•		•		•			•	•	
4243	Kings Kamp RV Park & Marina, Key Largo	154 C4	62	•	•		•	•		•		•			•		
4244	Kissimmee RV Park, Kissimmee	100 C3	193					•		•	•	•	•	•		•	
4246	Kozy Kampers RV Park, Fort Lauderdale	147 A6	103					•		•	•	•		•		•	
4249	LaBontes Garden RV Park, North Fort Myers	129 C6	28					•		•		•					
4252	Lake Bonnet Village Mobile Home & RV Resort, Avon Park	116 C3	175		•		•	•		•		•		•		•	
4253	Lathrom's Landing RV Park South, Mims	94 C2	60				•	•		•		•				•	
4255	Lazy Days RV Resot, Seffner	106 B1	300					•		•		•		•		•	
4258	Lazy J Mobile Home & RV Park, Fort Myers	129 D7	58				•	•		•		•					
4261	Lazy Lakes RV Resort, Sugarloaf Key	157 C6	99				•	•		•		•		•		•	•
4267	Leisure Days RV Resort, Zephyrhills	98 D2	240					•		•		•		•		•	
4270	Lelynn RV Resort, Polk City	107 A7	360		•		•	•		•		•		•		•	
4273	Lone Pine RV Park, Ruskin	113 A7	68					•		•		•					
4276	Mango/Oak Manor, Cape Canaveral	103 C5	50					•		•		•					•
4278	Mexico Beach RV Resort, Mexico Beach	54 C4	32			•	•	•		•		•		•		•	
4279	Miami Everglades RV Resort, Miami	150 C3	267					•		•		•		•		•	
4285	Morgan's RV Park, Lakeland	107 B6	30					•		•		•					
4291	Naples/Marco Island KOA, Naples	142 B4	140			•		•		•	•	•		•		•	•
4294	Navarre Beach Camping Resort, Navarre	36 B2	105	•	•	•	•	•		•		•		•		•	•
4300	New Smyrna Beach RV Park & Campground, New Smyrna Beach	94 A1	202					•		•		•		•		•	
4303	North Beach Camp Resort, Usinas Beach	67 C5	150	•			•	•		•		•		•		•	
4309	Nova Family Campground, Port Orange	86 C4	351				•			•		•		•		•	
4312	Ocala RV Camp Resort, Ocala	83 C6	186					•		•		•		•		•	
4315	Ocean Grove RV Resort, Butler Beach	67 D5	208		•			•		•		•		•		•	
4318	Ocklawaha Canoe Outpost & Resort, Eureka	84 A2	14				•			•		•					
4321	Okeechobee KOA, Okeechobee	125 B7	750				•	•		•		•	•	•		•	
4324	Okeechobee Landings RV Resort, Clewiston	132 C2	270					•		•		•		•		•	
4327	Orange City RV Resort, Orange City	93 A5	525					•		•		•		•		•	
4333	Orlando/Kissimmee KOA, Kissimmee	100 C3	70					•		•		•		•		•	
4336	Orlando NW/Orange Blossom KOA, Apopka	92 D2	92					•		•		•		•		•	
4337	Orlando RV Resort, Clermont	99 C8	1017		•		•	•		•		•		•		•	
4342	Orlando Southwest KOA, Davenport	100 D1	203					•		•		•		•		•	
4344	Outdoor Resorts of Chokoloskee, Chokoloskee	143 D8	283		•		•	•		•		•		•		•	
4346	Palm Bay RV Park & Mobile Home, Palmetto	113 C6	103					•		•		•					
4347	Palm Beach Traveler RV Park, Lantana	141 A7	102					•		•		•		•		•	
4351	Parramore's Fish Camp & RV Resort, Astor	85 C6	72		•		•	•		•	•	•				•	•
4354	Peace River Campground, Arcadia	122 B2	225	•	•		•	•		•		•				•	•
4363	PepperTree RV Resort, Butler Beach	67 D5	17					•		•		•		•		•	
4366	Perry KOA, Perry	60 B2	115			•		•		•		•		•		•	•
4369	Pine Lake RV Park, Fountain	40 A4	135			•	•	•		•		•		•		•	
4372	Pioneer Creek RV Resort, Bowling Green	115 B7	377					•		•		•		•		•	
4375	Pioneer Village RV Resort, Fort Myers	129 C7	505					•		•		•		•		•	
4378	Ponderosa RV Park, Kissimmee	100 C4	200					•		•		•		•		•	•
4384	Quail Run RV Resort, Wesley Chapel	97 D8	292					•		•	•	•		•		•	
4386	Ragans Family Campground, Madison	46 C4	160	•		•		•		•		•	•	•		•	•
4390	Rainbow Village of Zephyrhills, Zephyrhills	98 D2	382					•		•		•		•		•	
4393	Raintree RV Resort, North Fort Myers	129 C6	340					•		•		•		•		•	
4396	Ramblers Rest RV Campground, Venice	121 D5	647		•		•	•		•		•		•		•	•
4399	Recreation Plantation RV Resort, Lady Lake	91 A5	1079					•		•		•		•		•	
4405	River Oaks RV Resort, Ruskin	113 B7	115		•			•		•		•					
4408	Riverside Lodge Resort, Inverness	90 B2	23		•		•			•		•					•
4409	River Vista RV Village, Ruskin	113 B7	400		•		•	•		•		•		•		•	
4411	Road Runner Travel Resort, Fort Pierce	119 D8	452				•	•		•		•		•		•	
4414	Royal Coachman RV Resort, Nokomis	120 C3	561				•	•		•		•		•		•	
4420	San Carlos RV Resort & Marina, Fort Myers Beach	136 B1	142		•		•	•		•		•		•		•	
4423	Sandy Oaks RV Resort, Beverly Hills	89 A7	185				•	•		•	•	•		•	•	•	

Continued on page 160

14

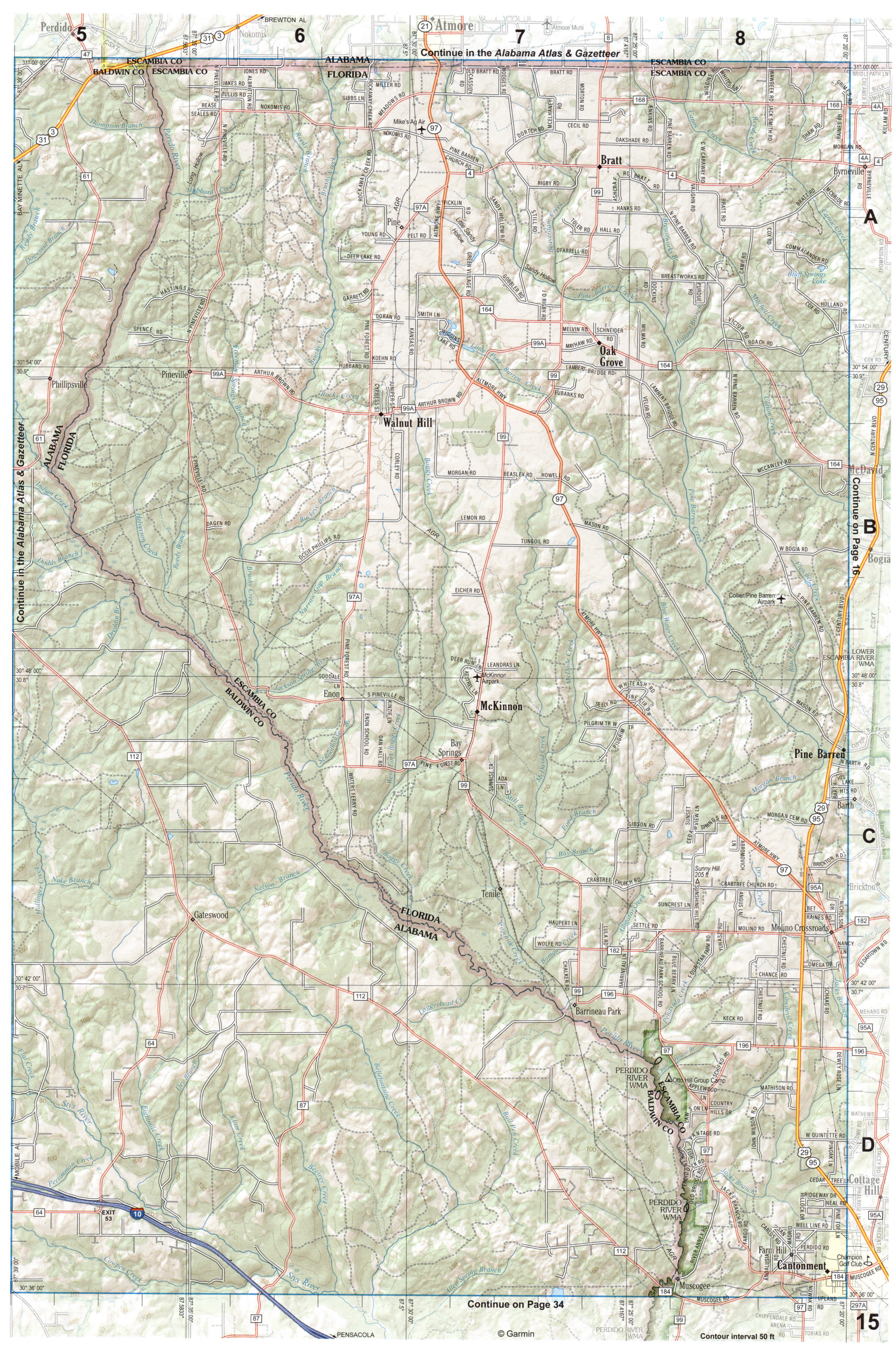

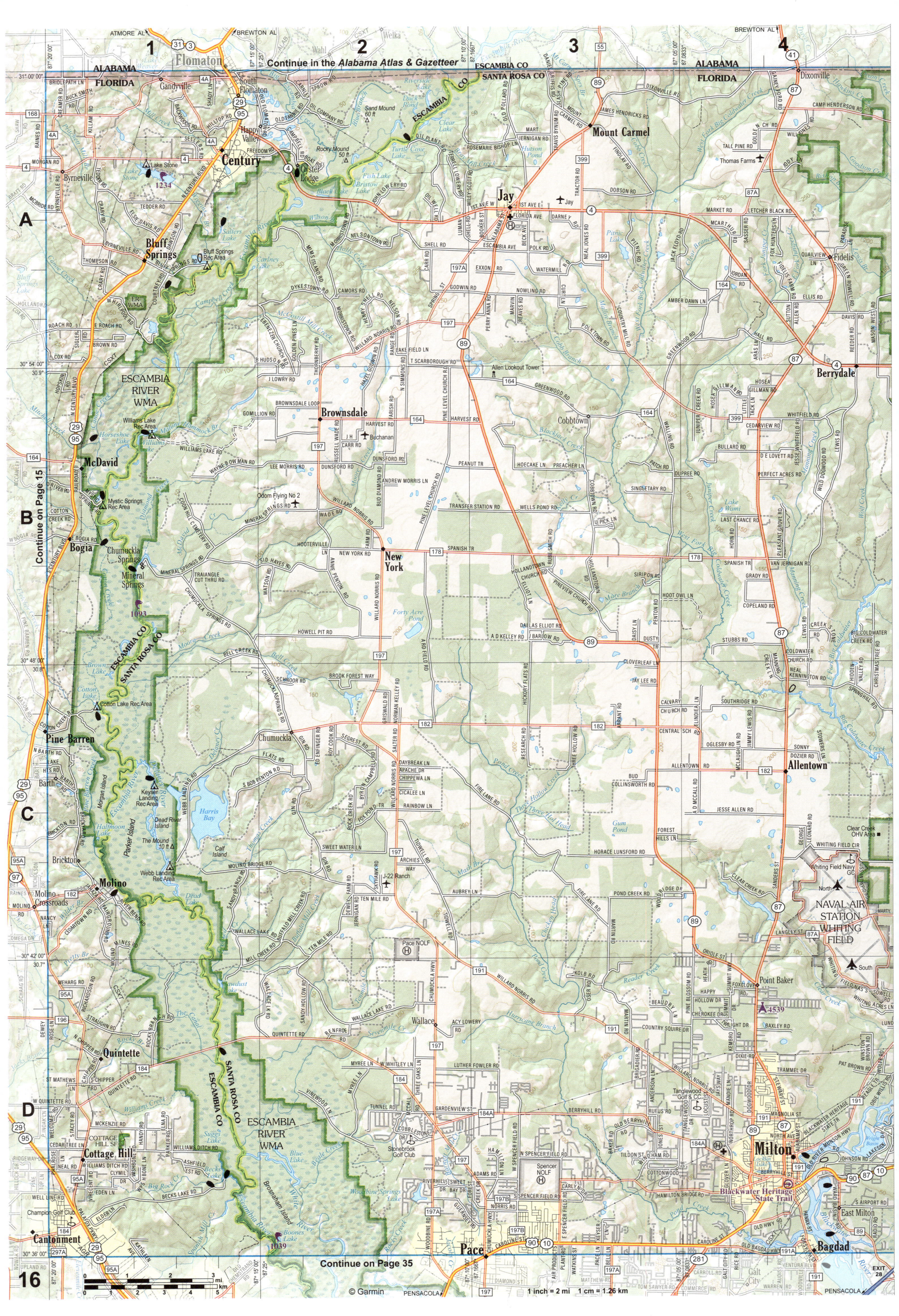

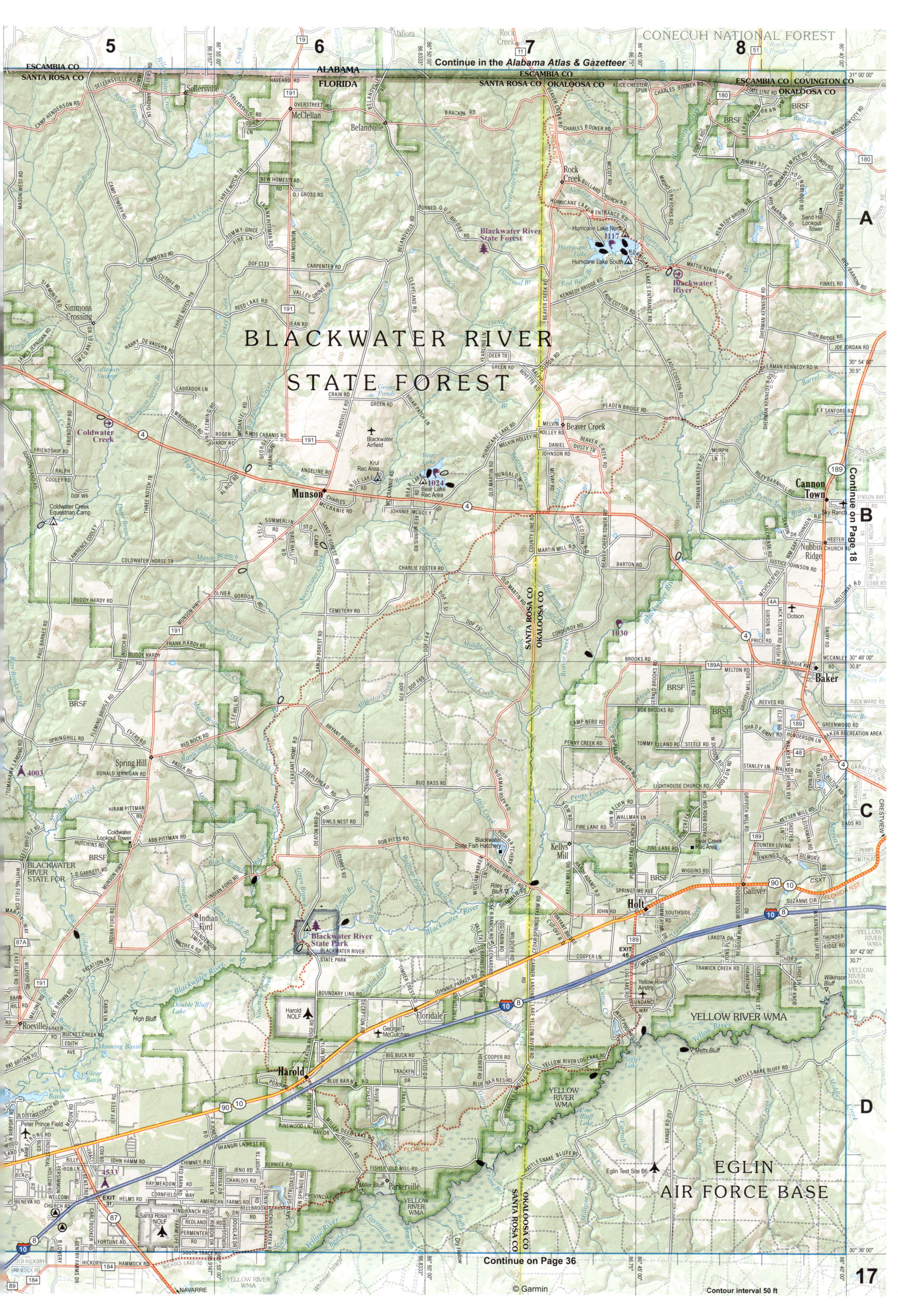

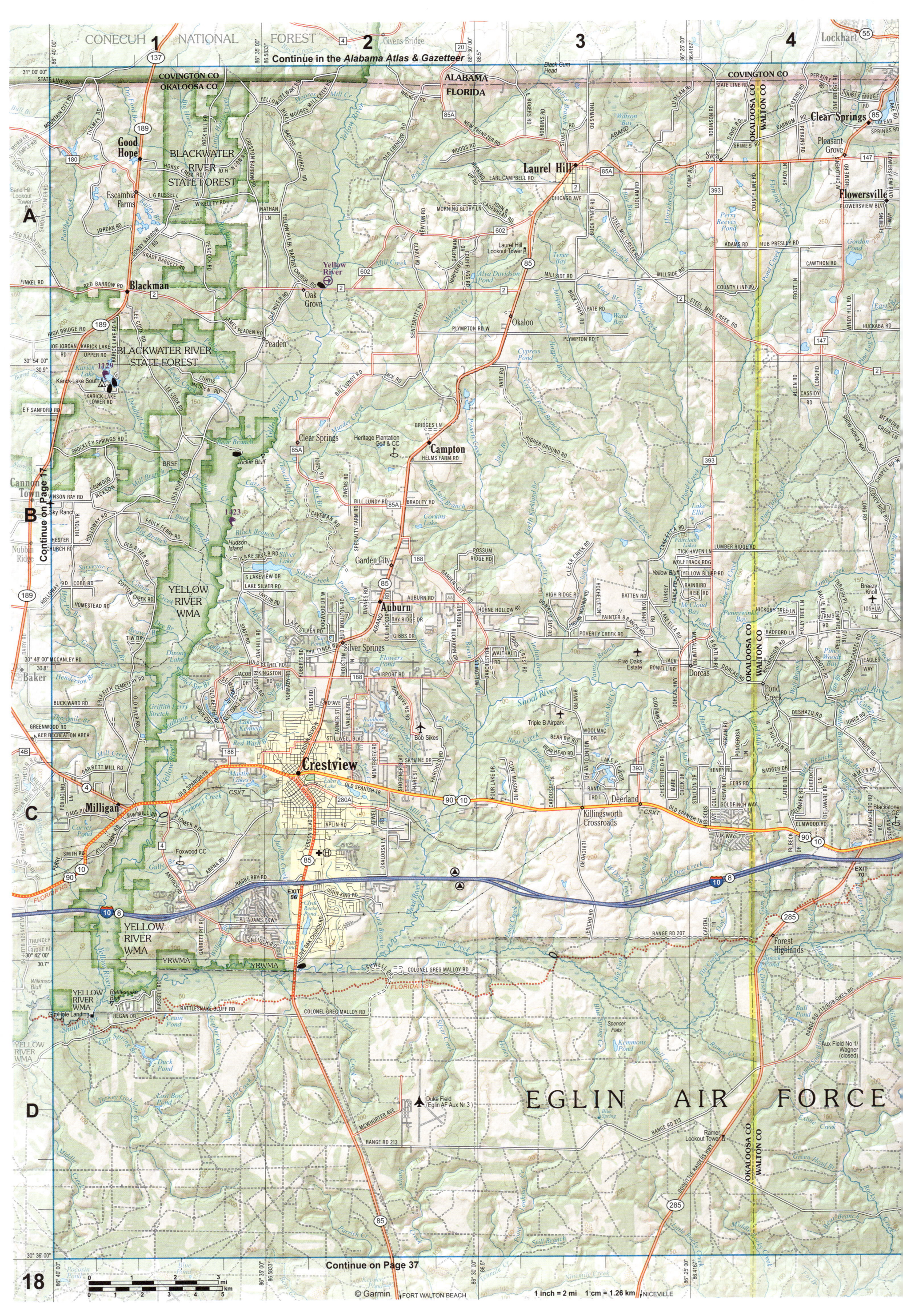

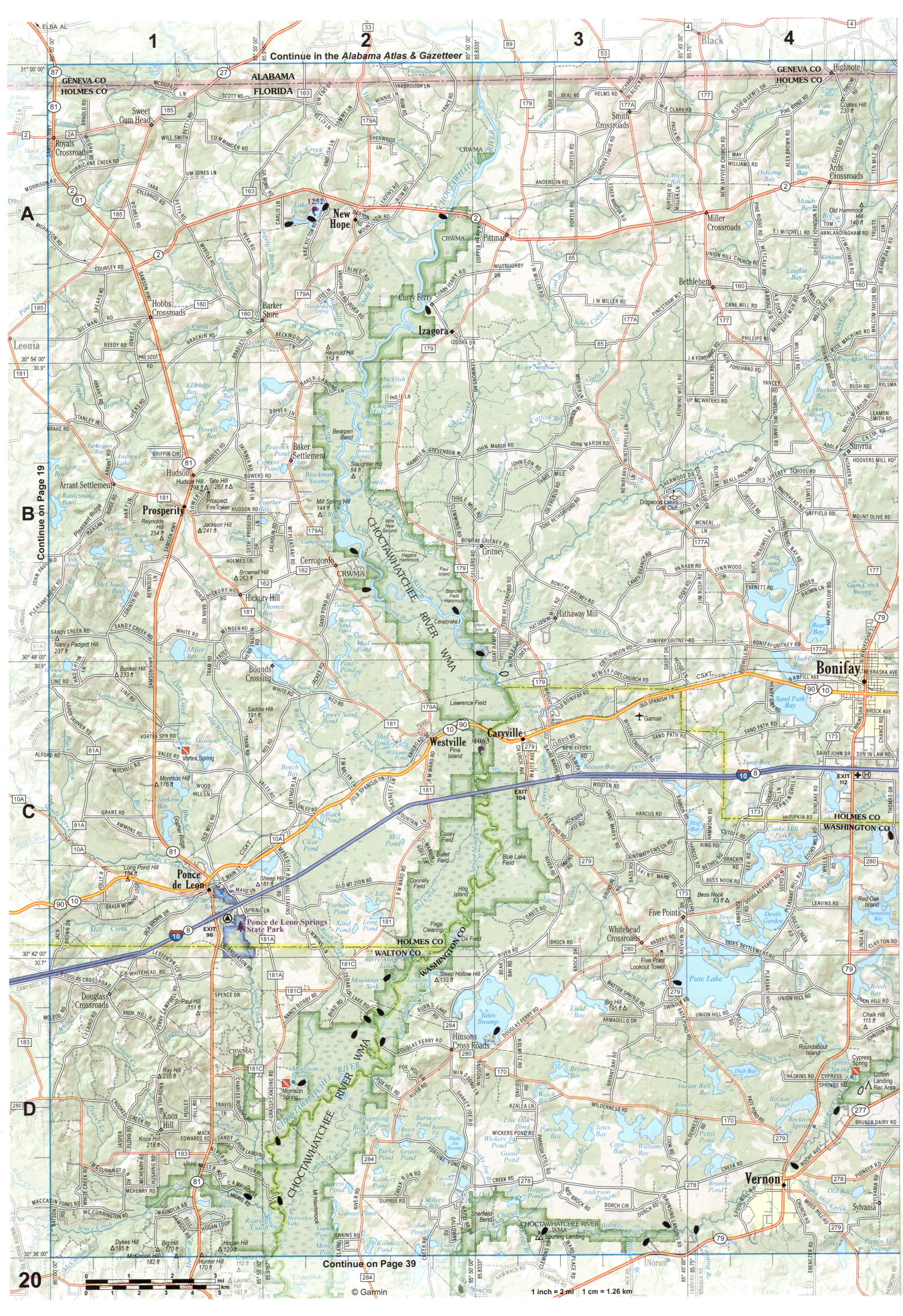

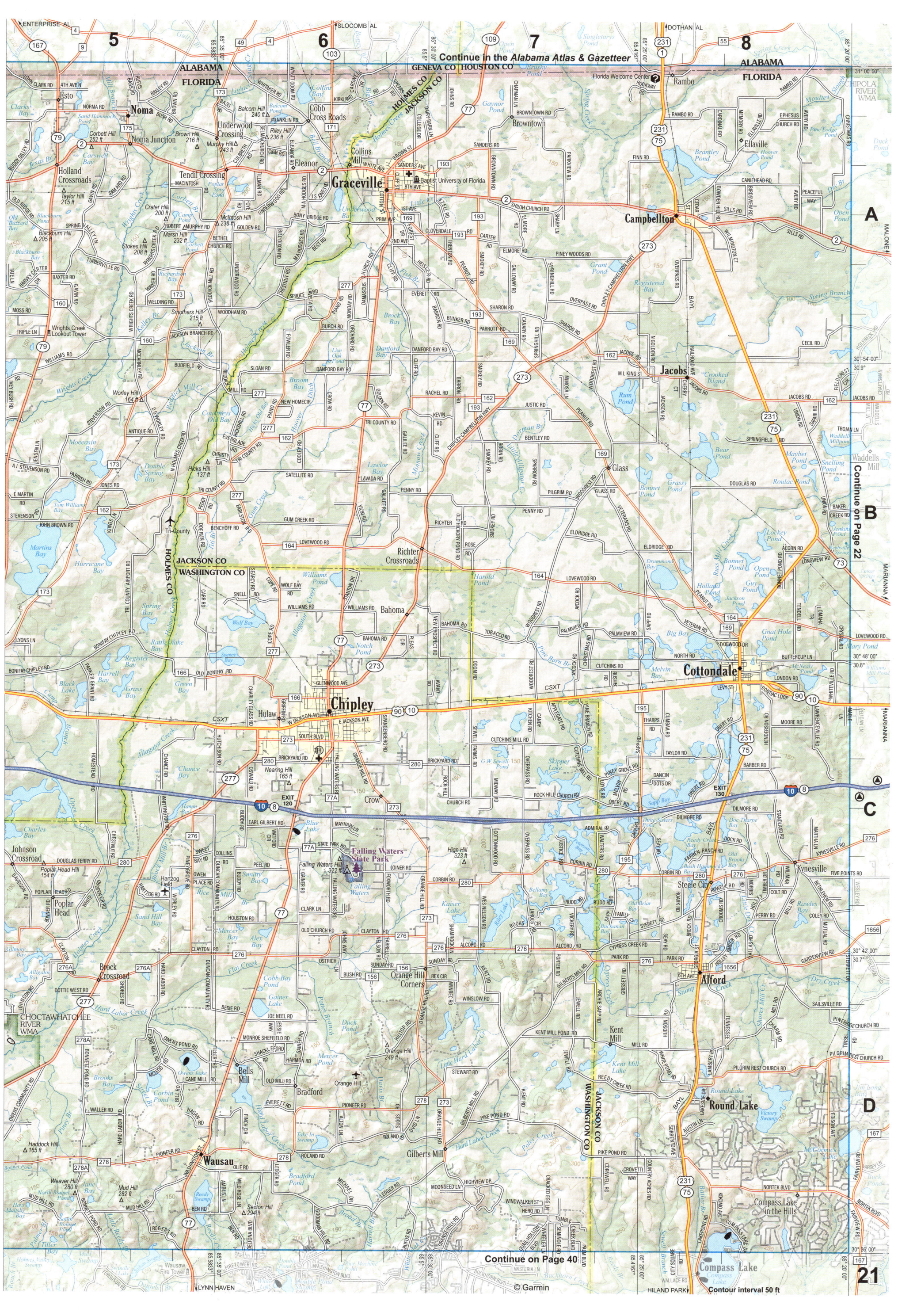

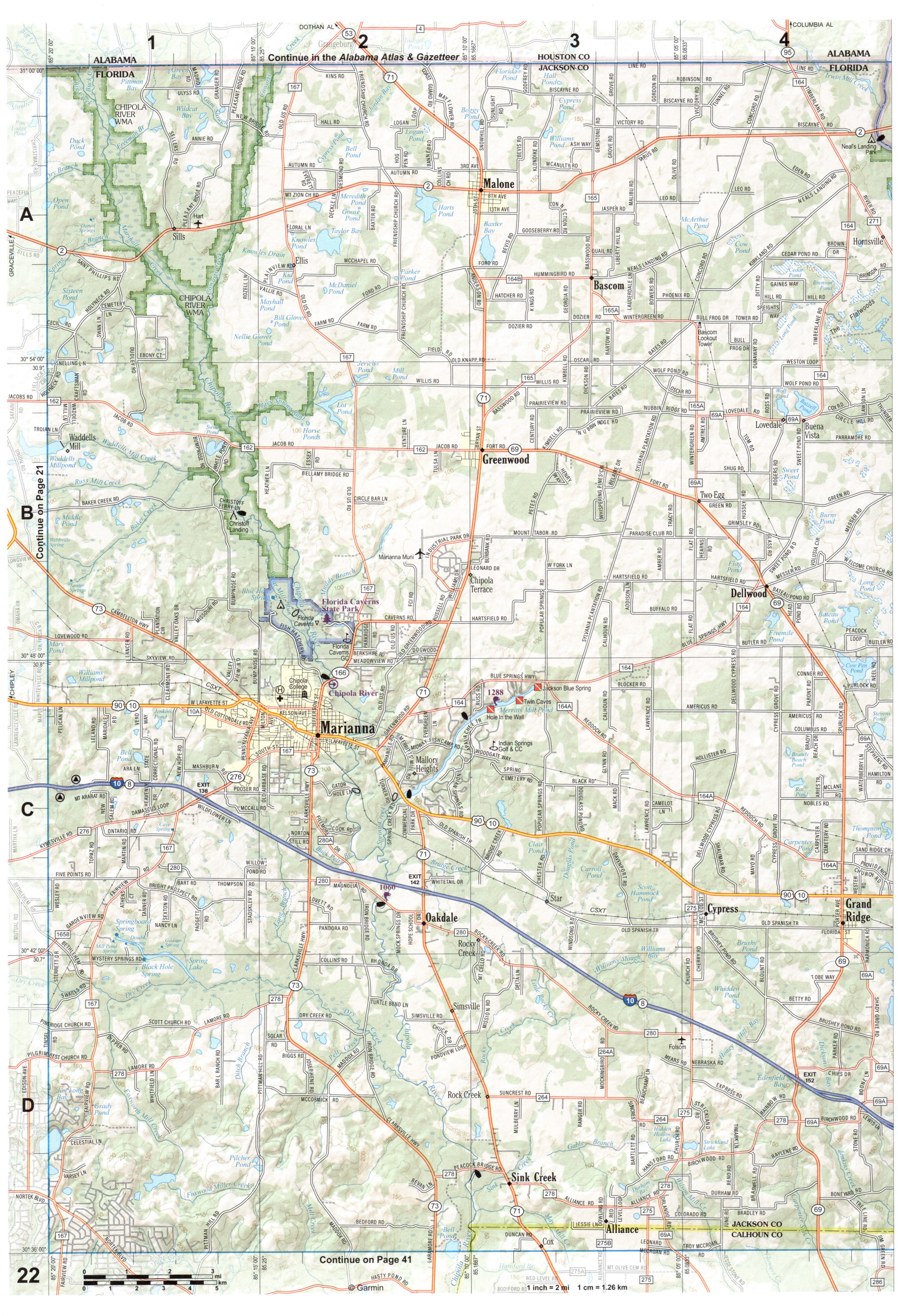

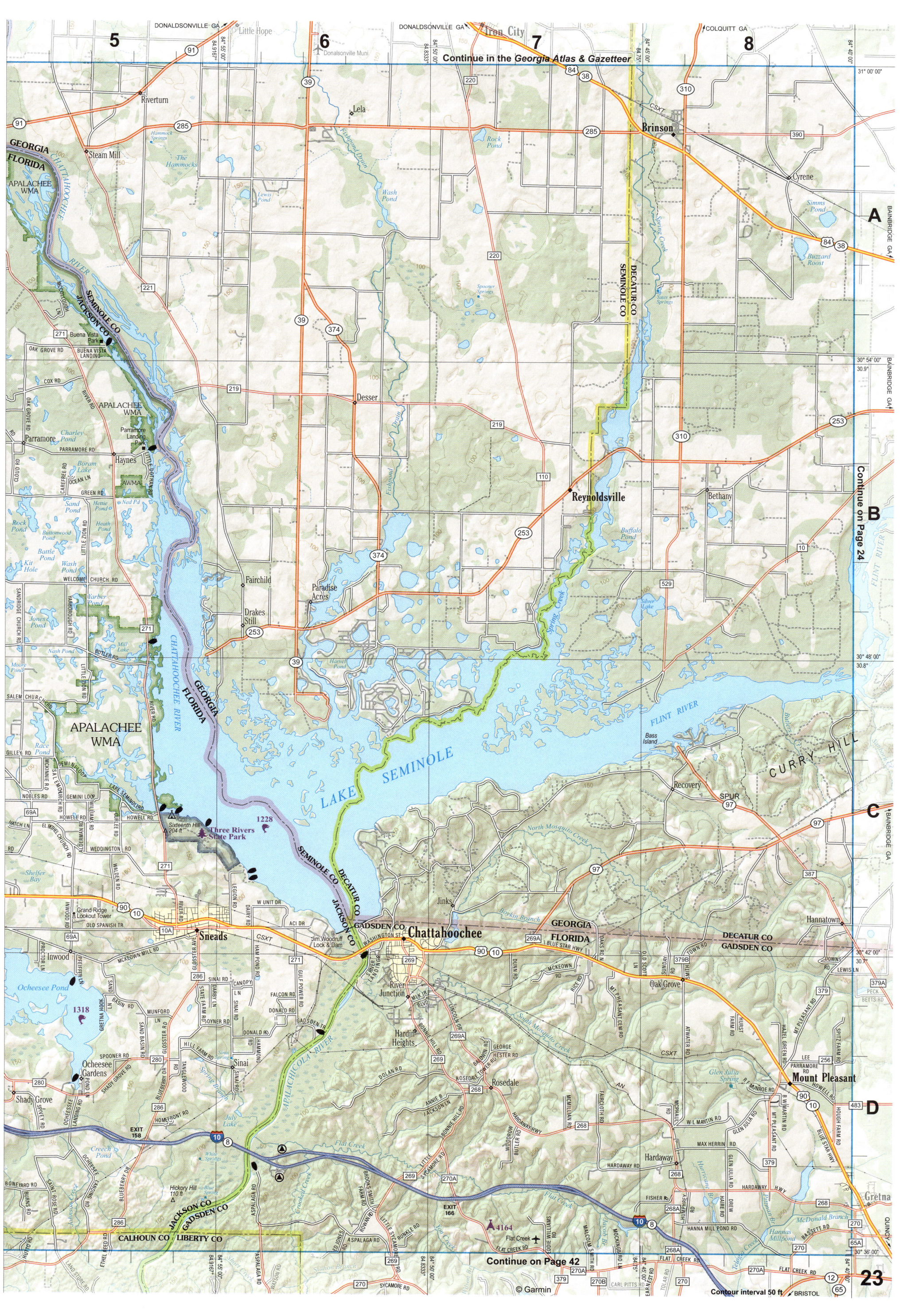

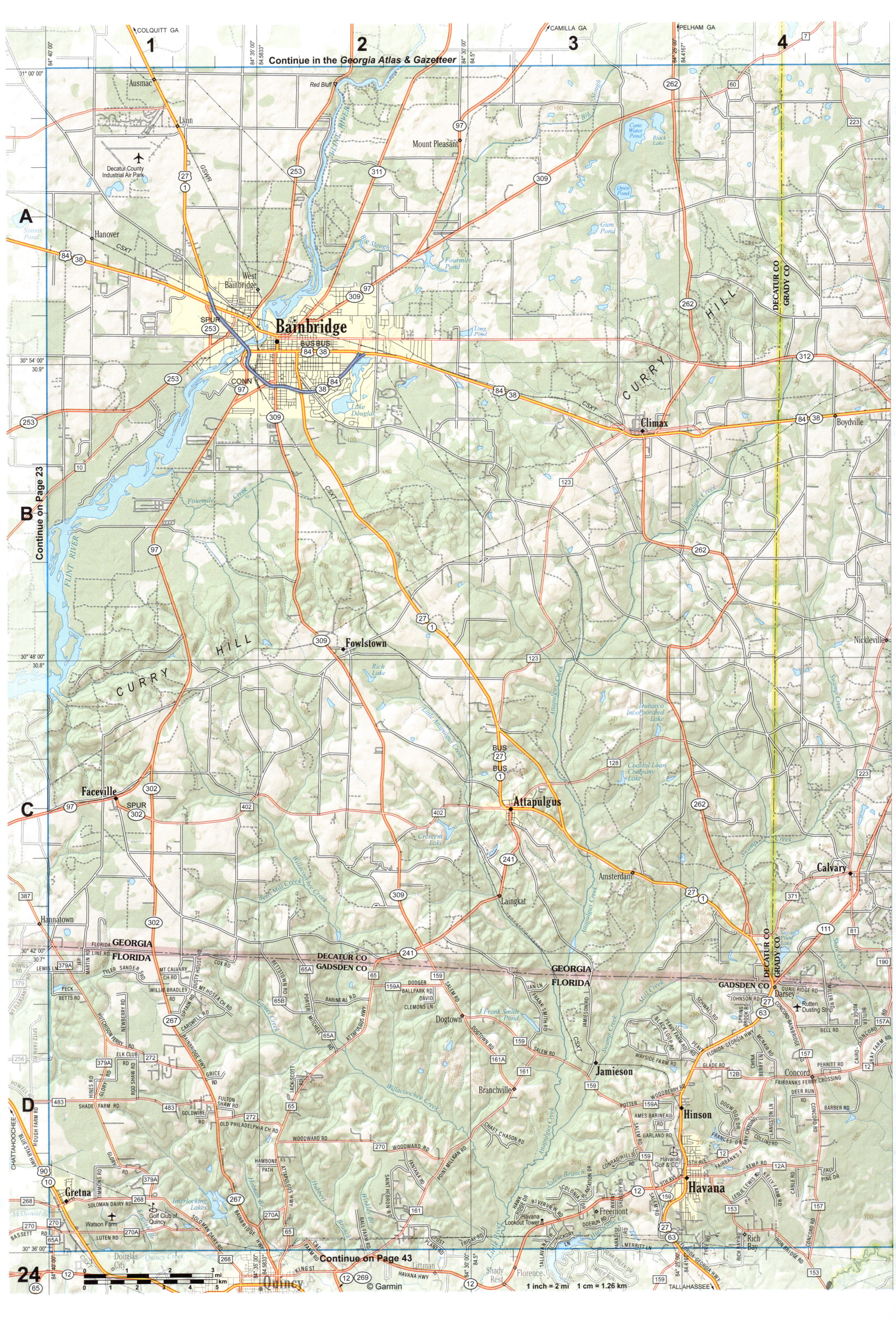

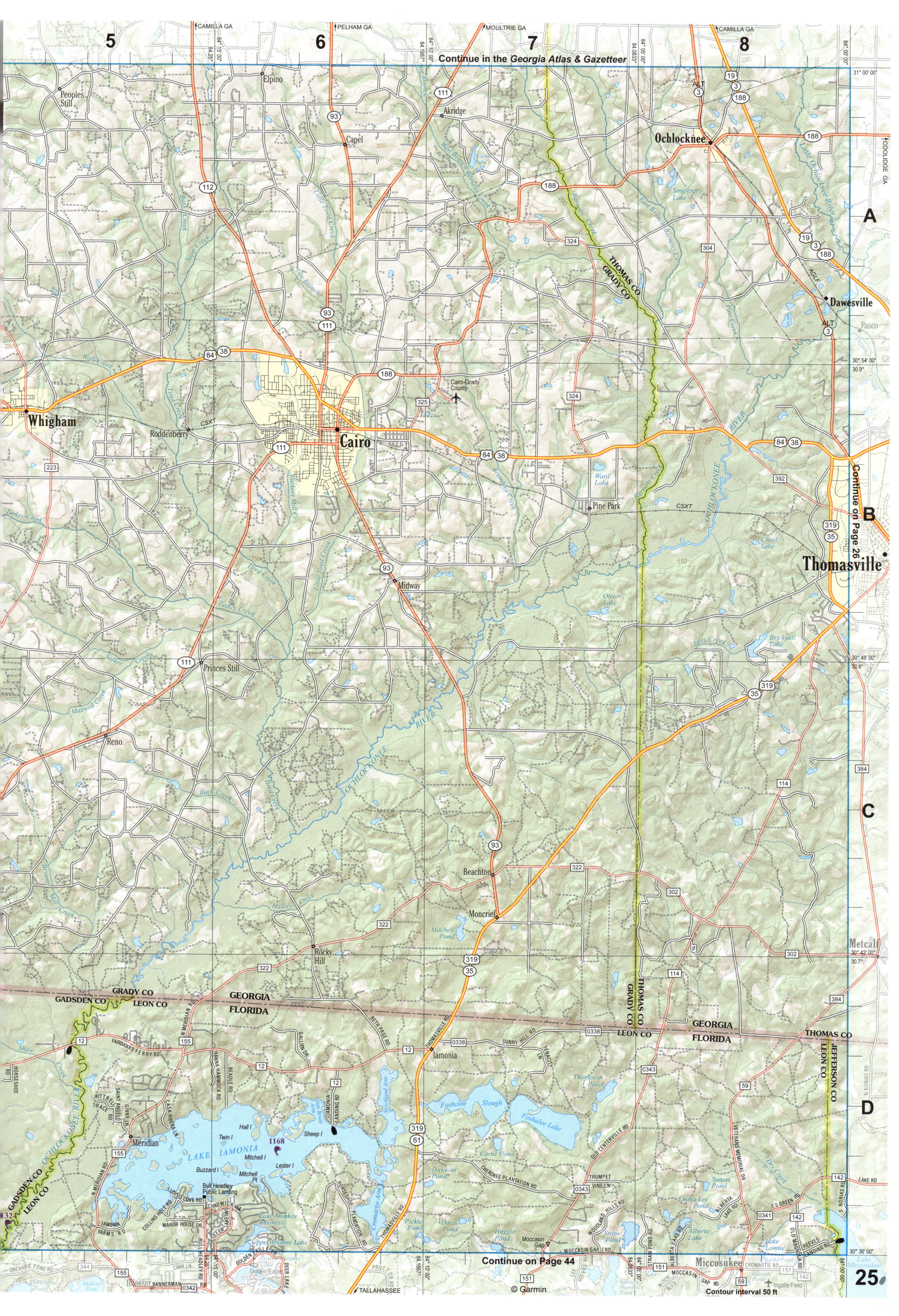

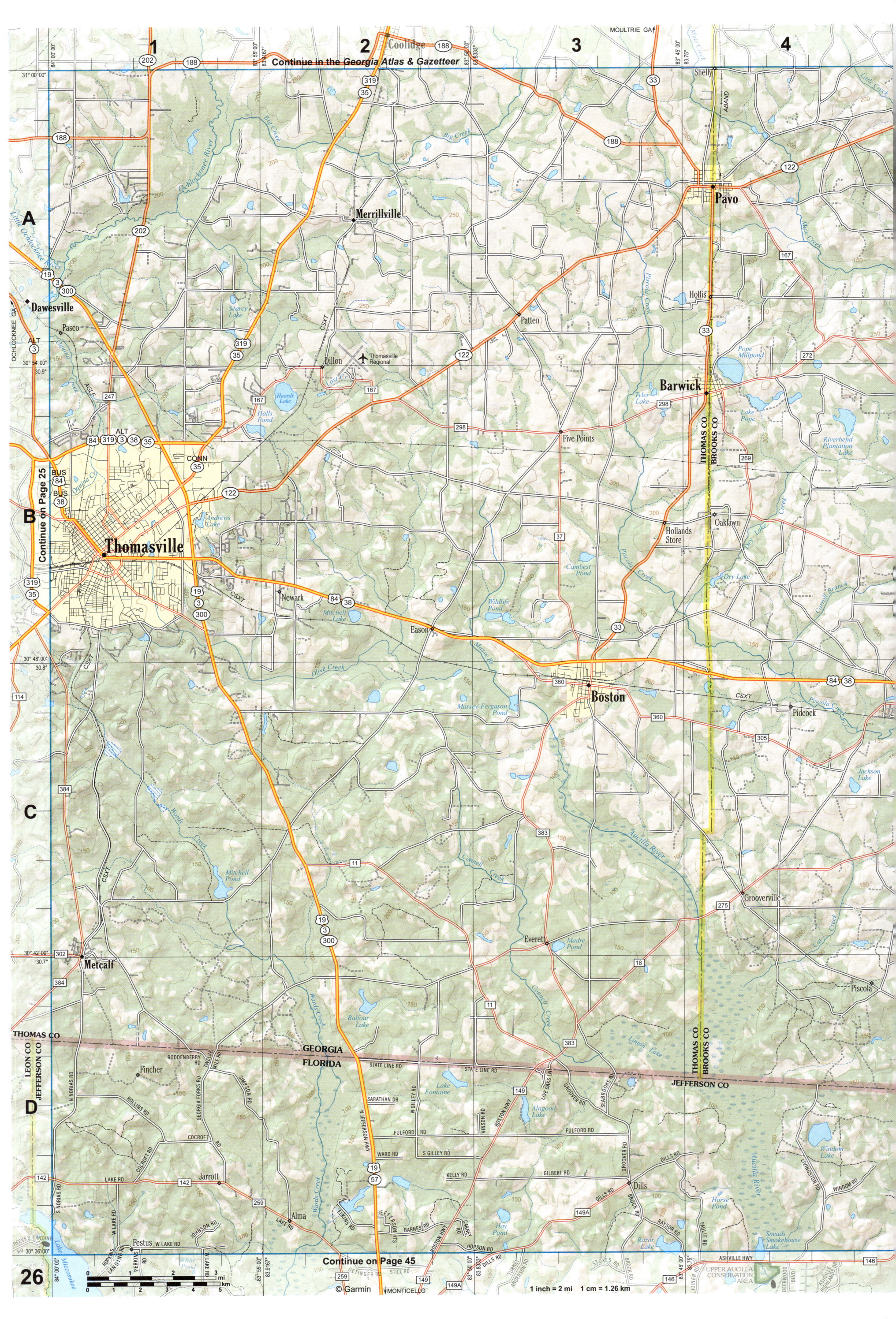

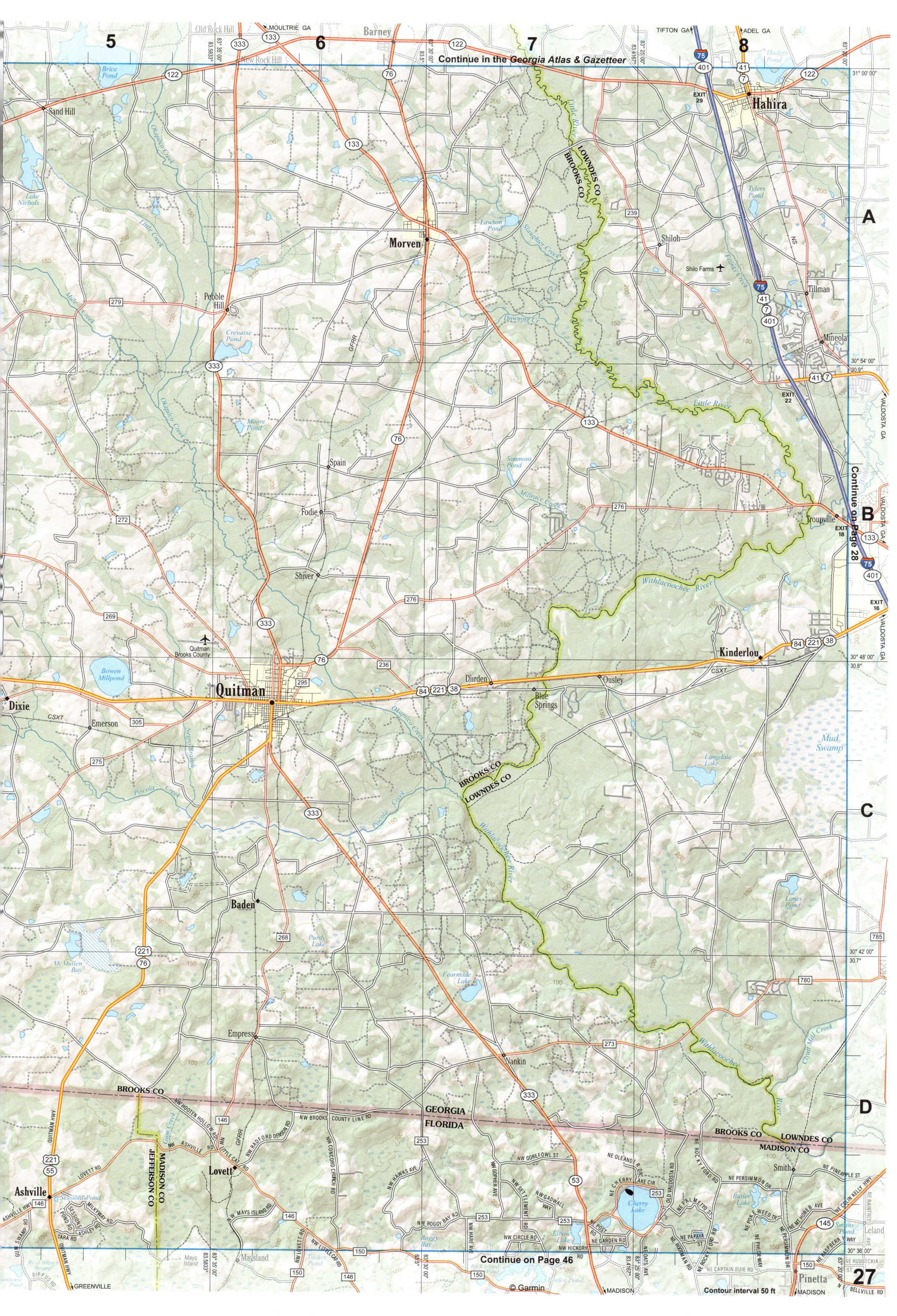

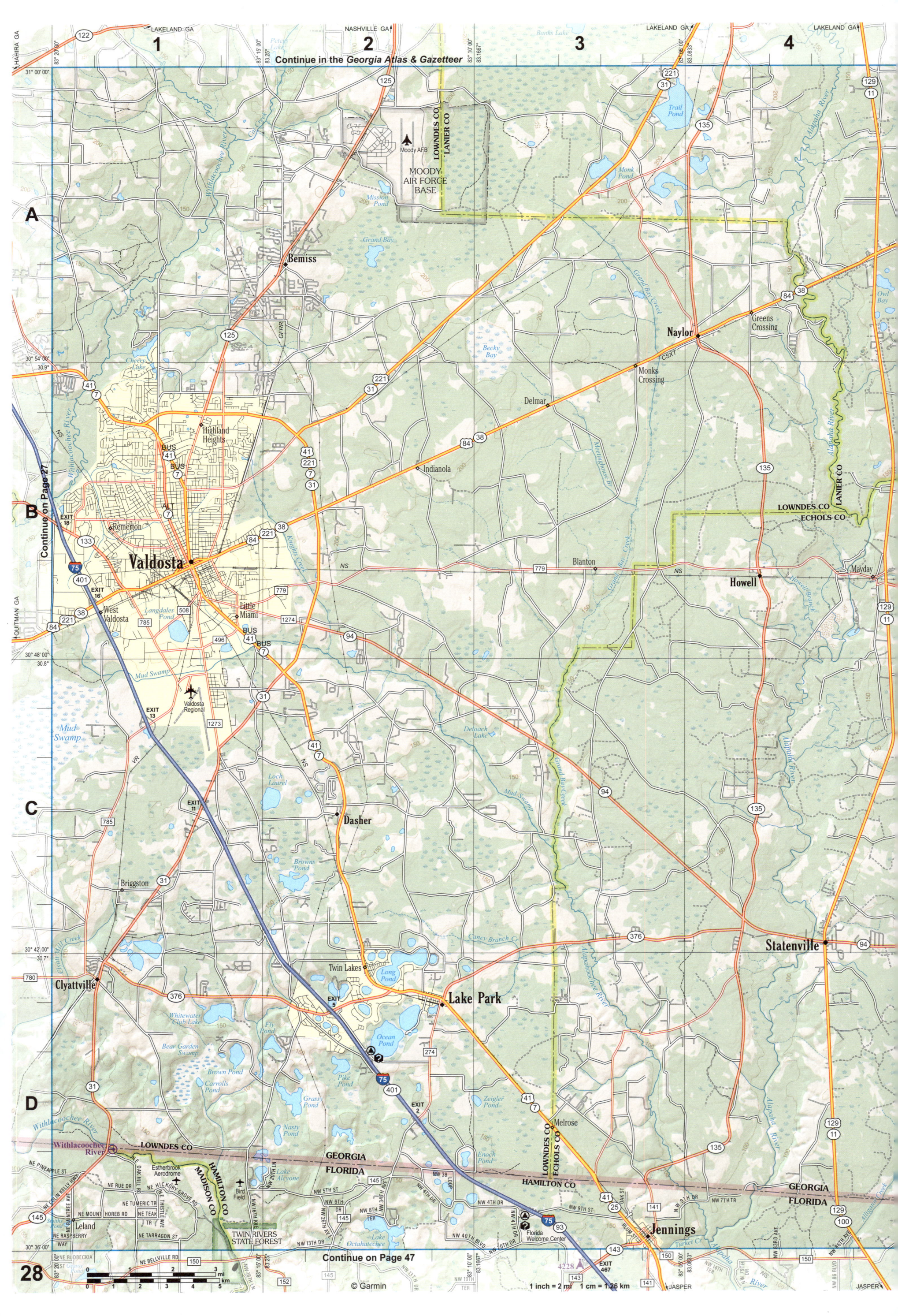

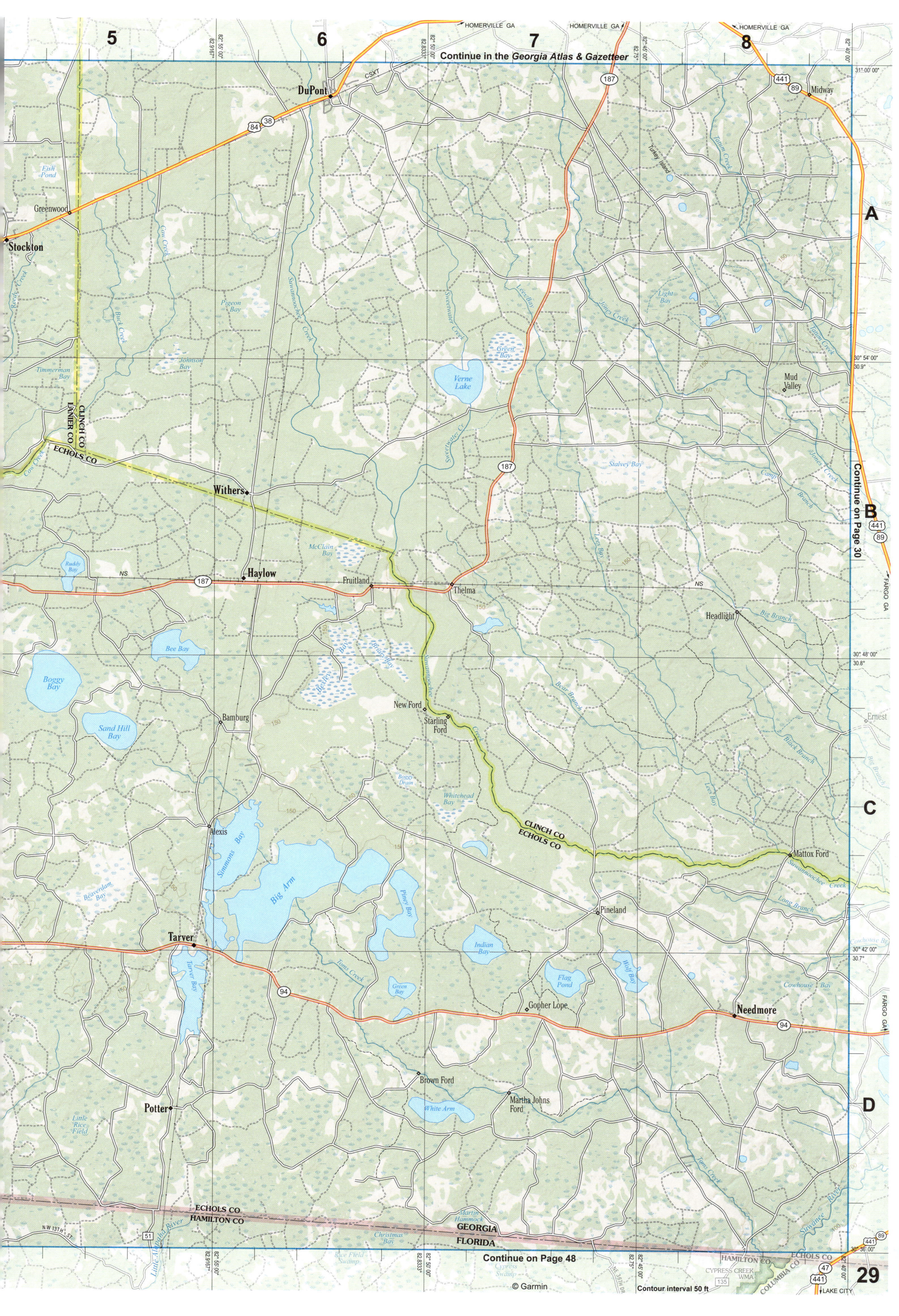

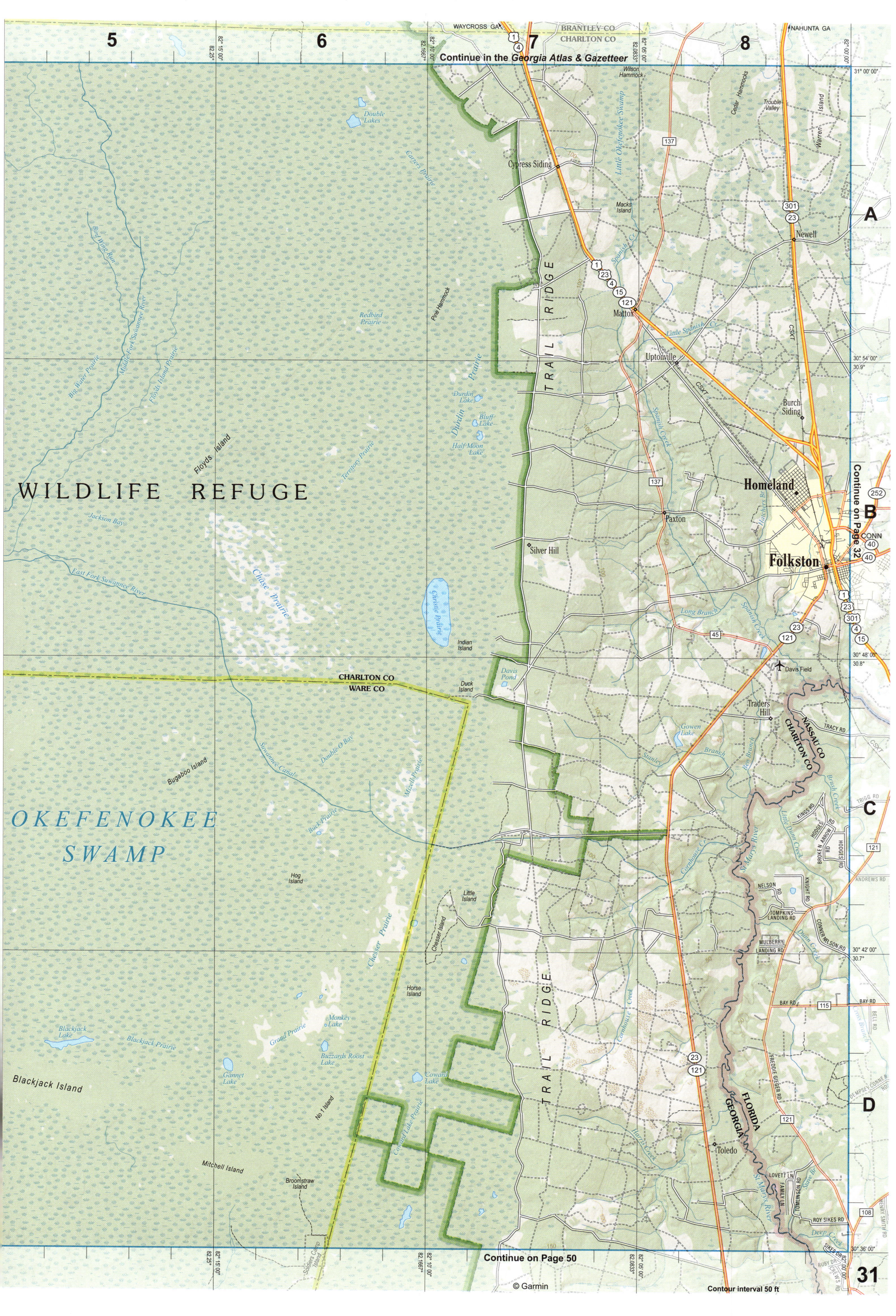

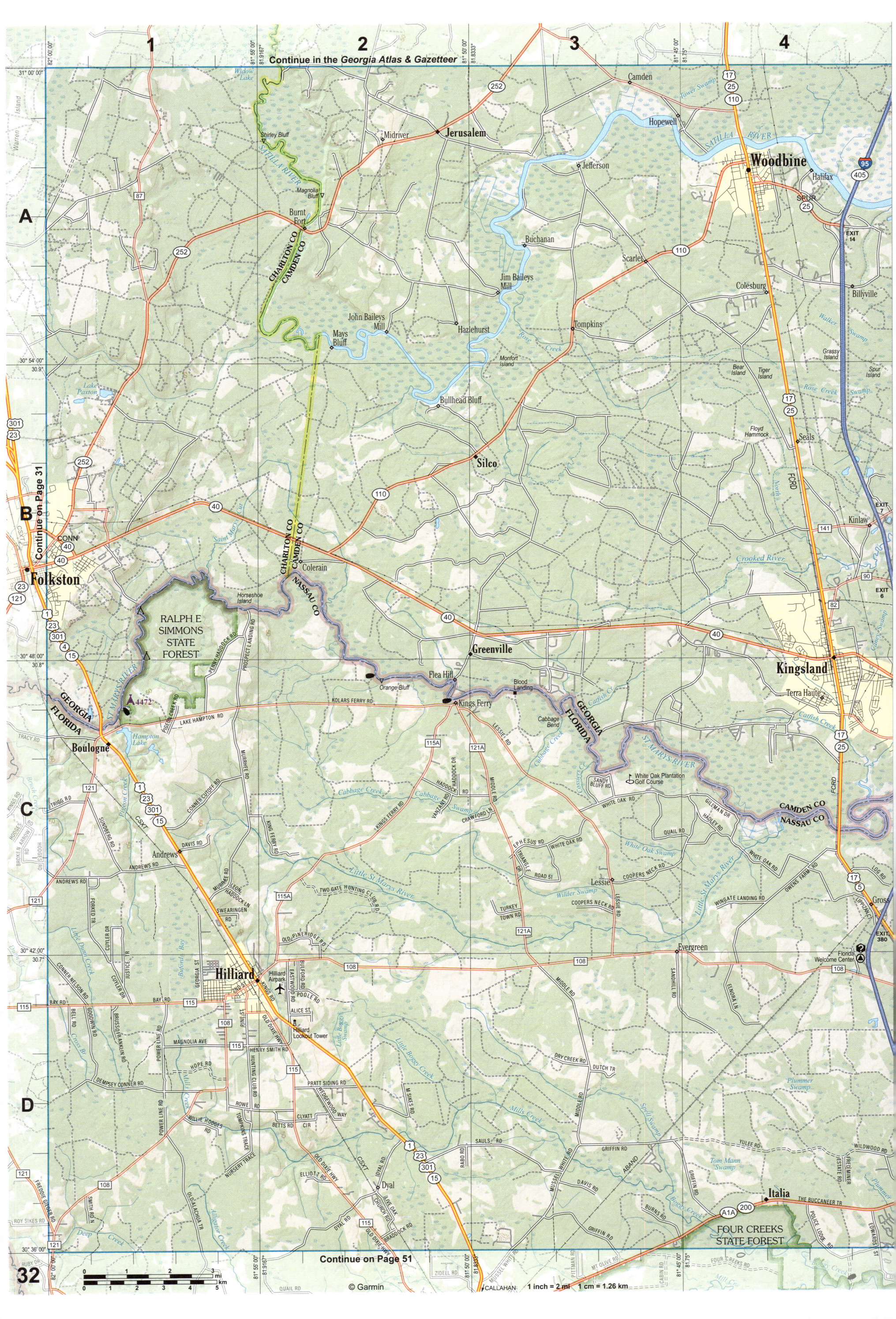

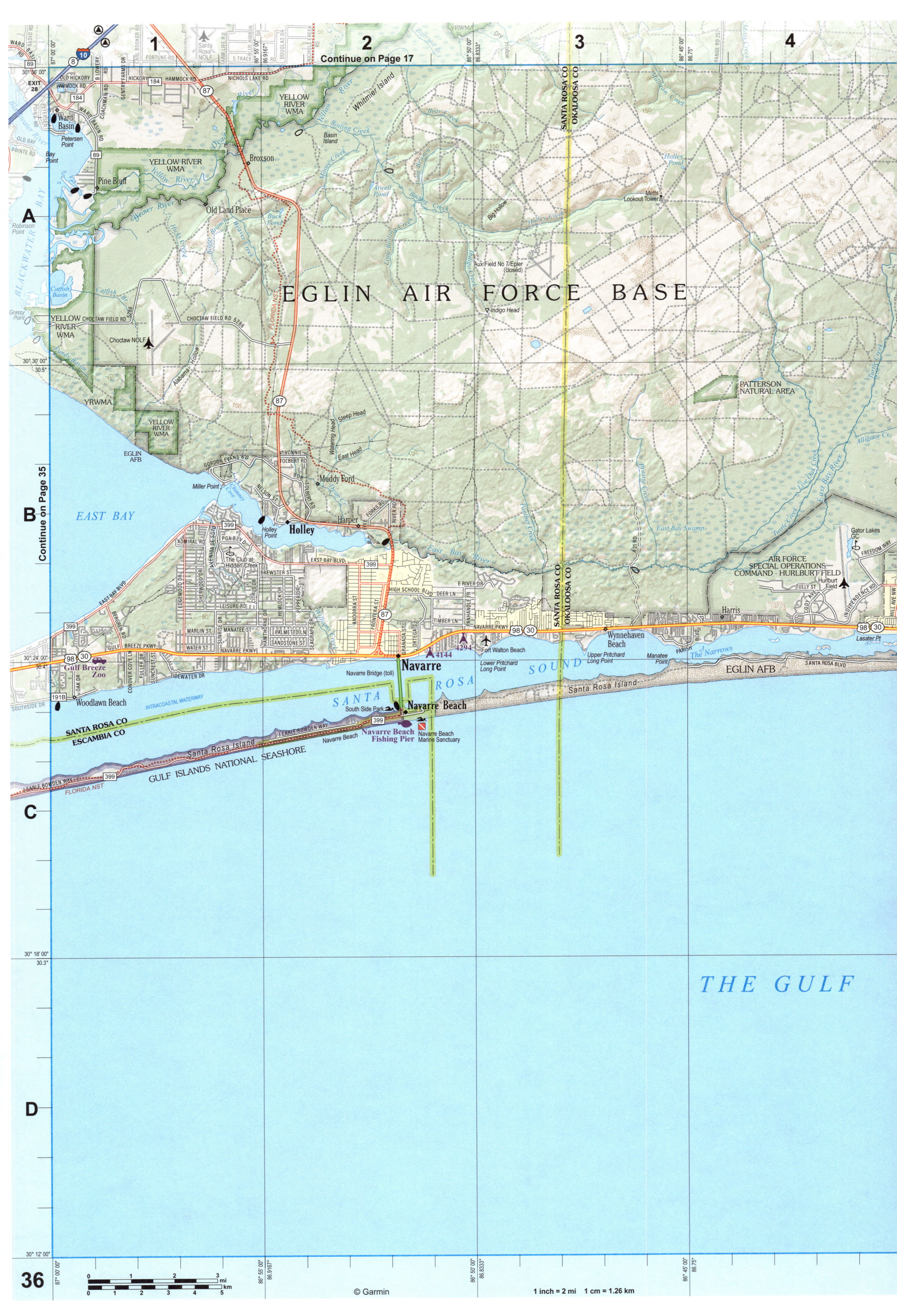

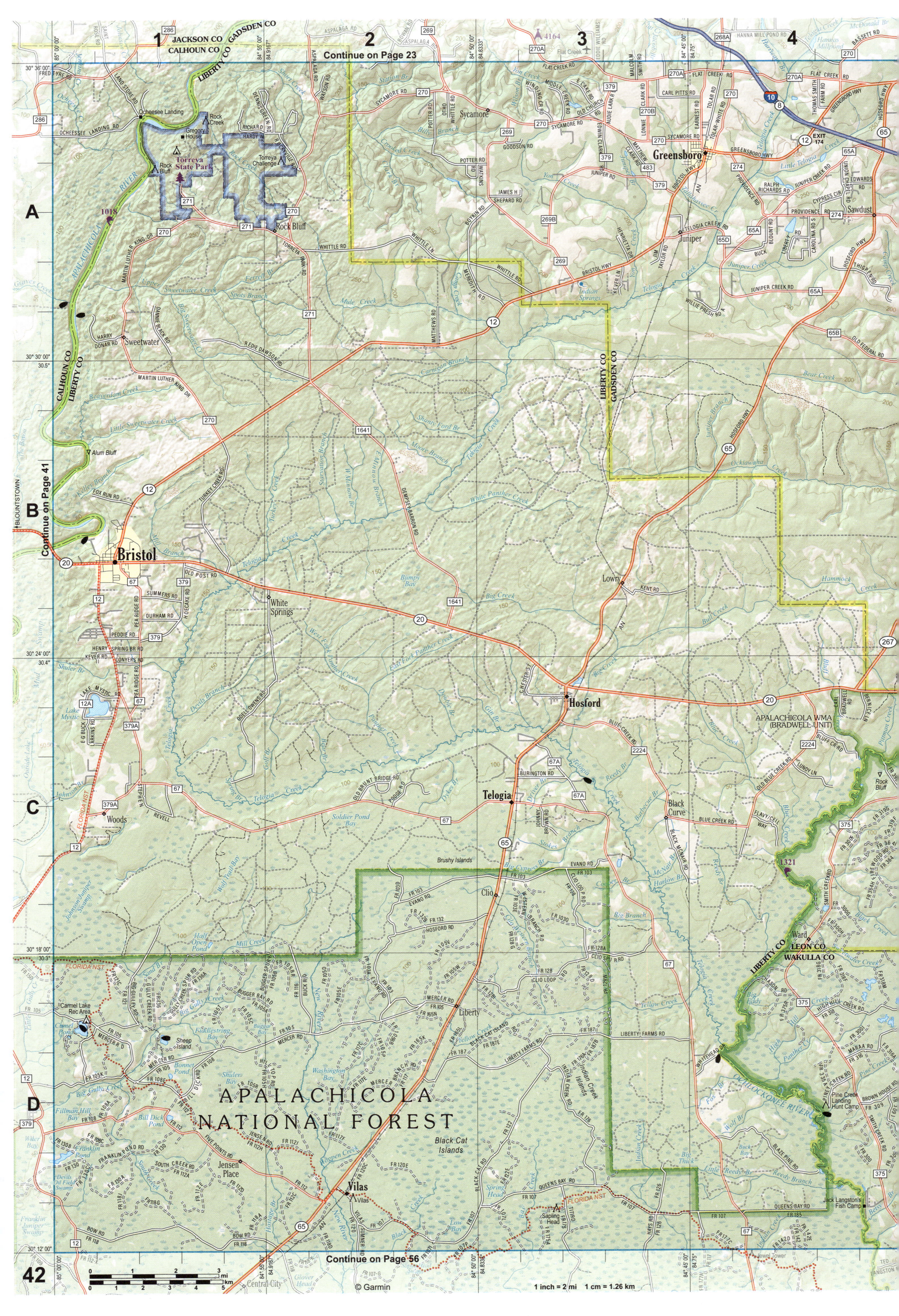

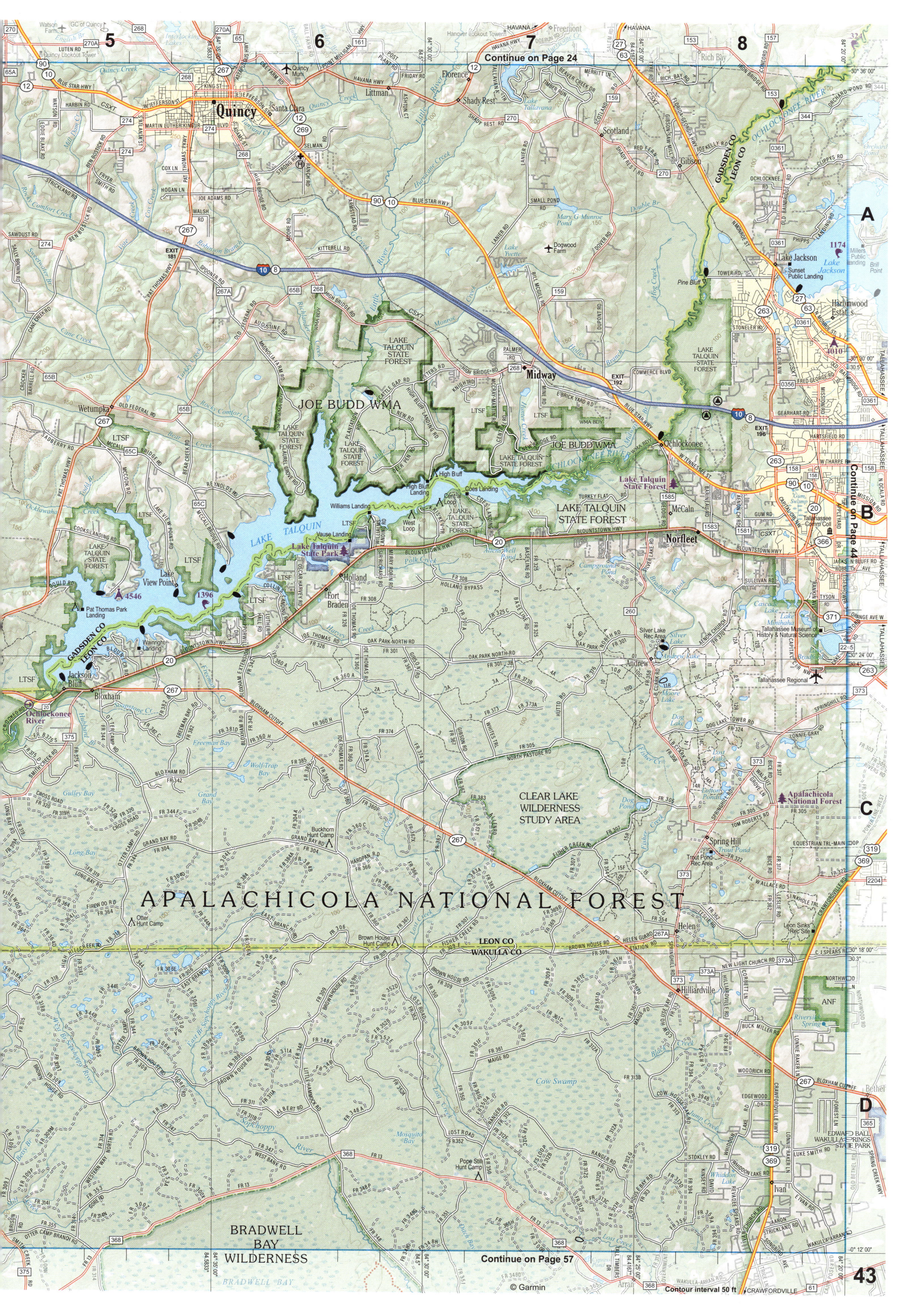

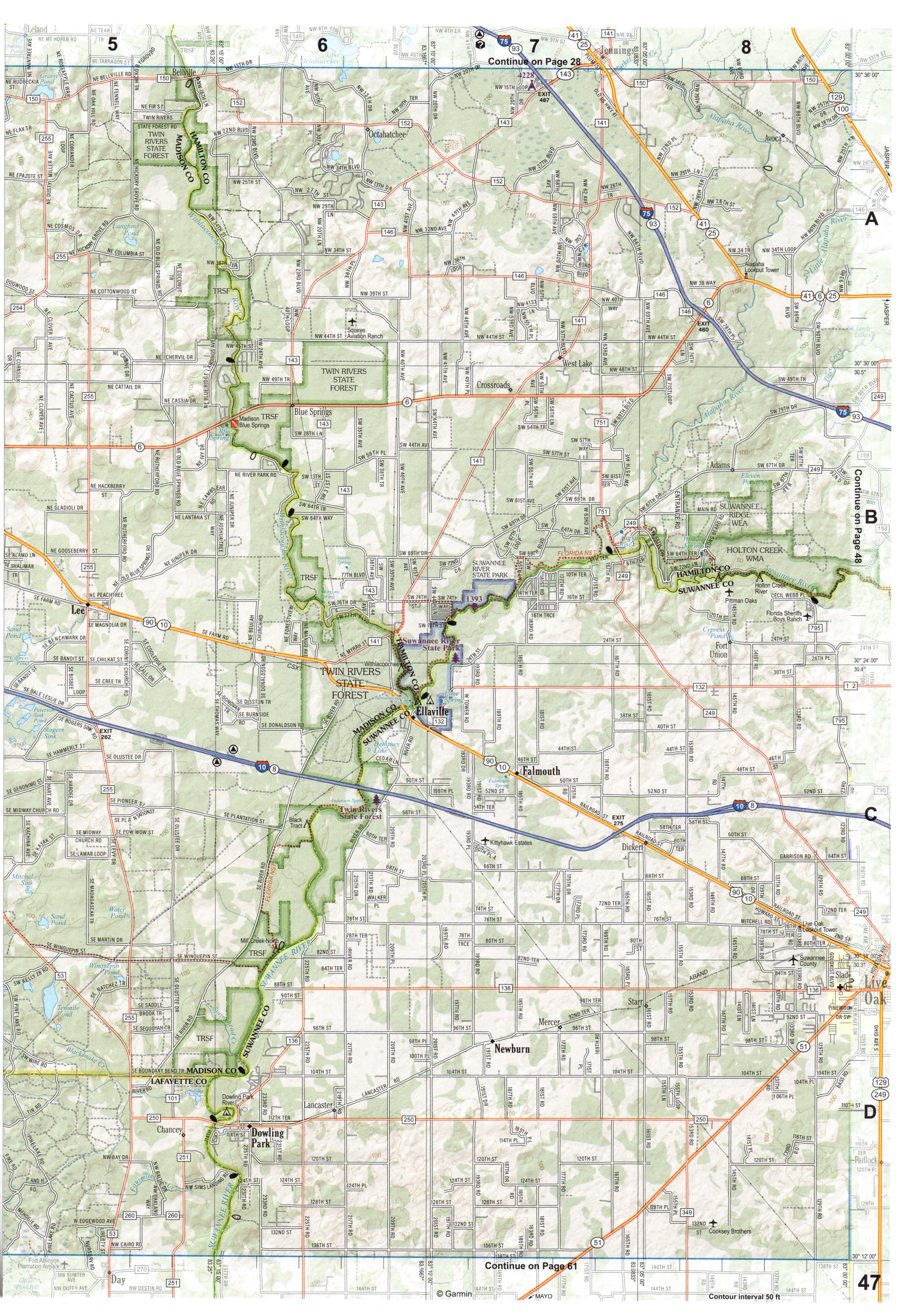

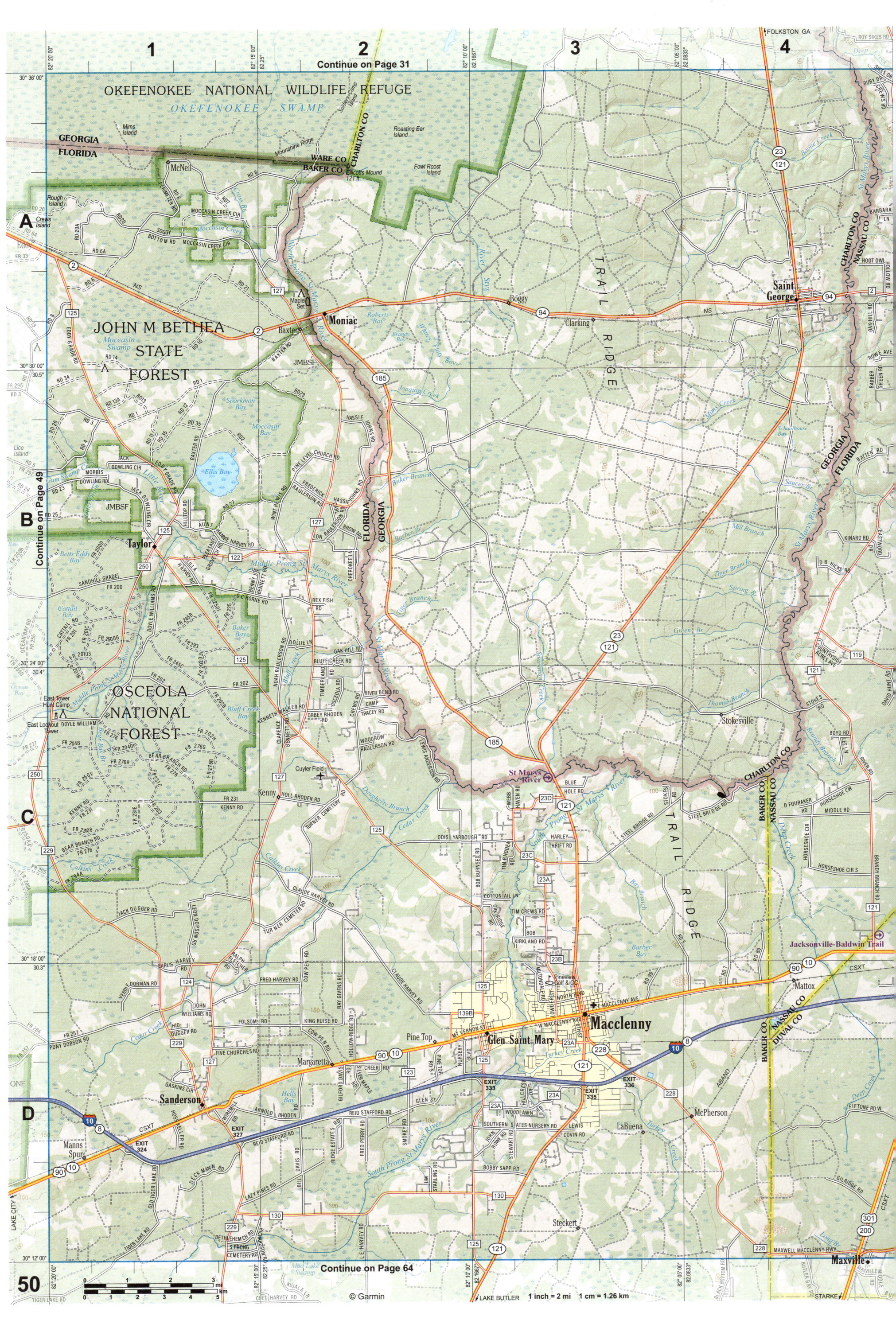

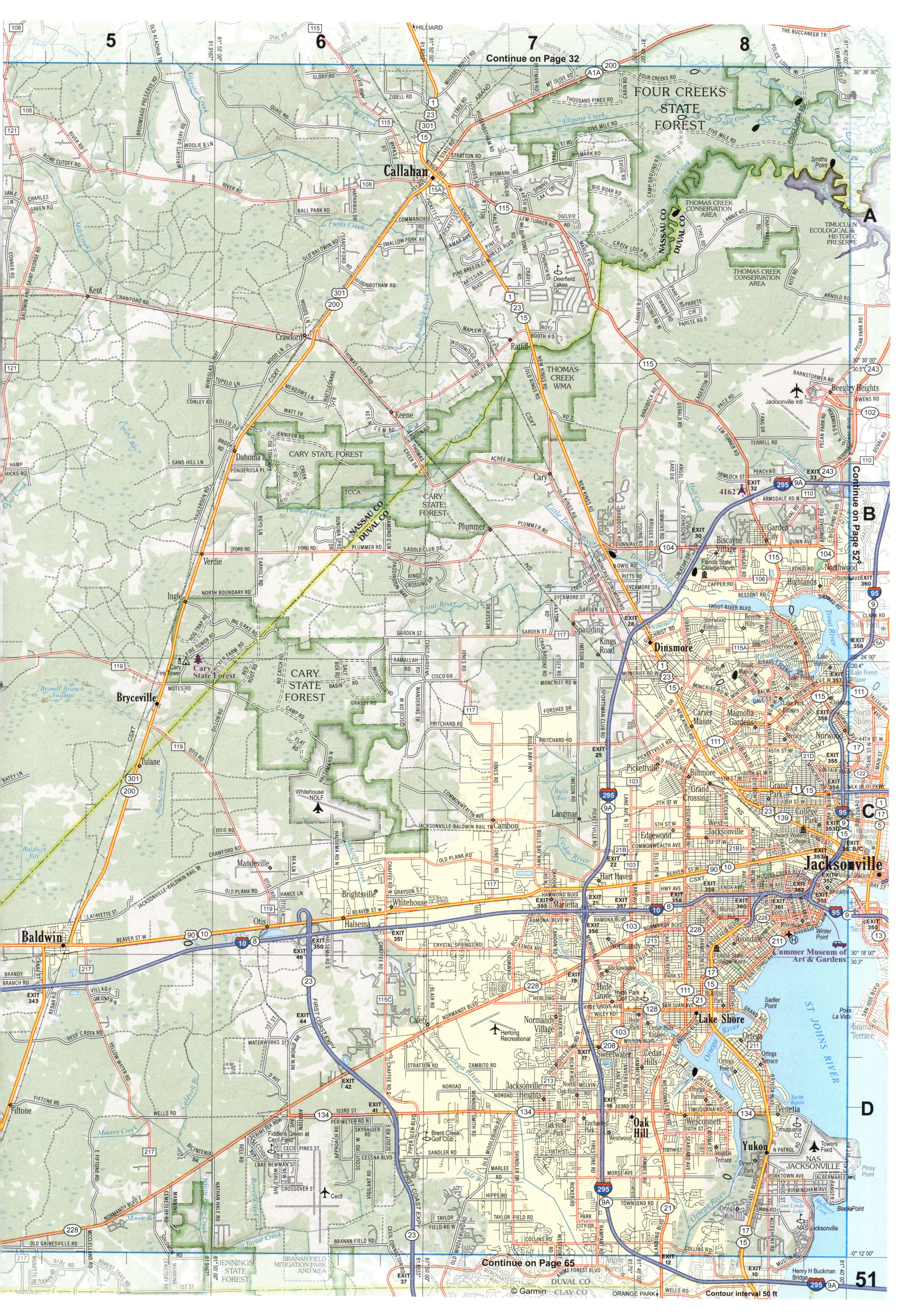

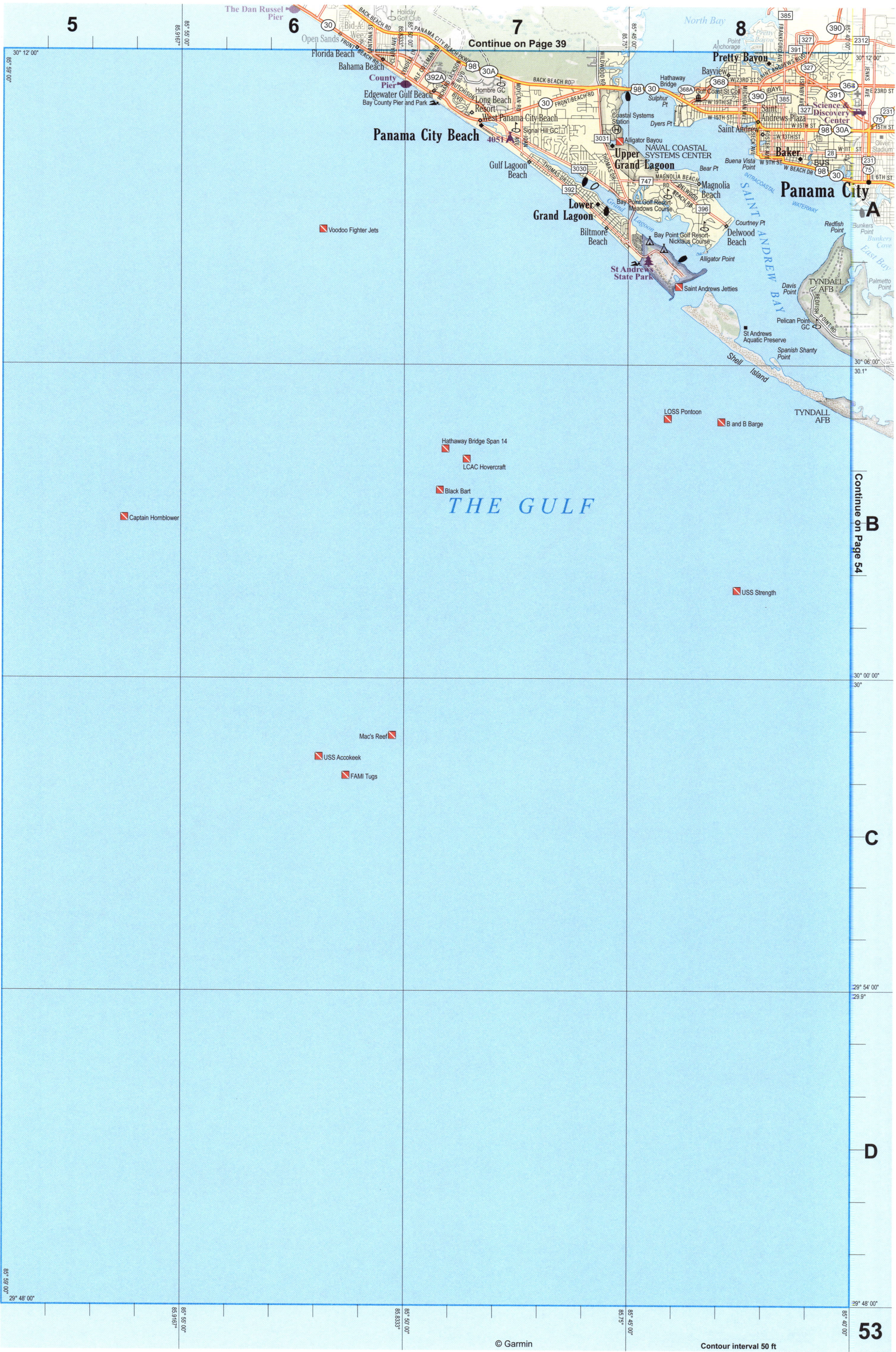

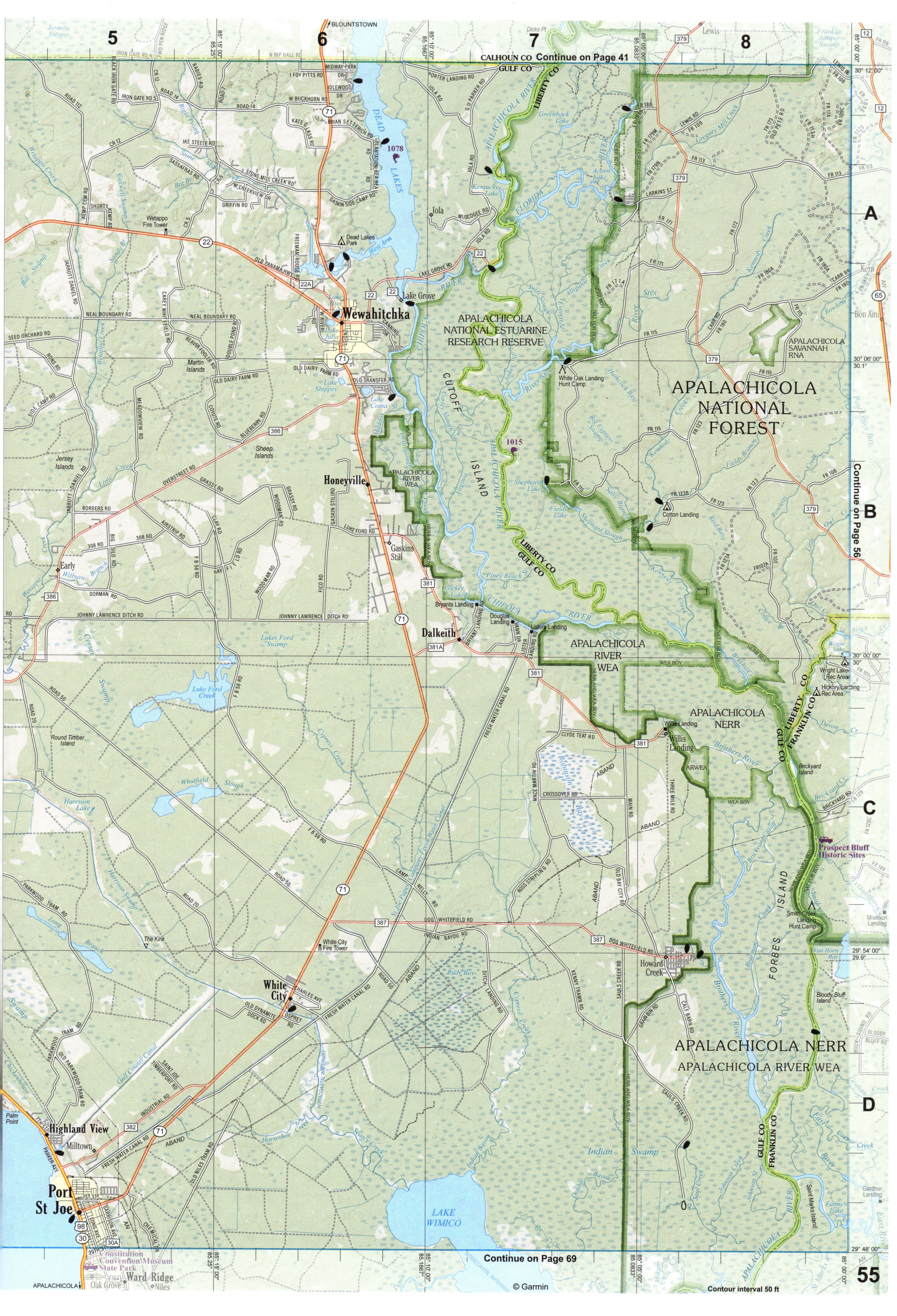

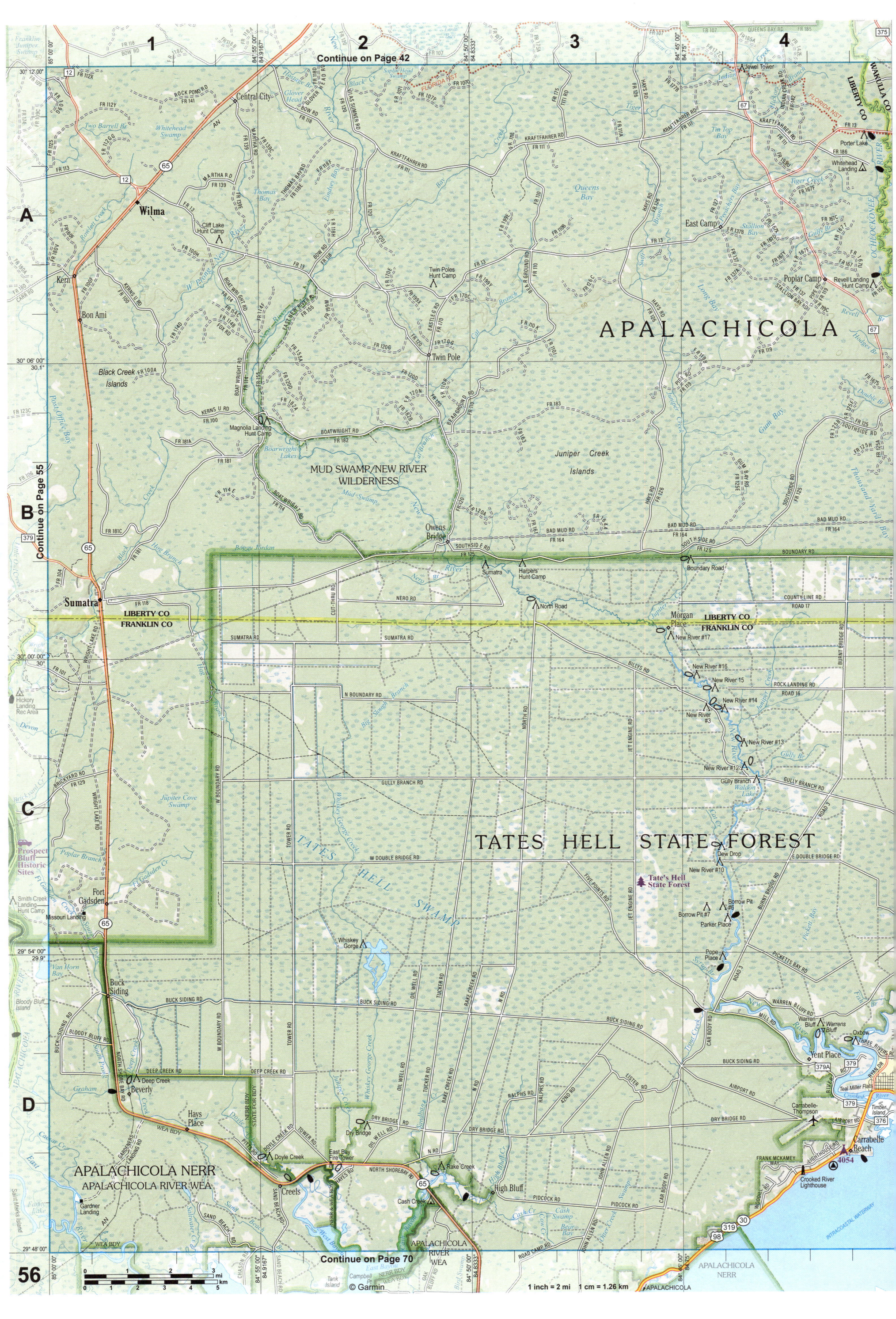

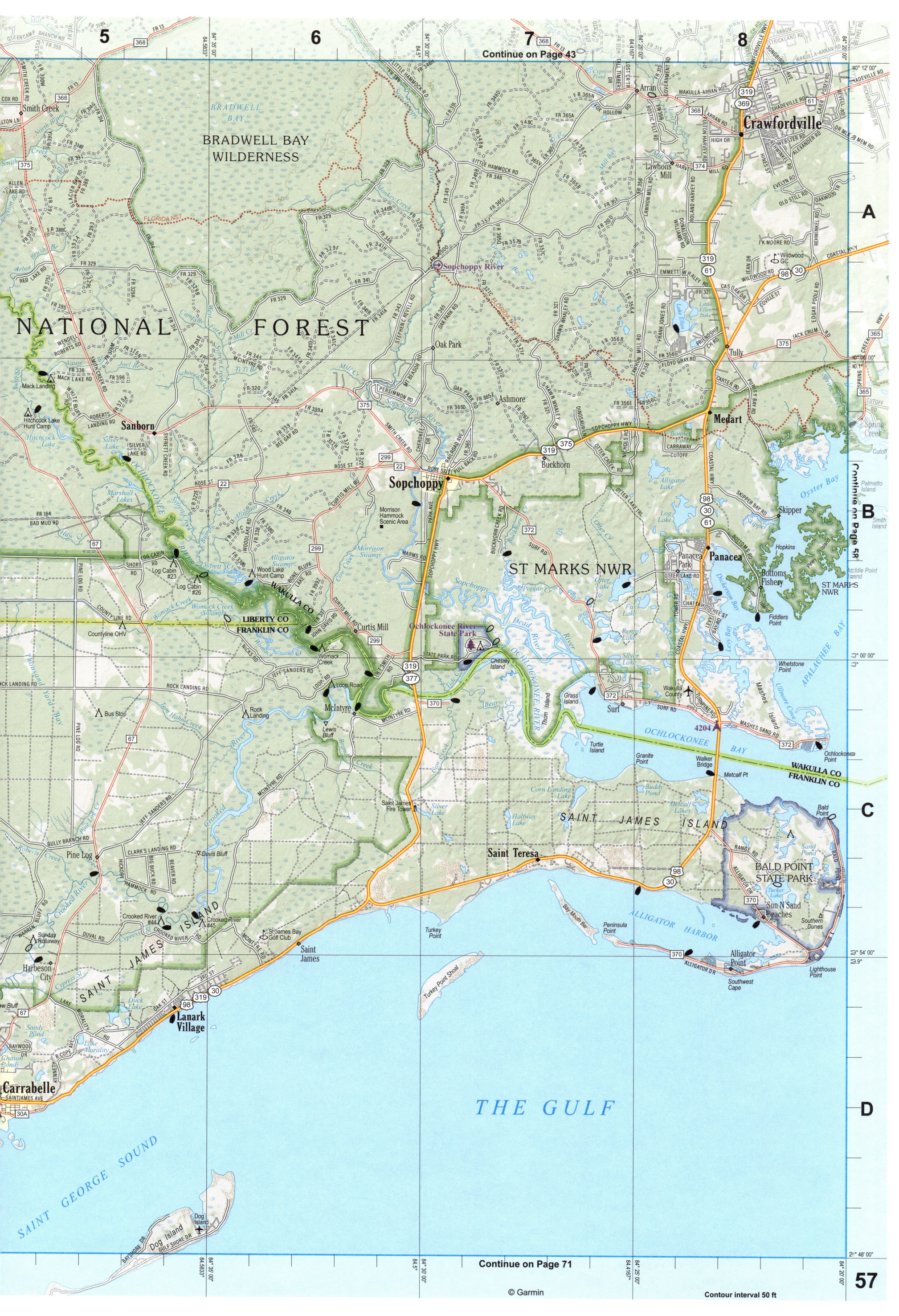

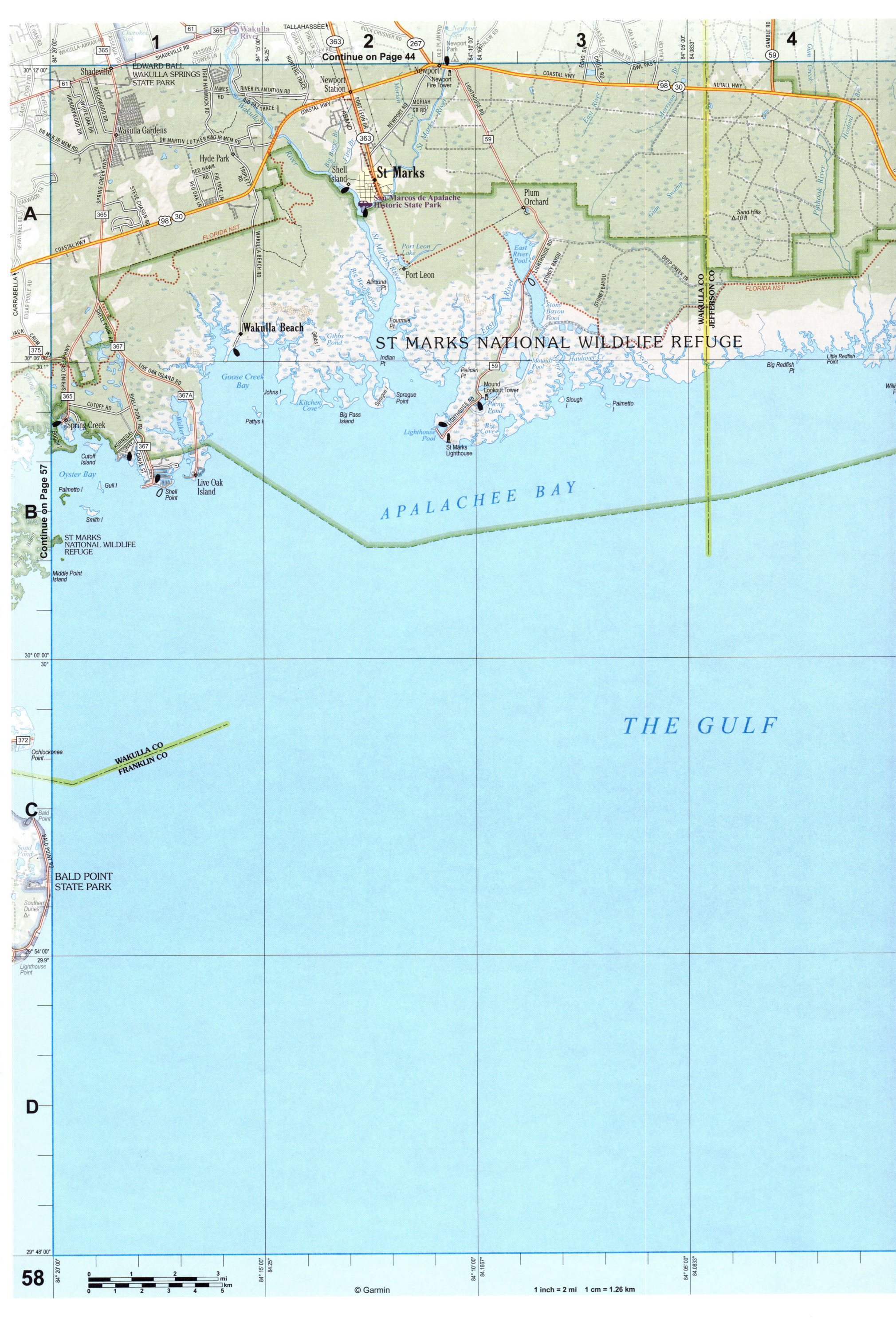

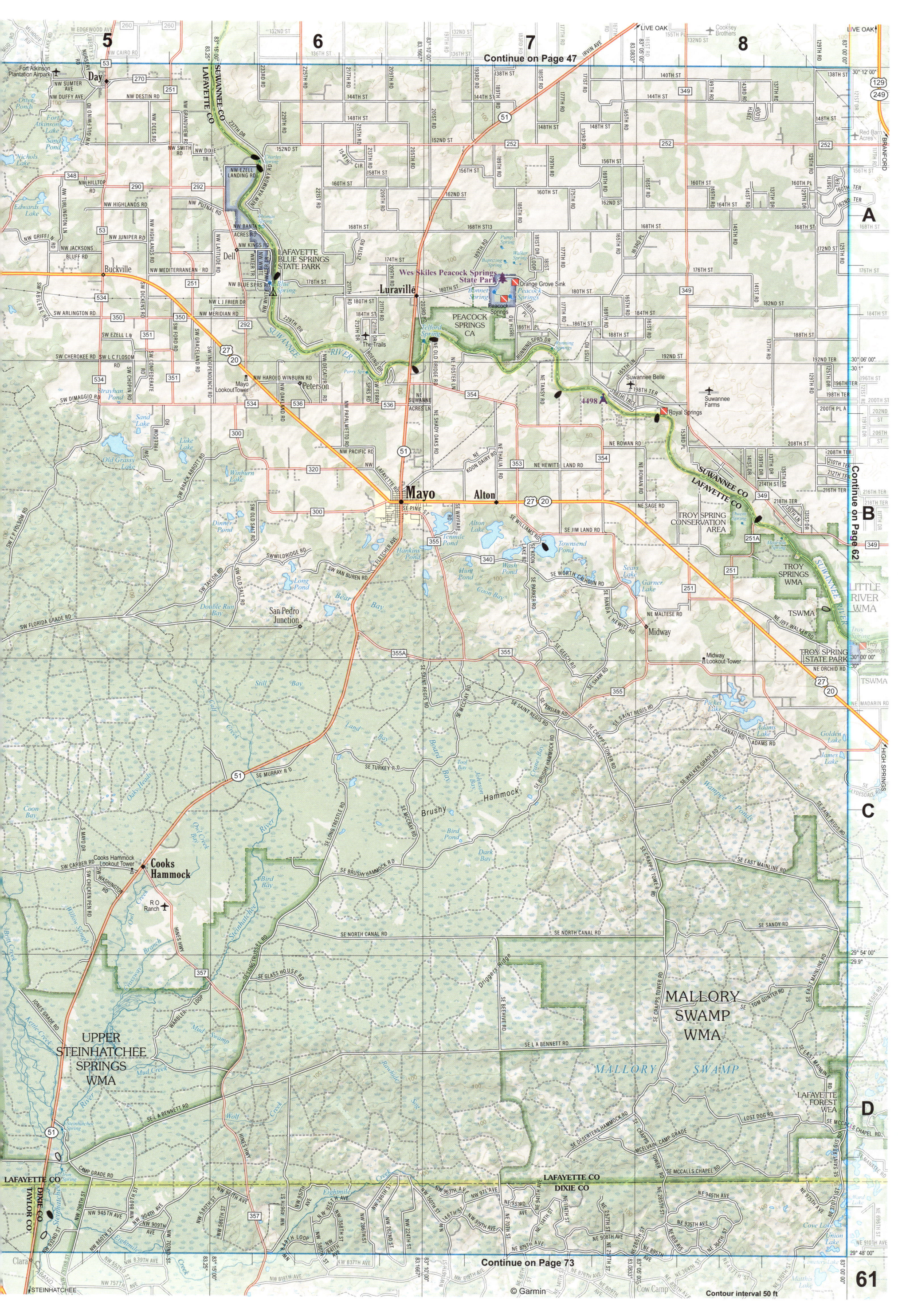

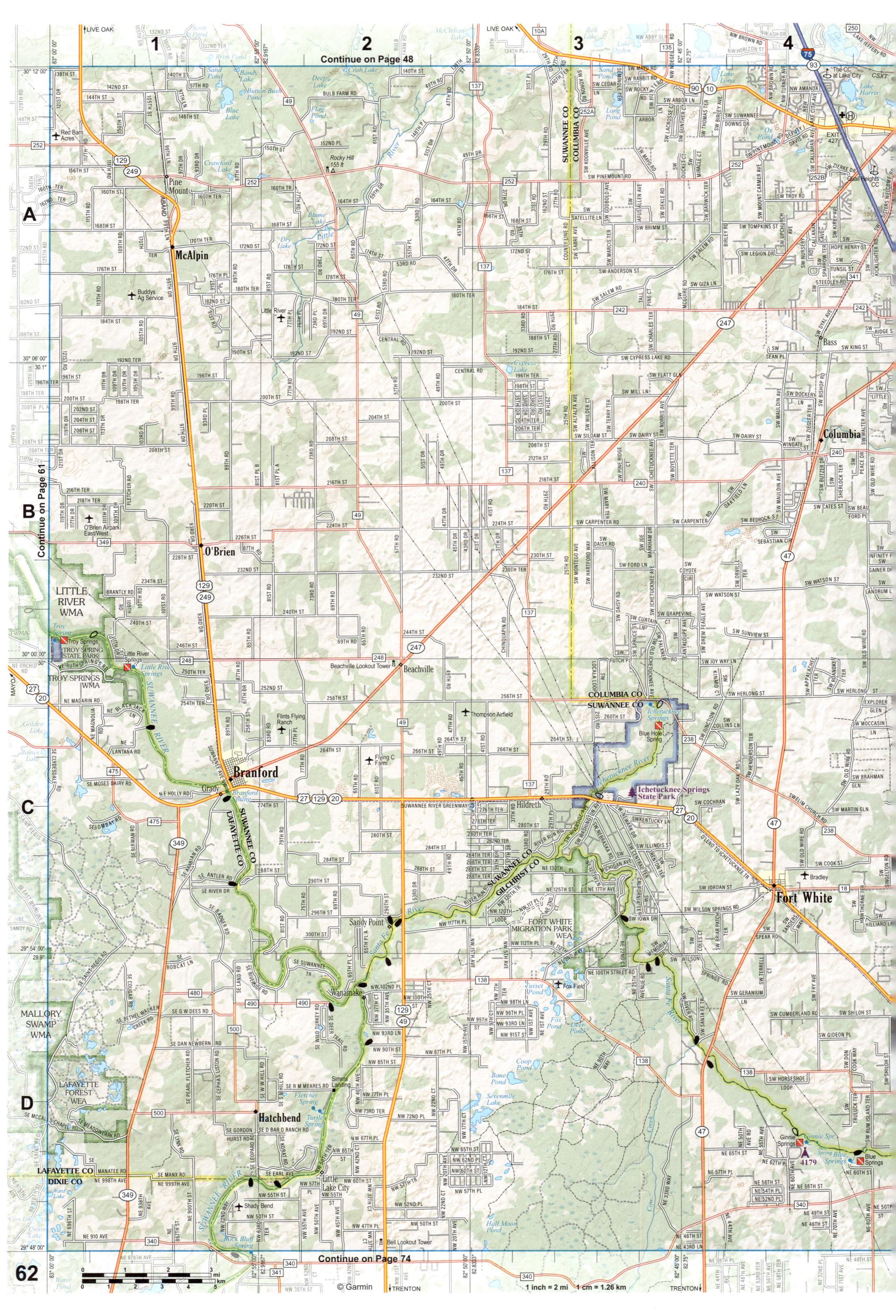

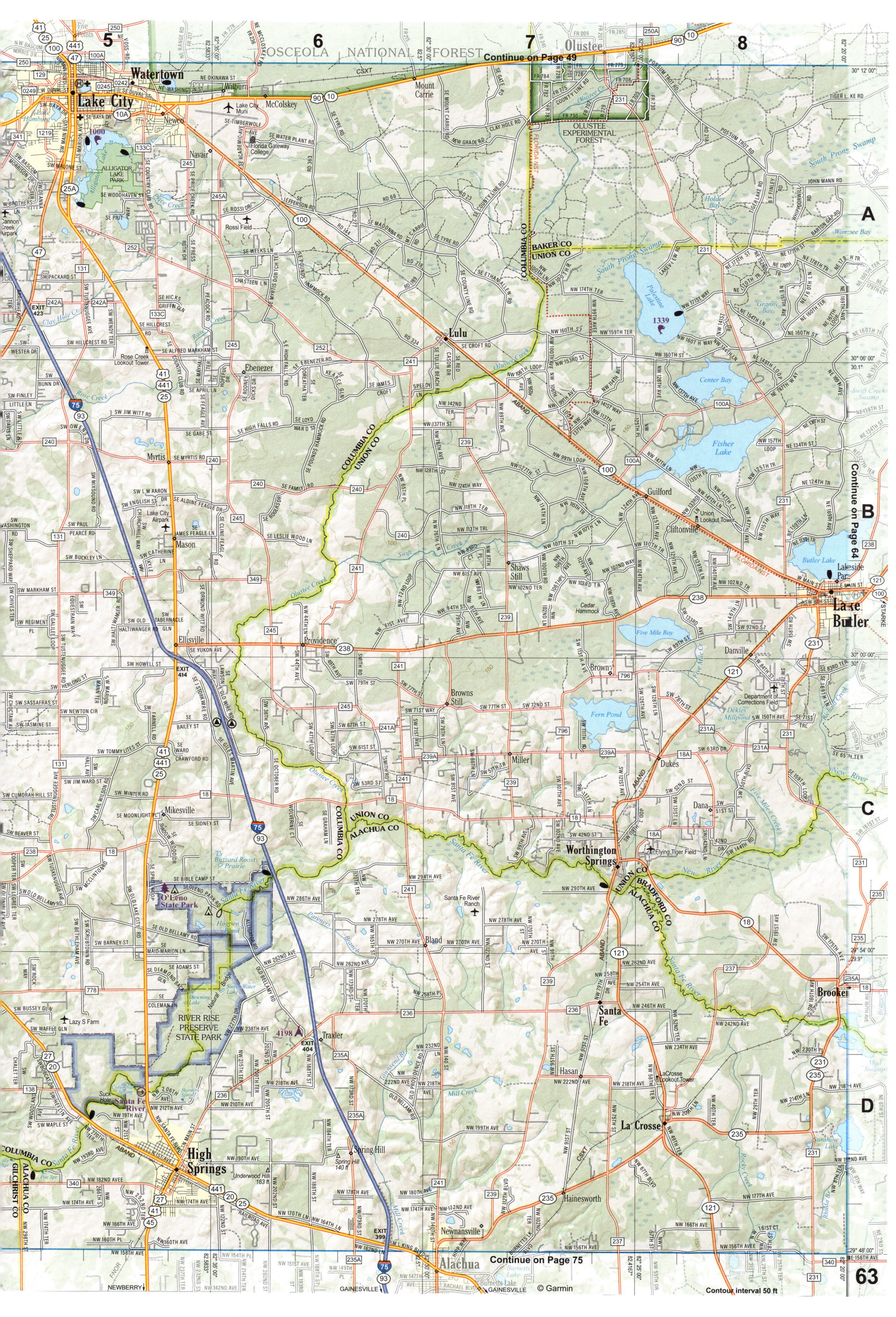

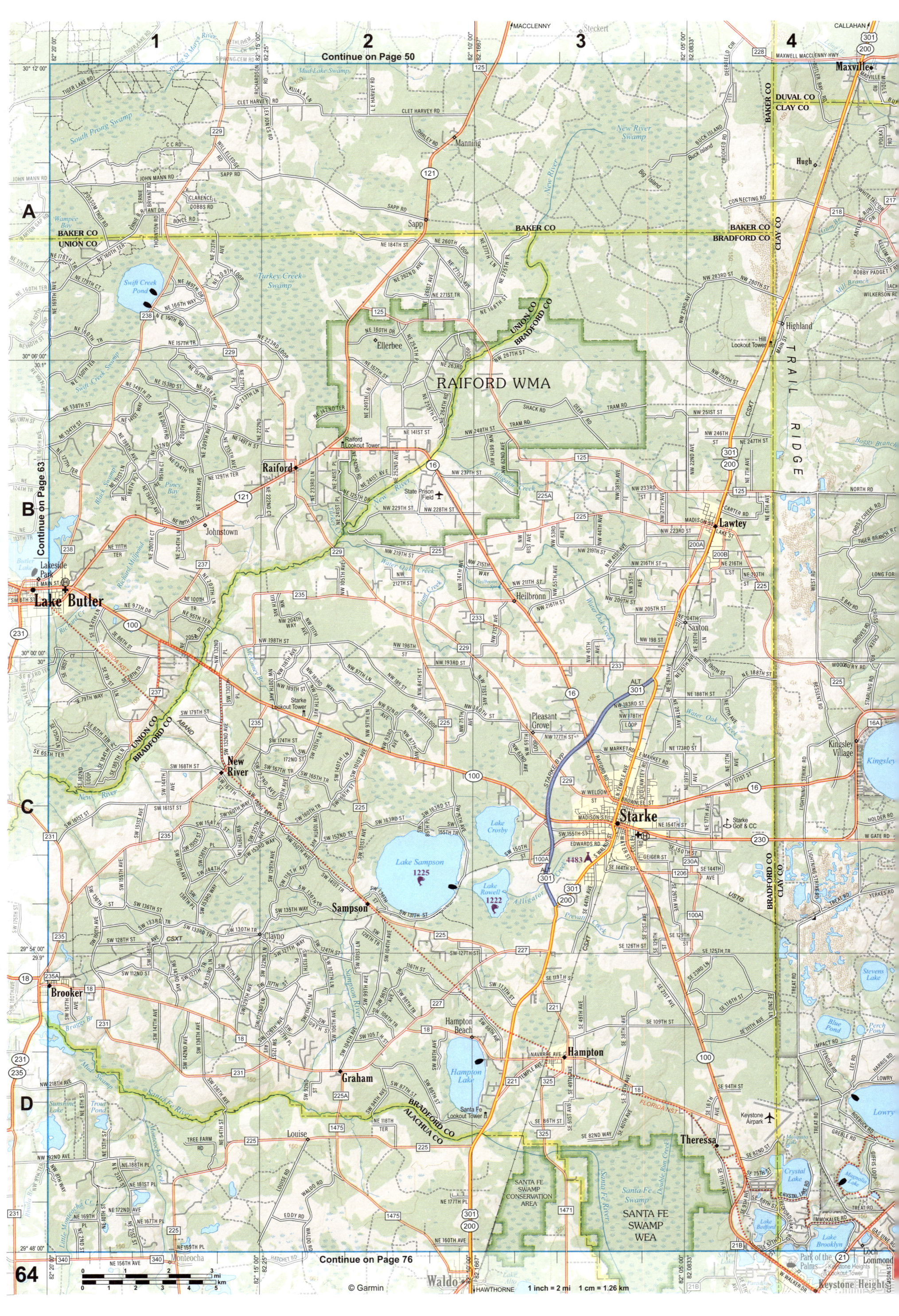

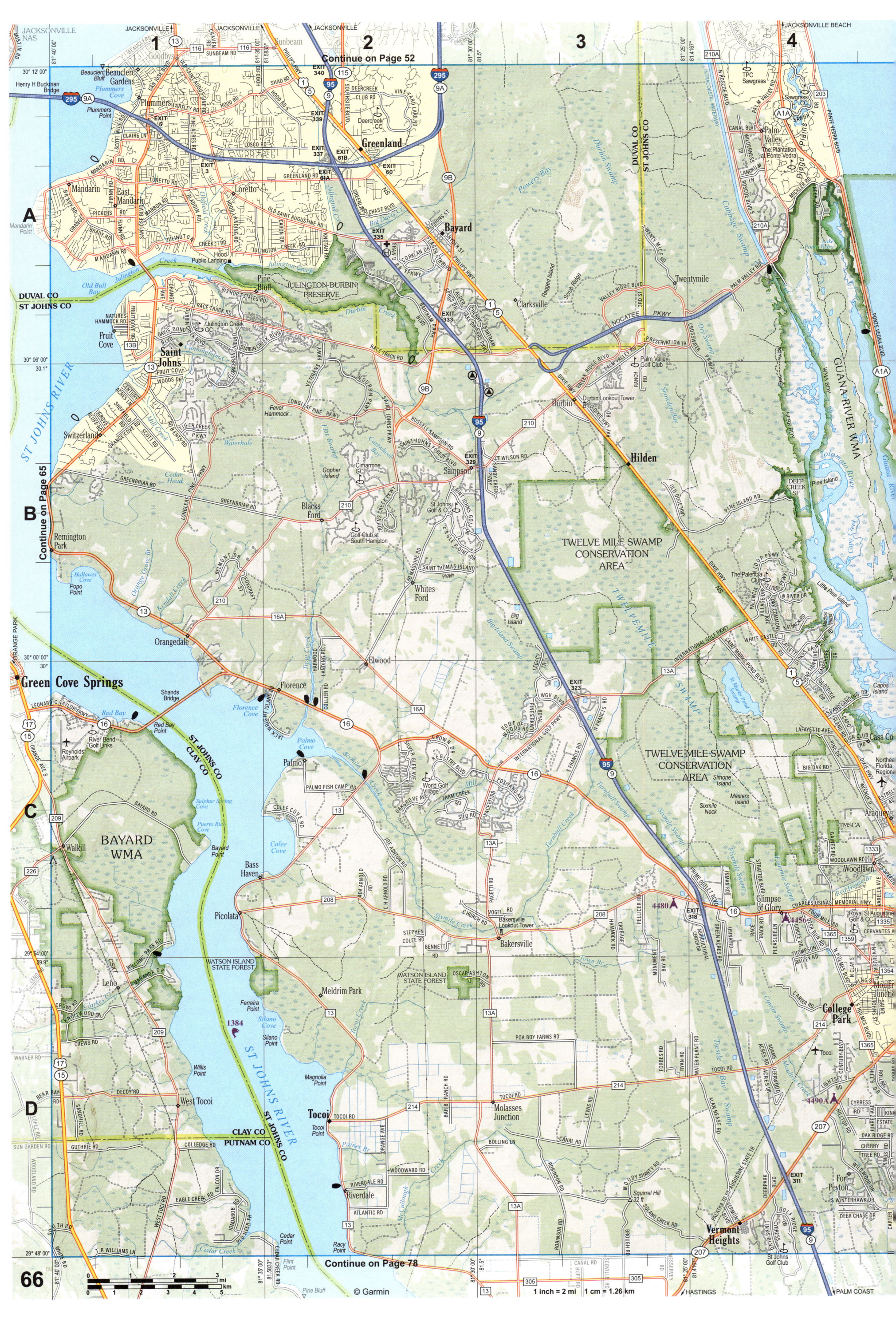

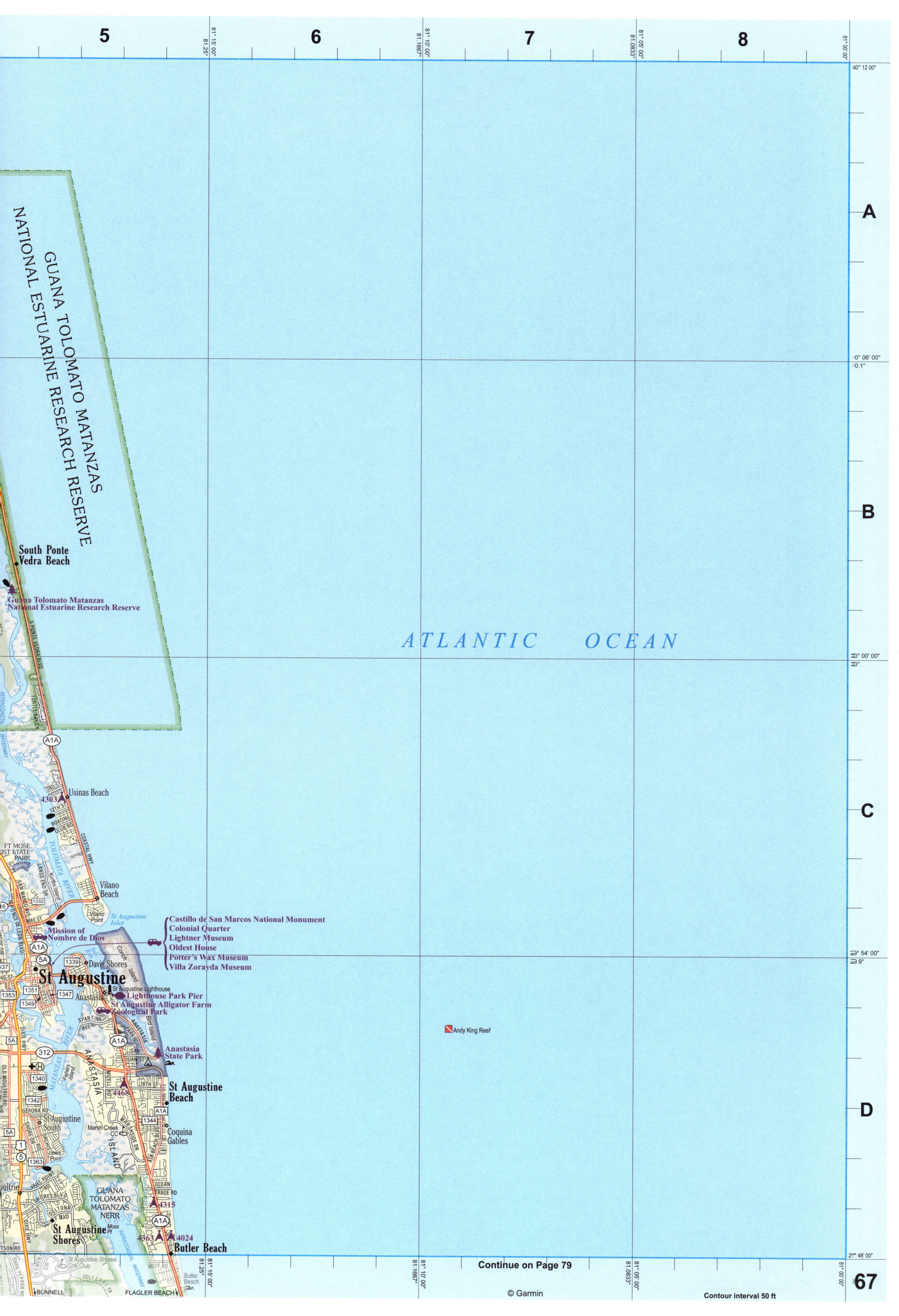

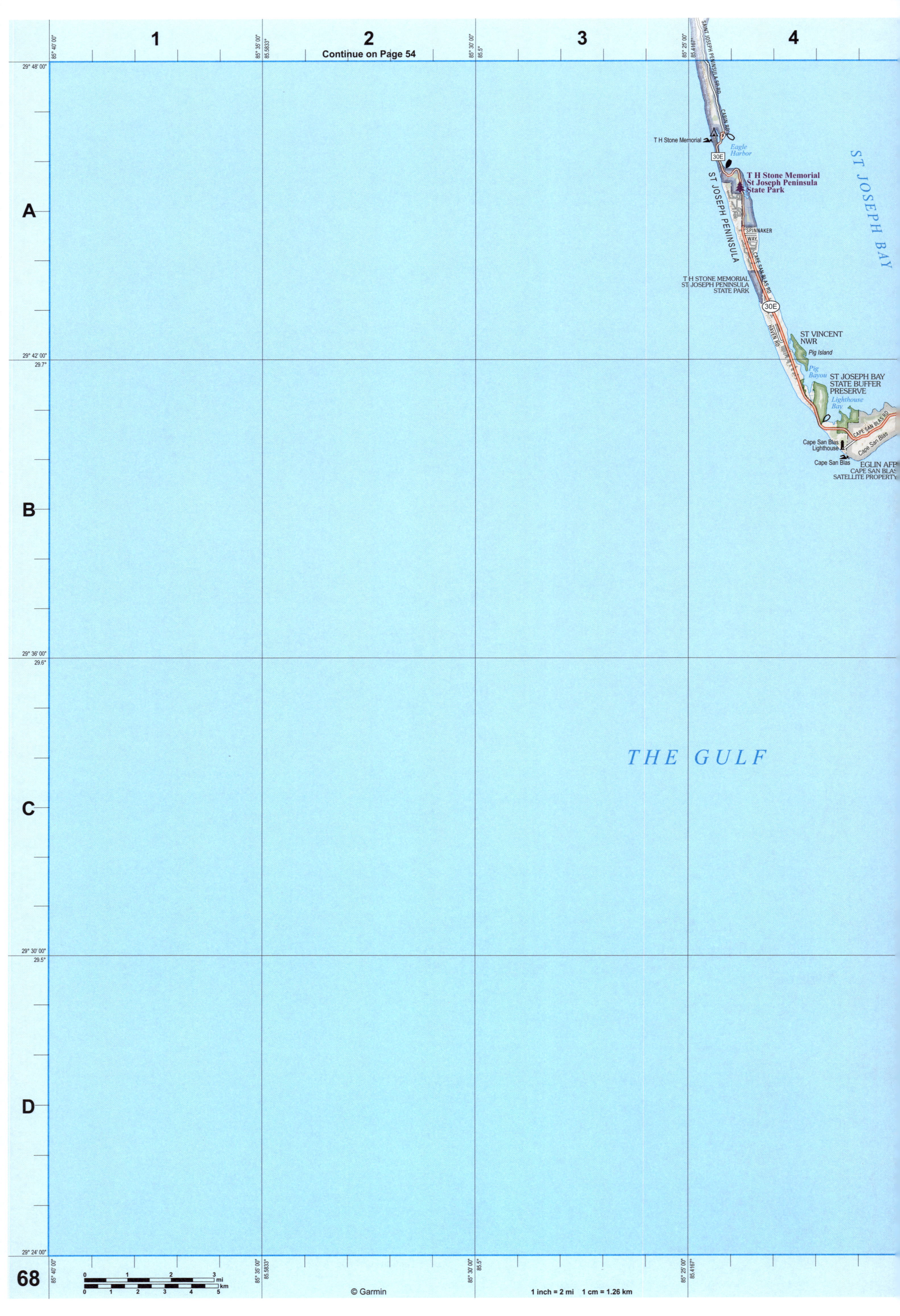

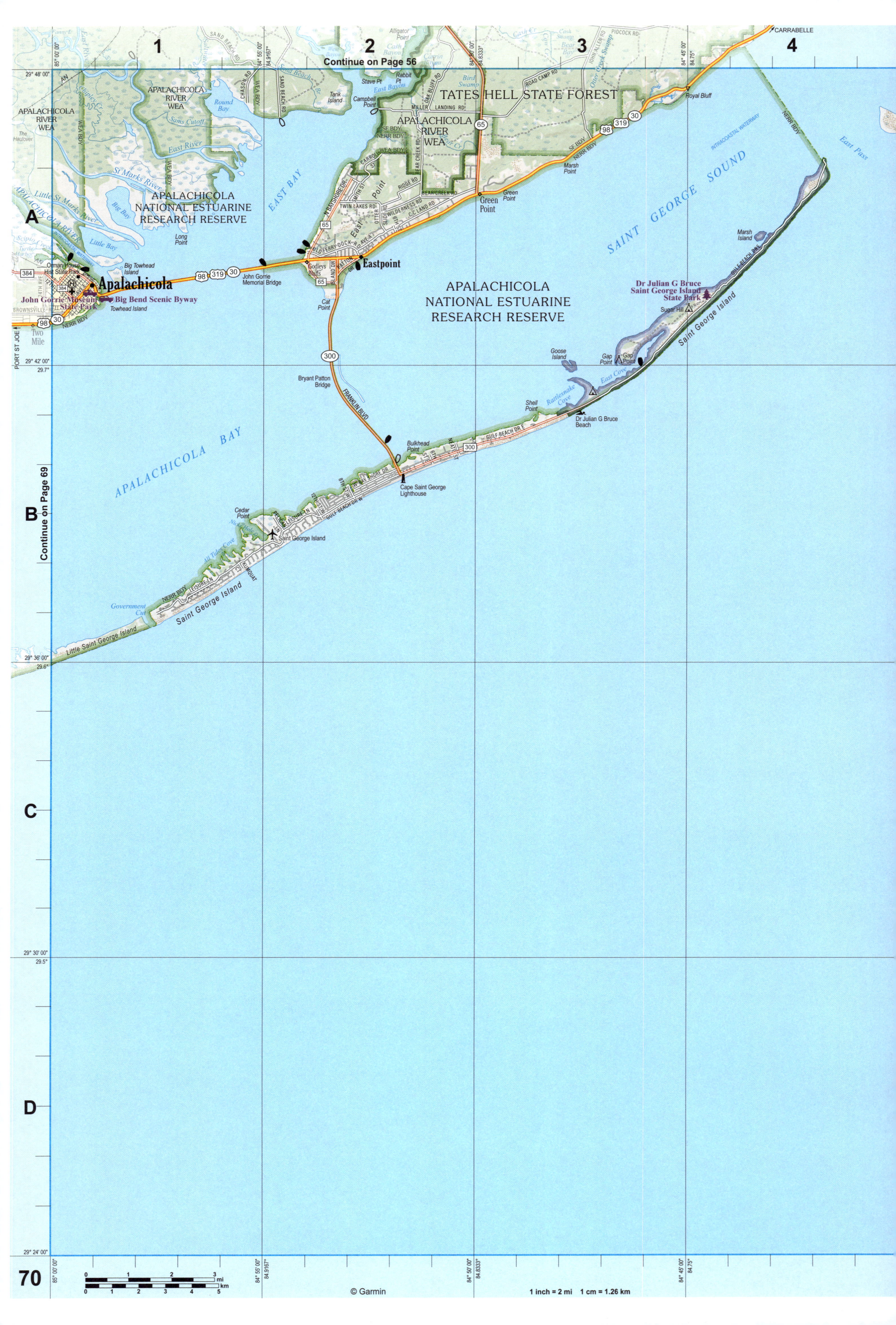

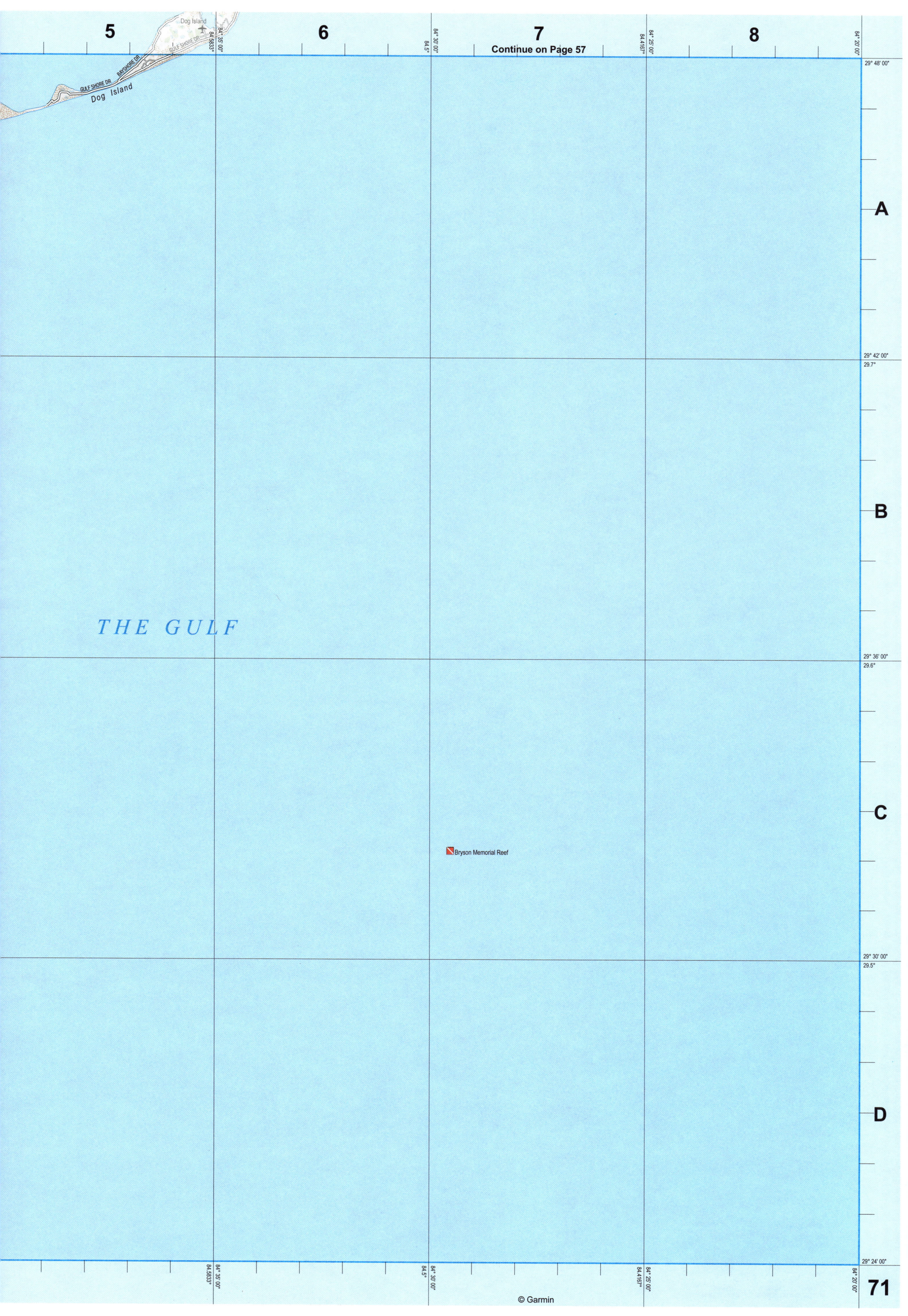

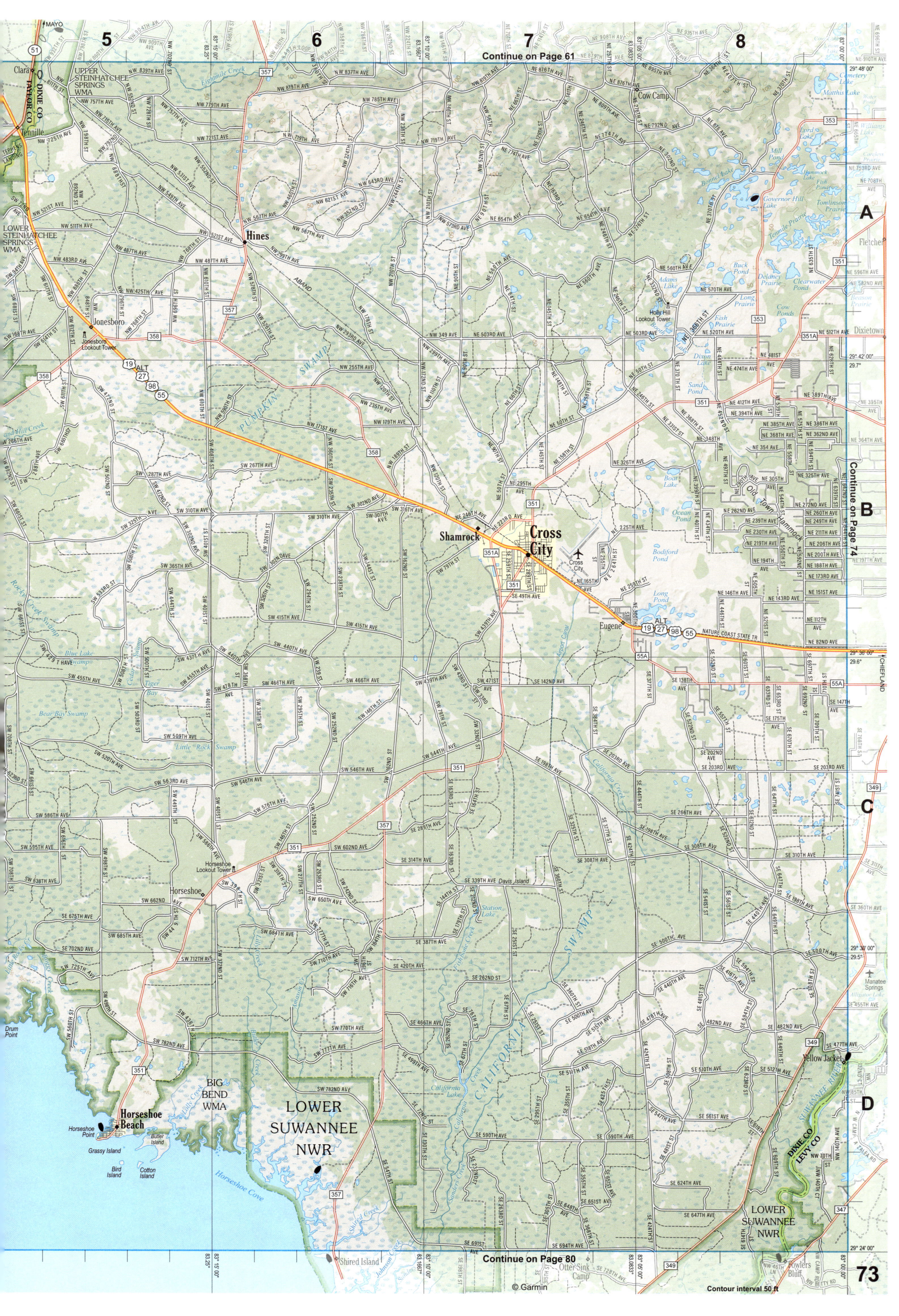

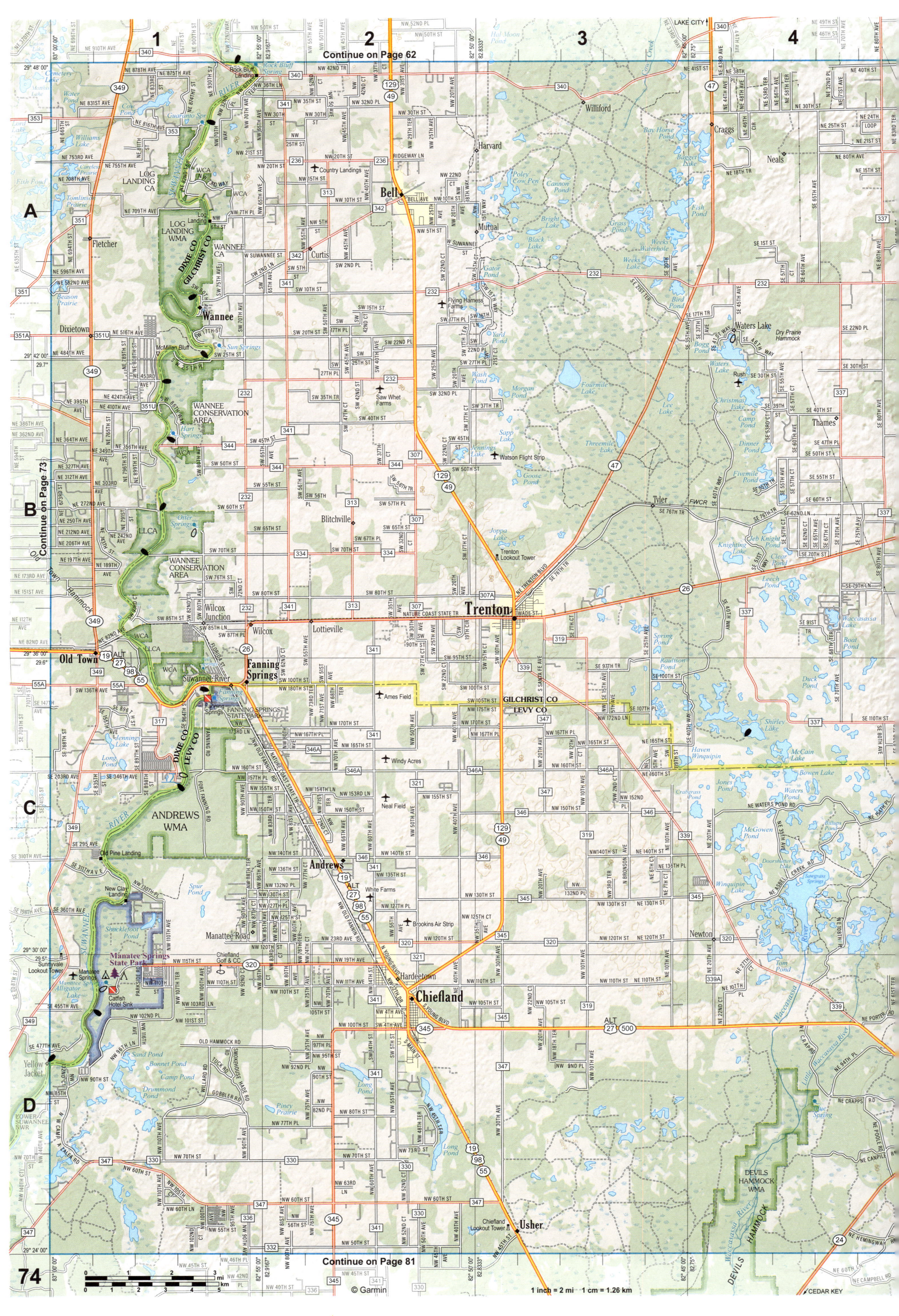

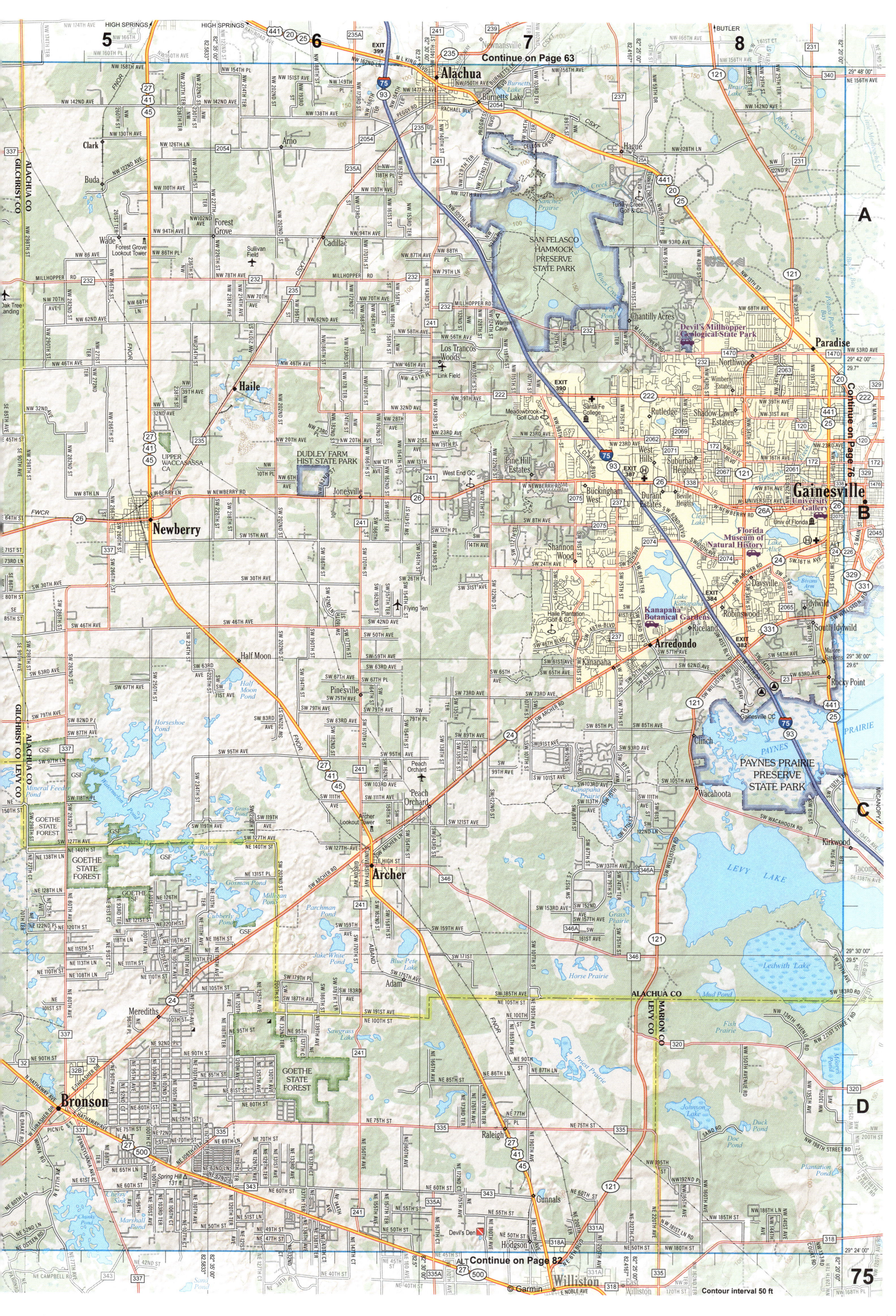

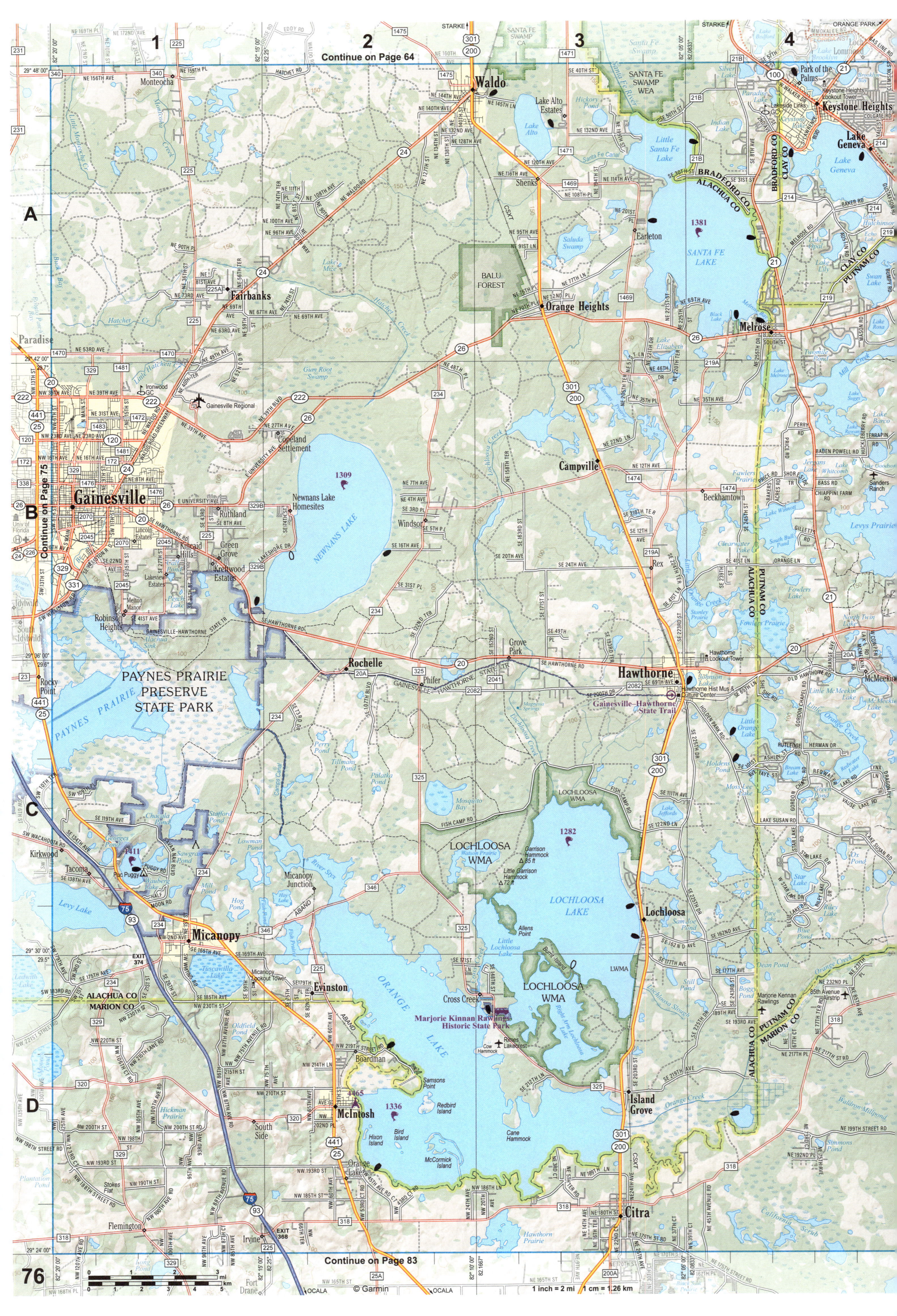

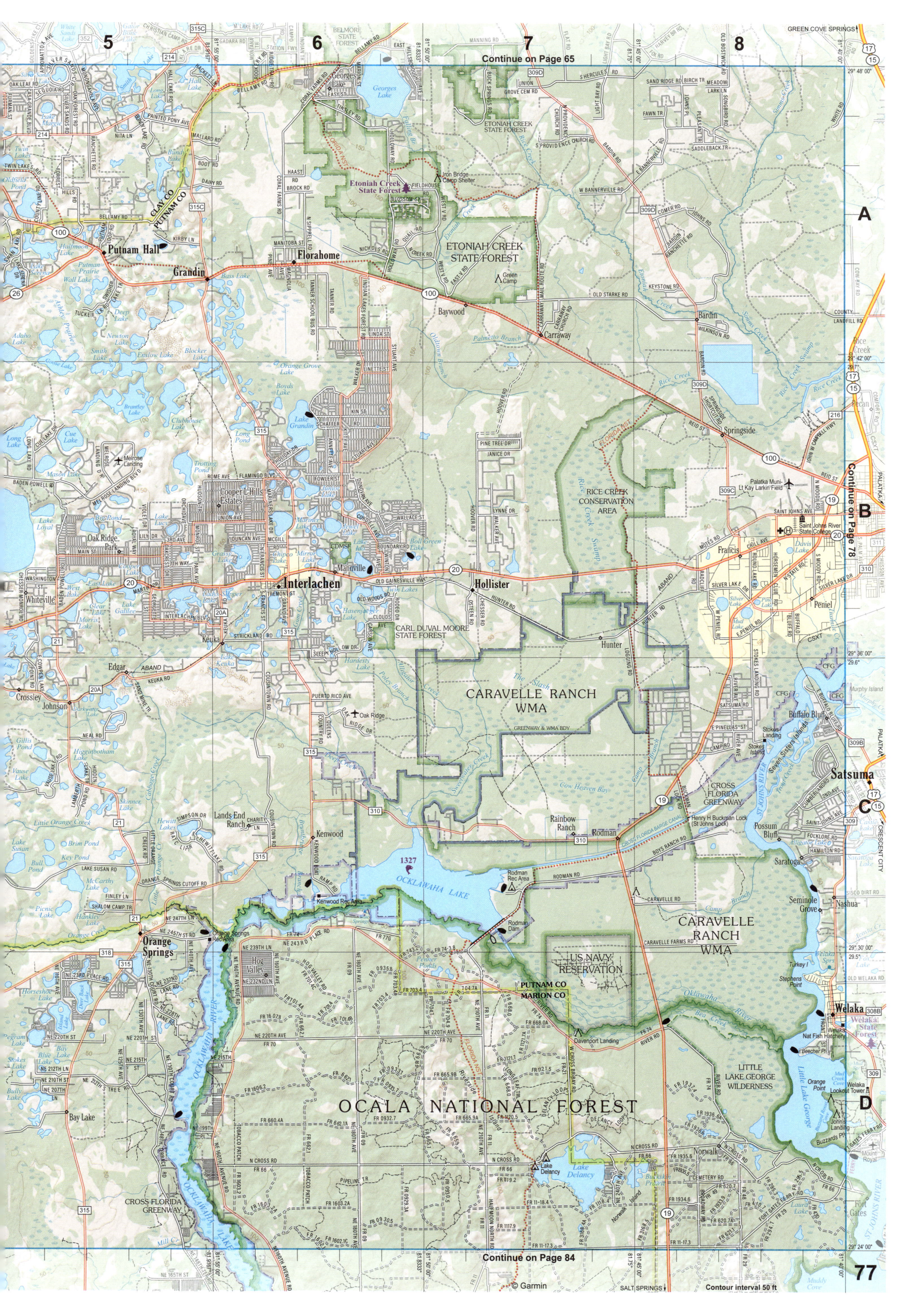

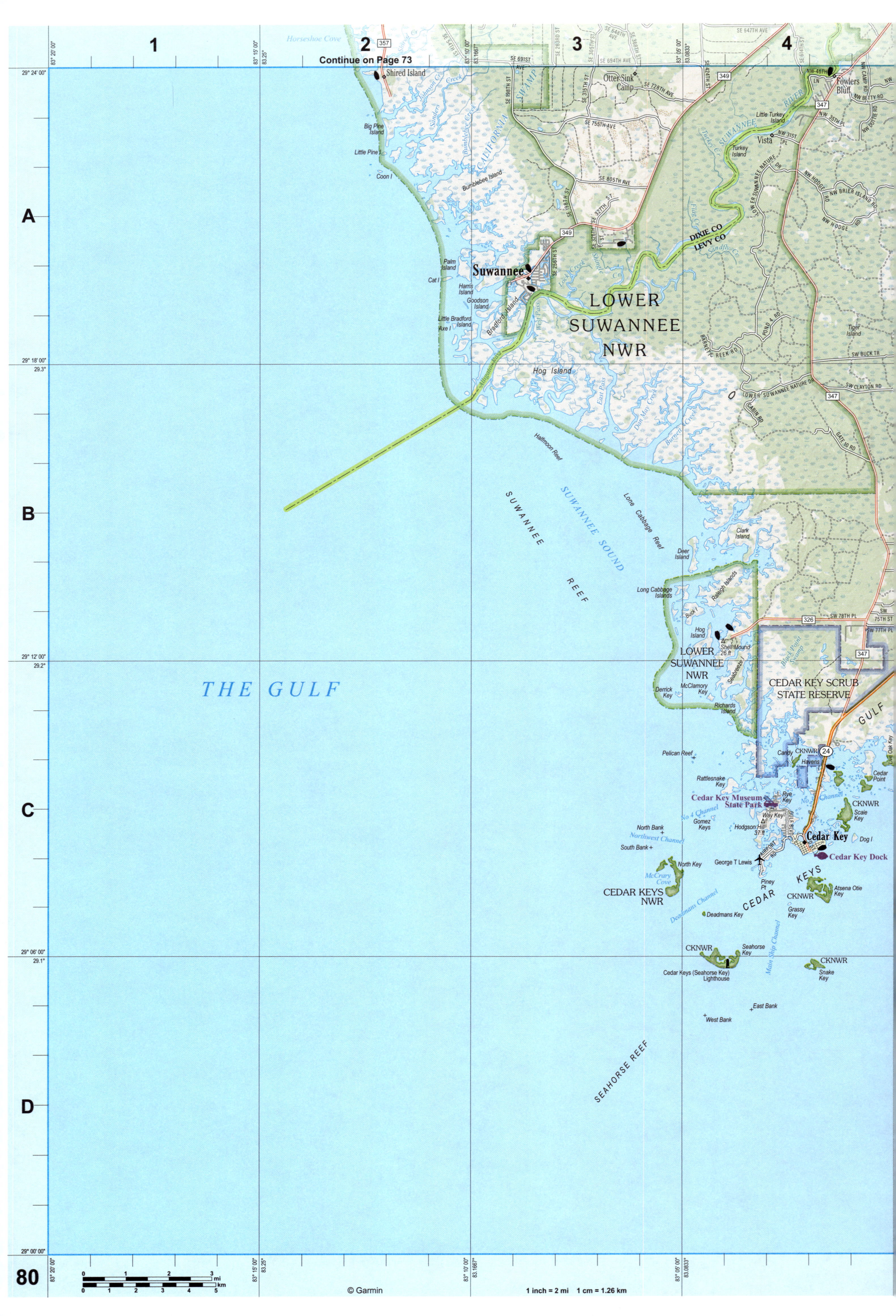

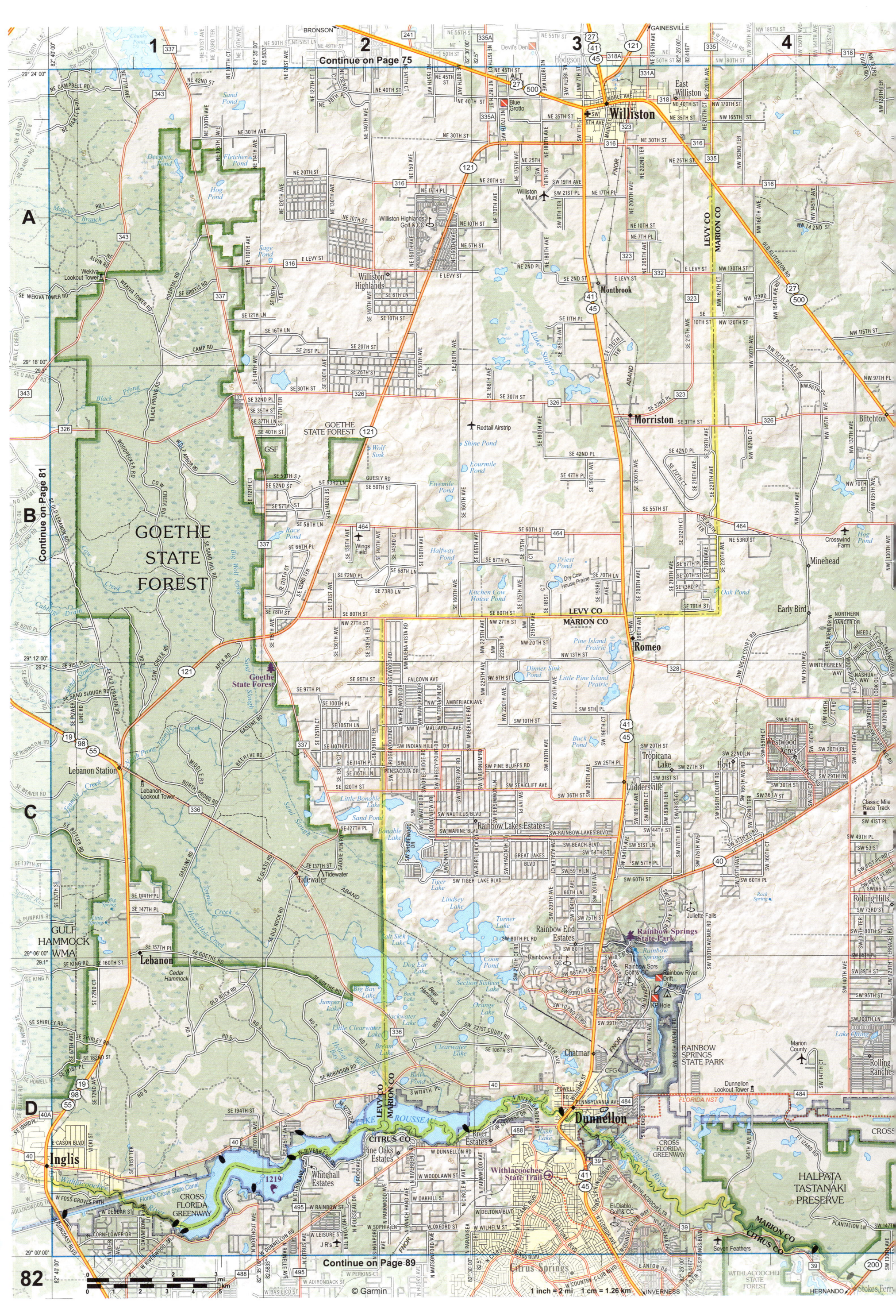

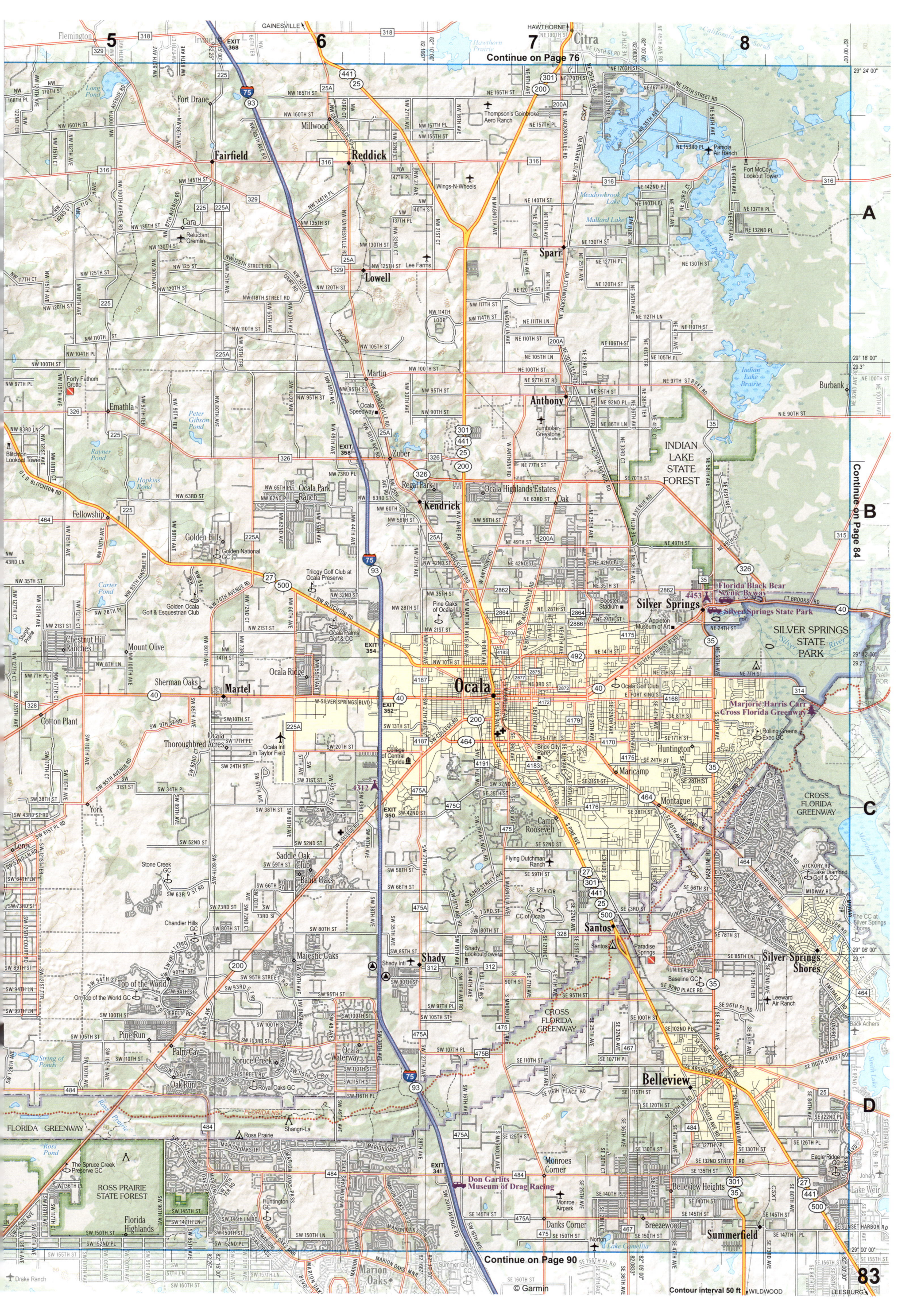

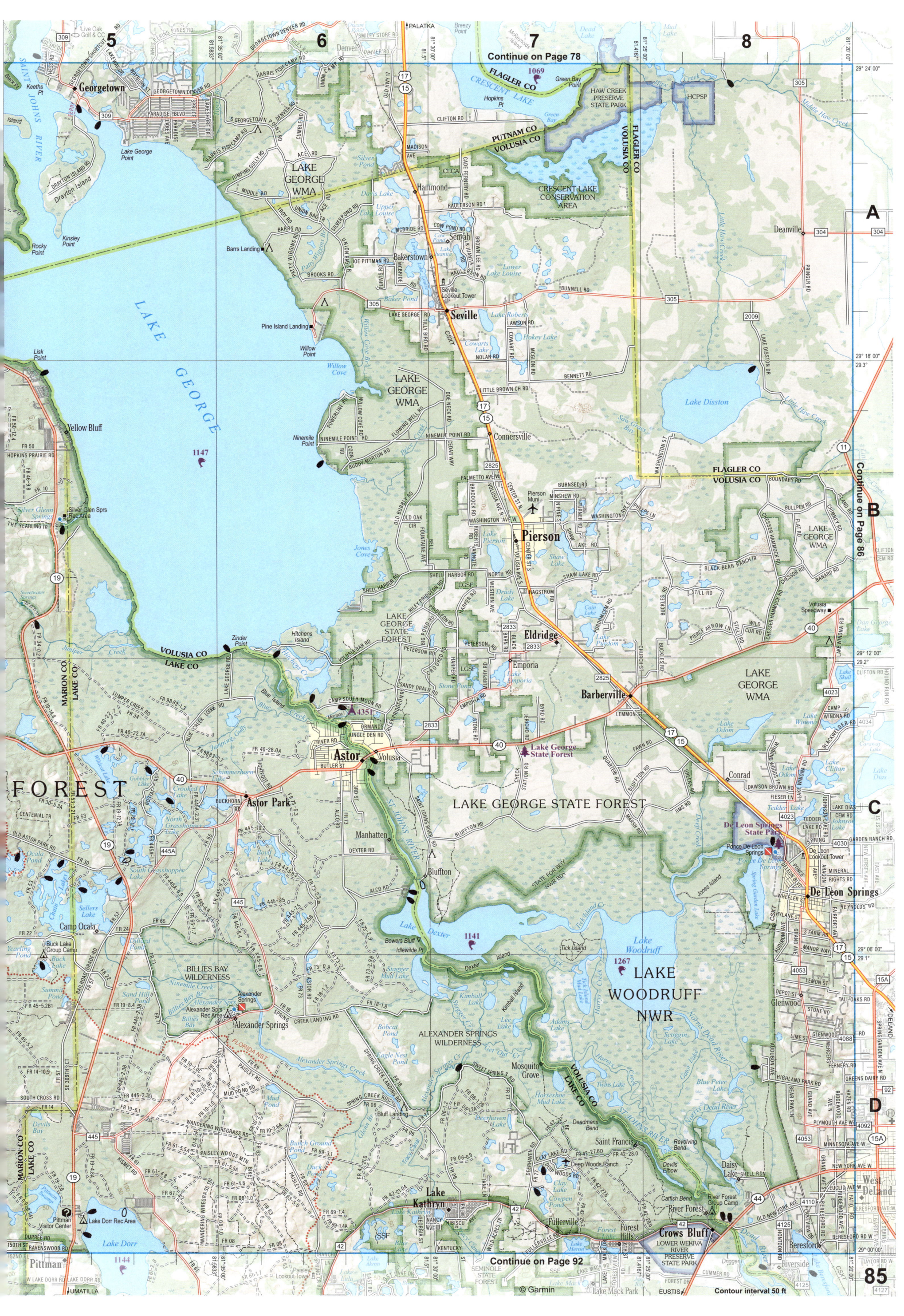

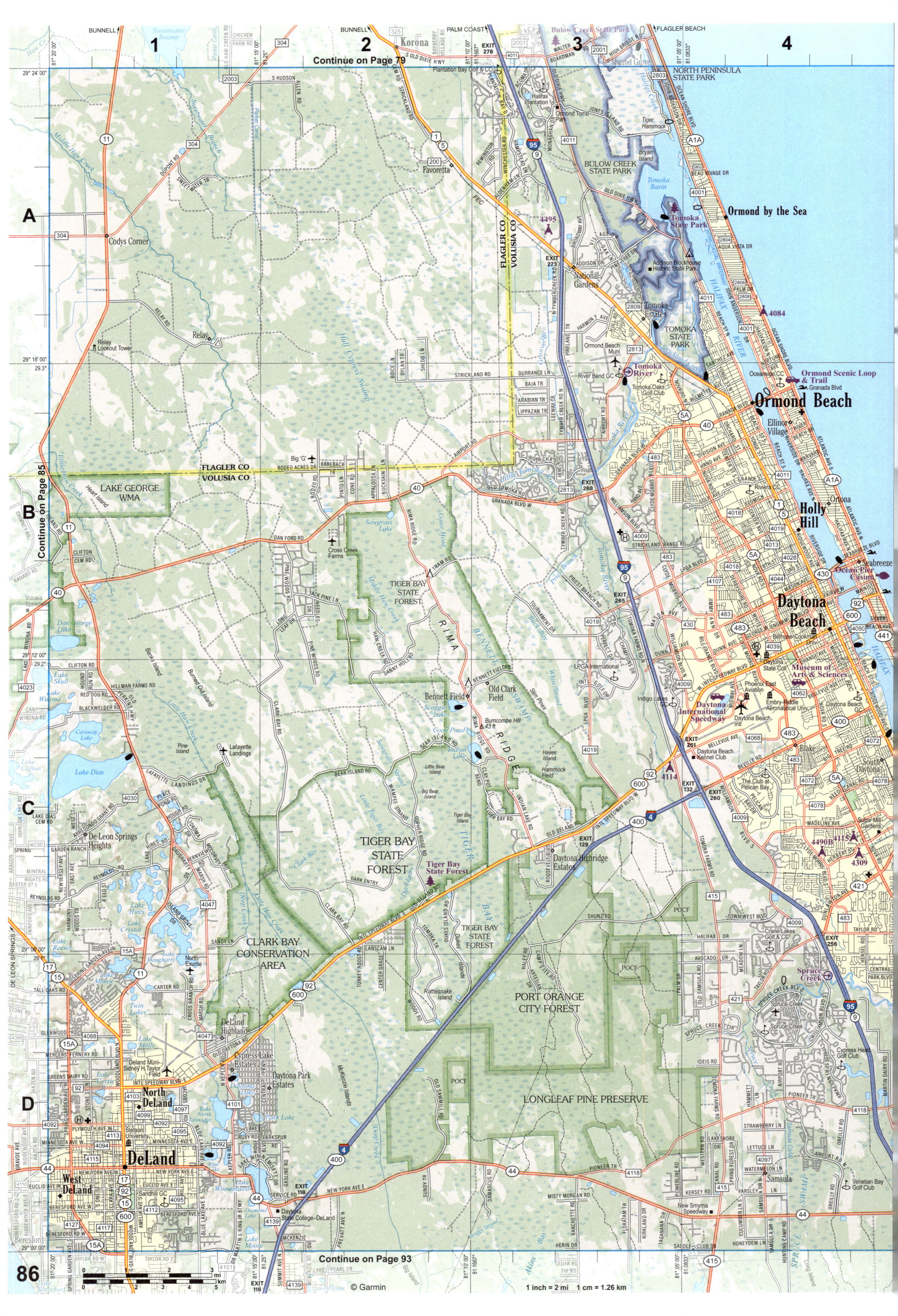

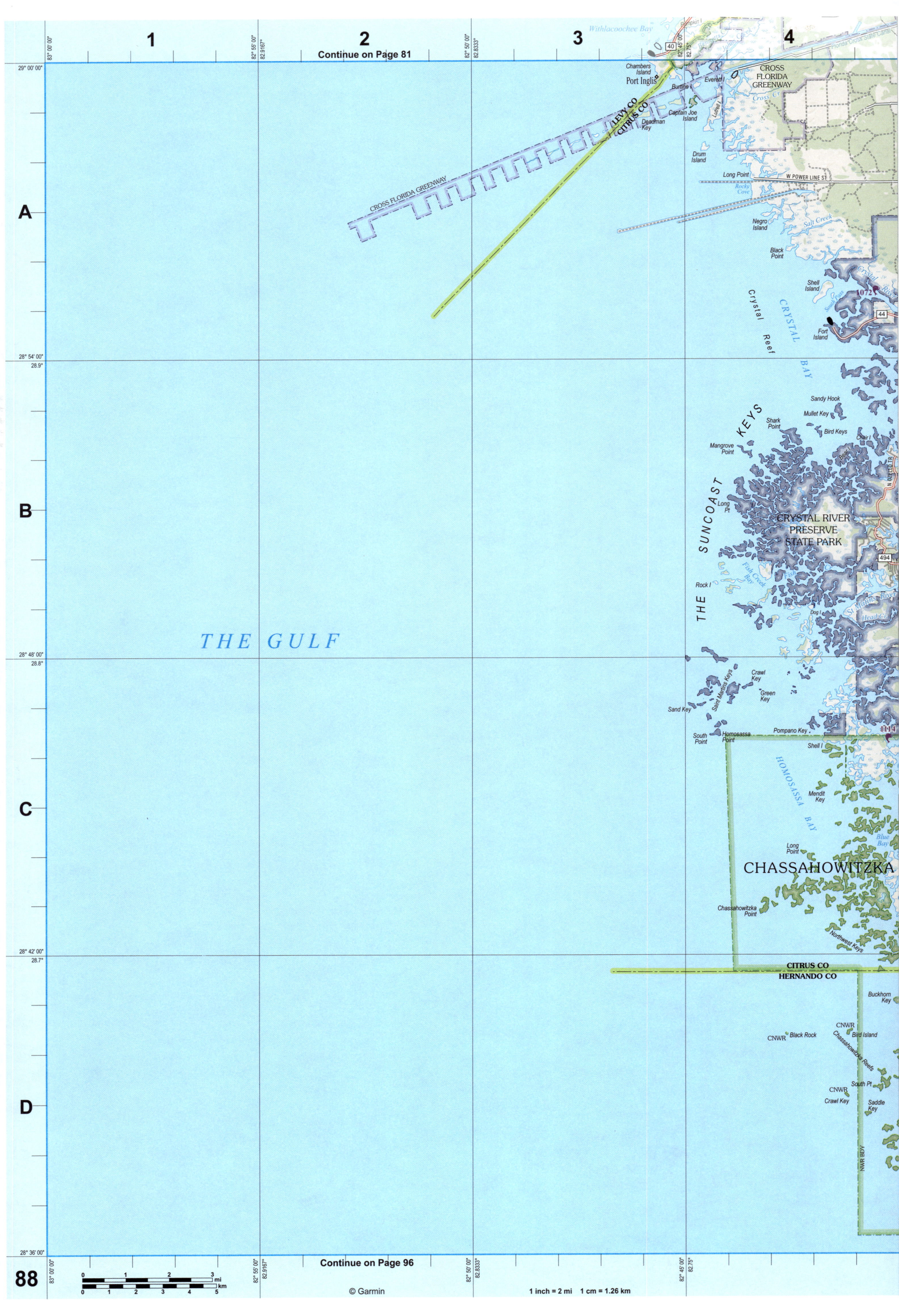

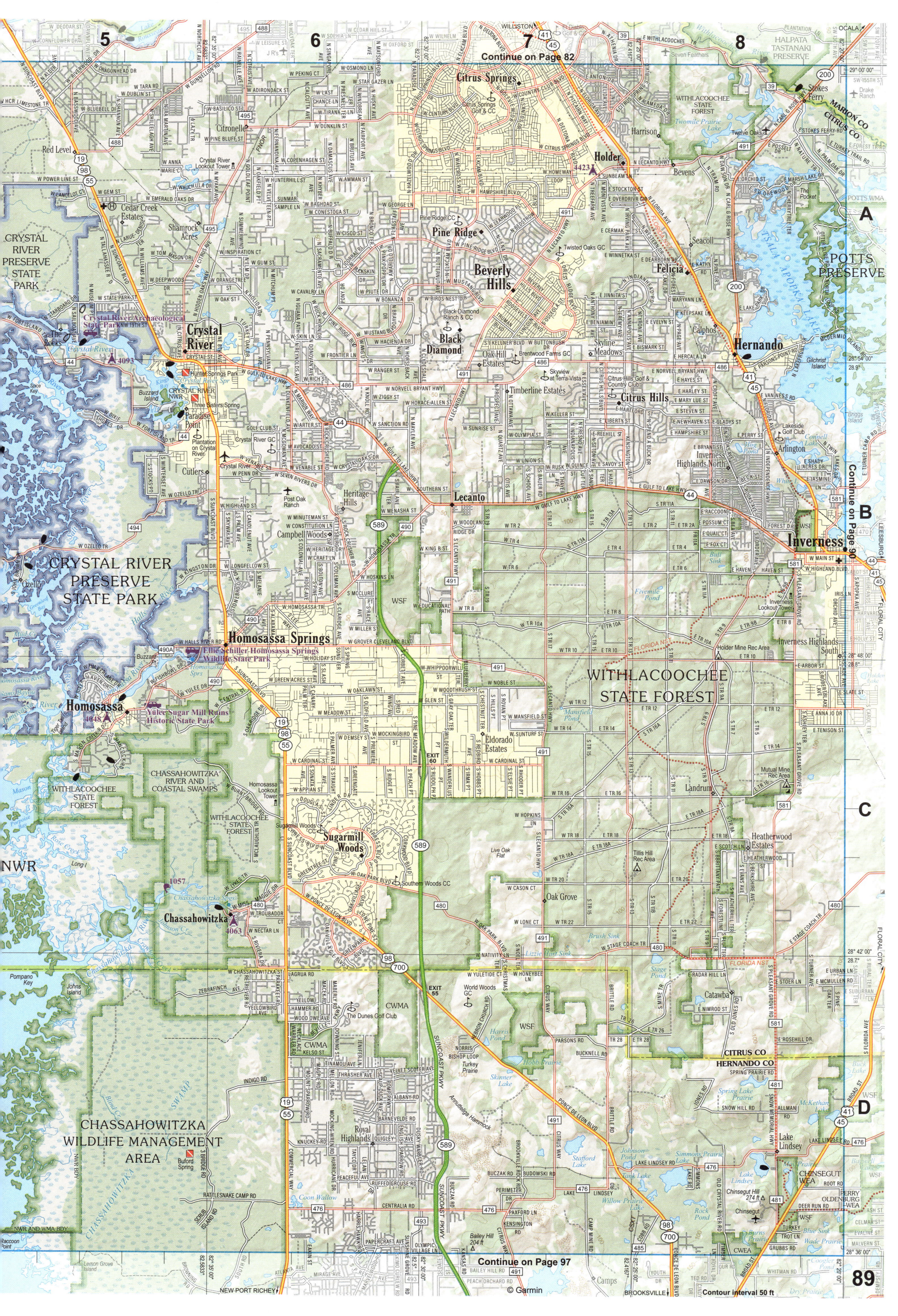

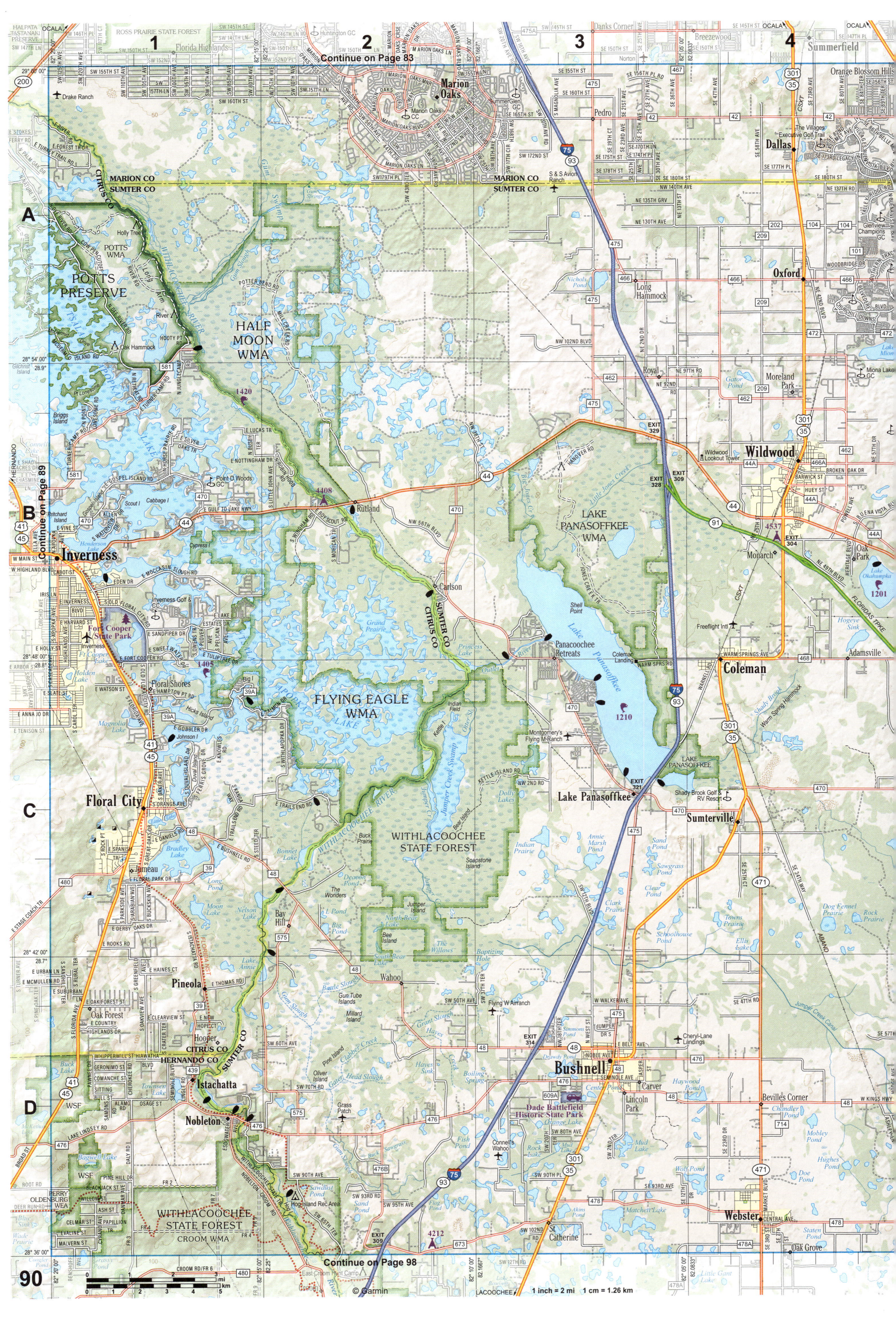

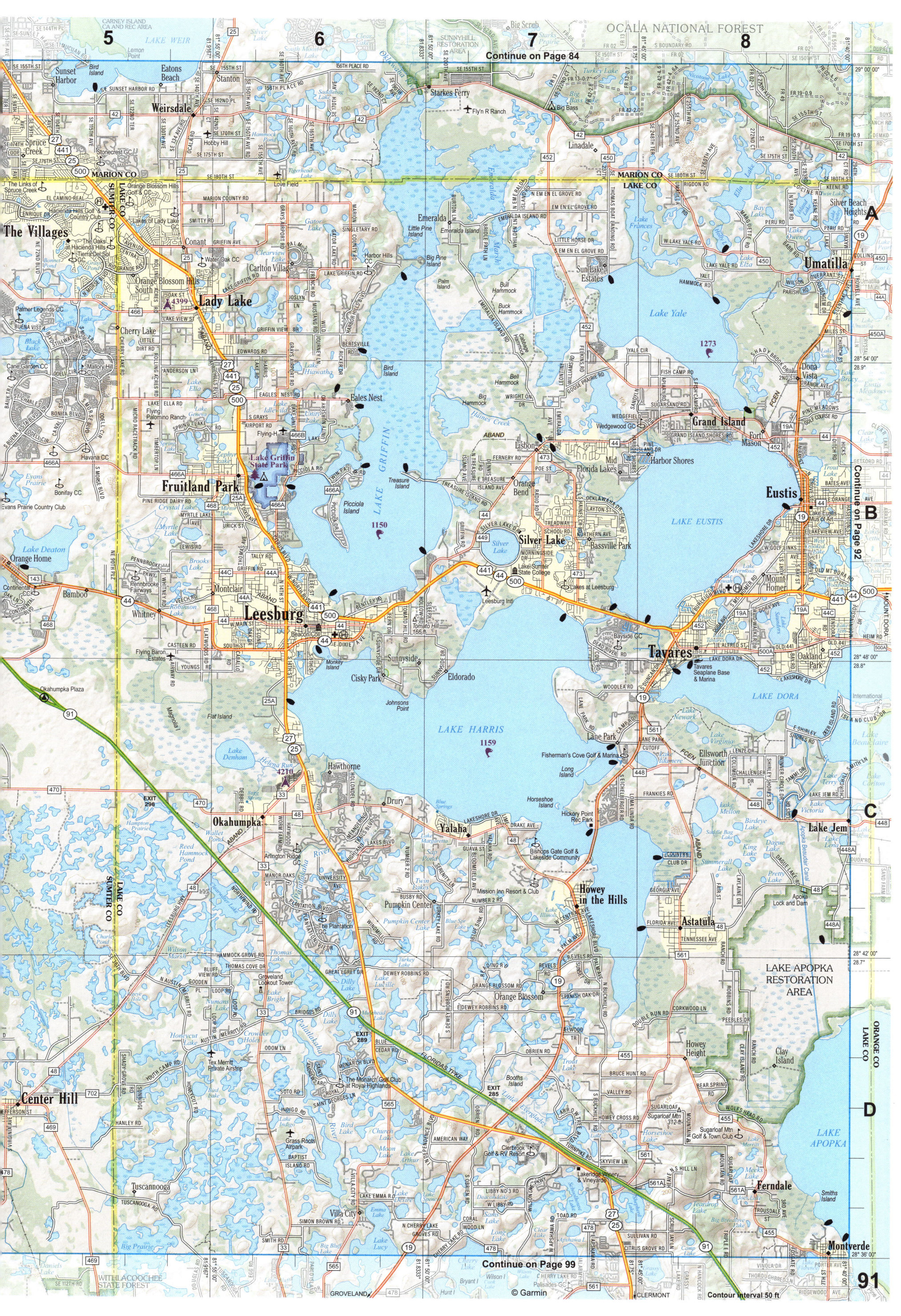

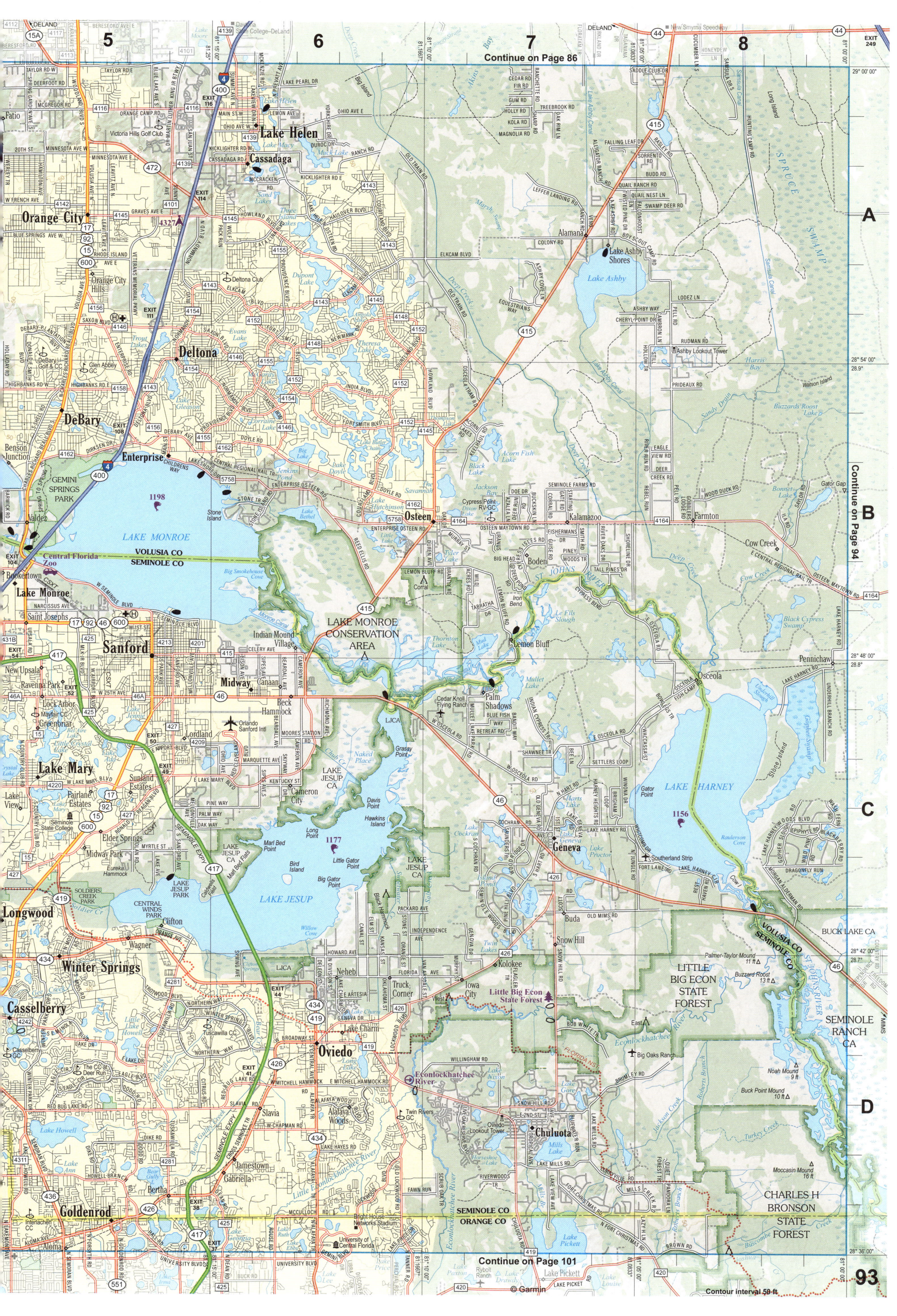

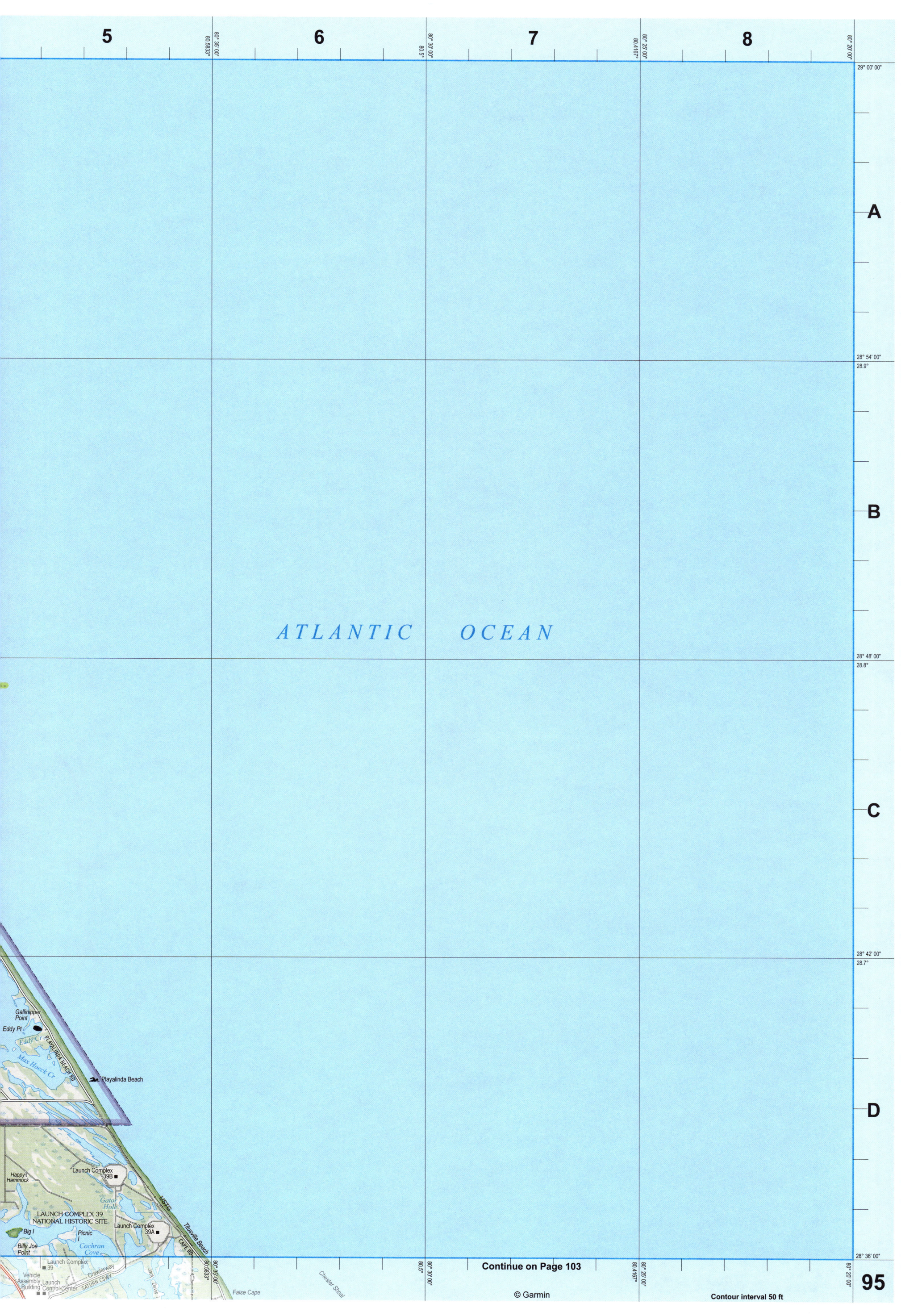

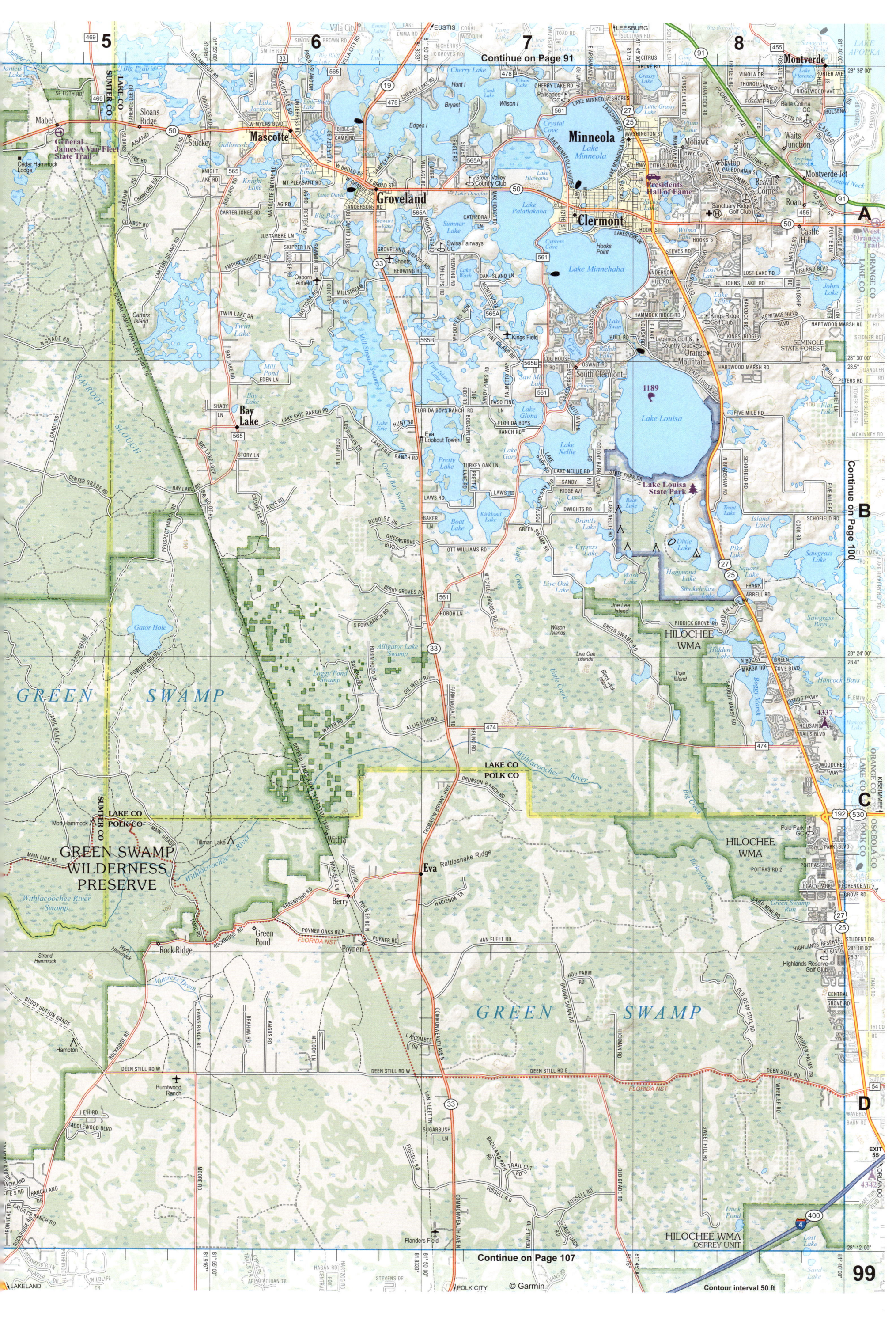

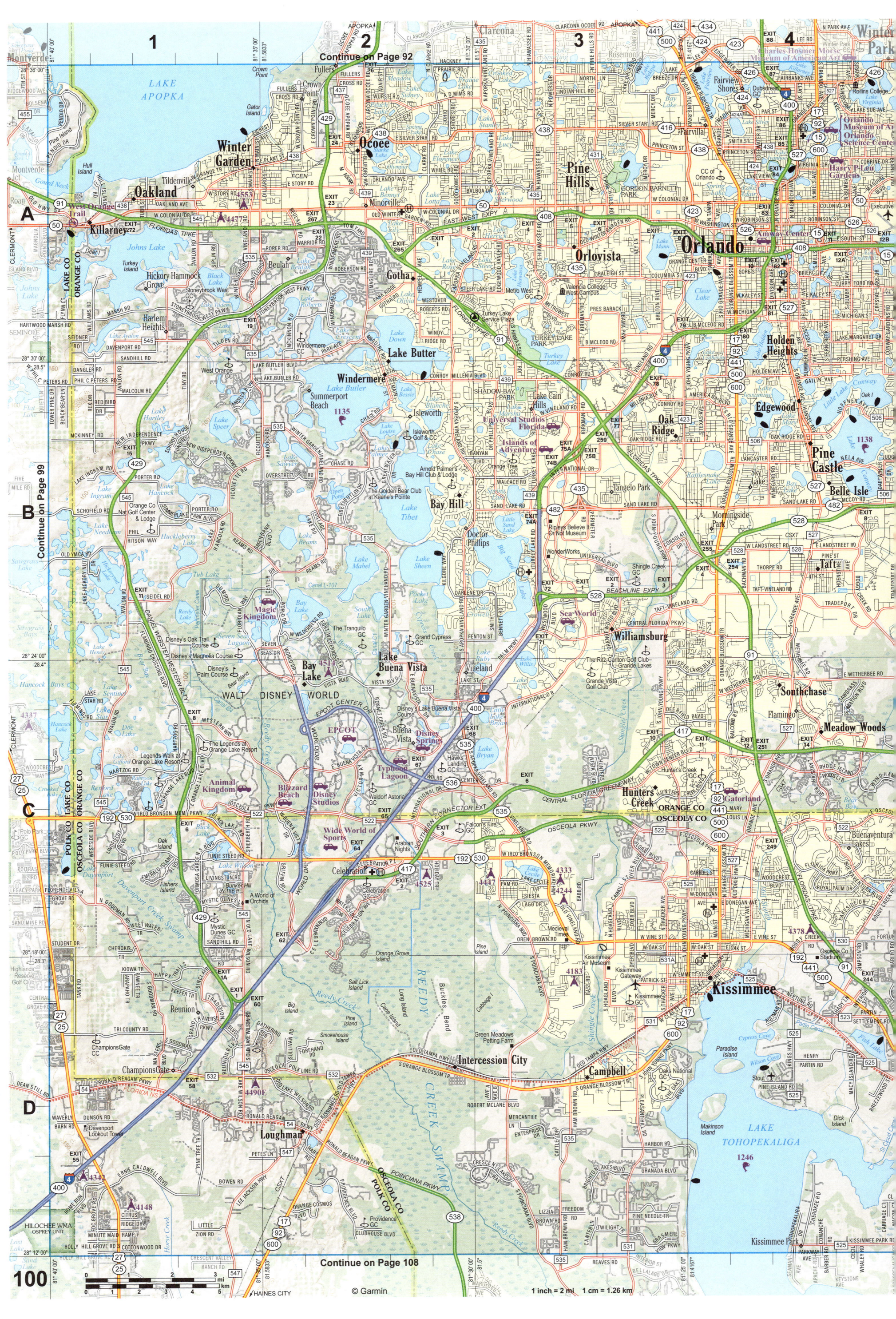

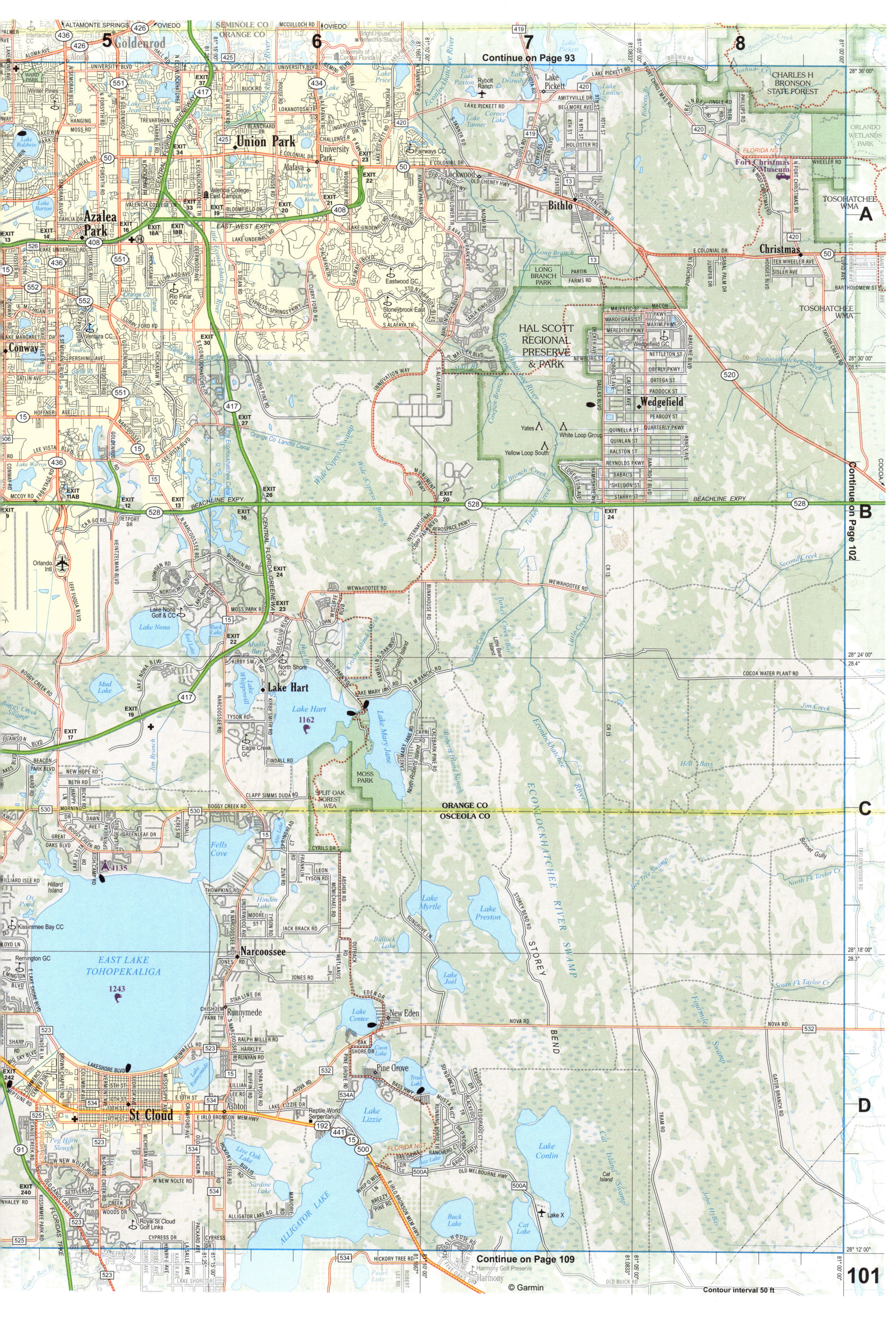

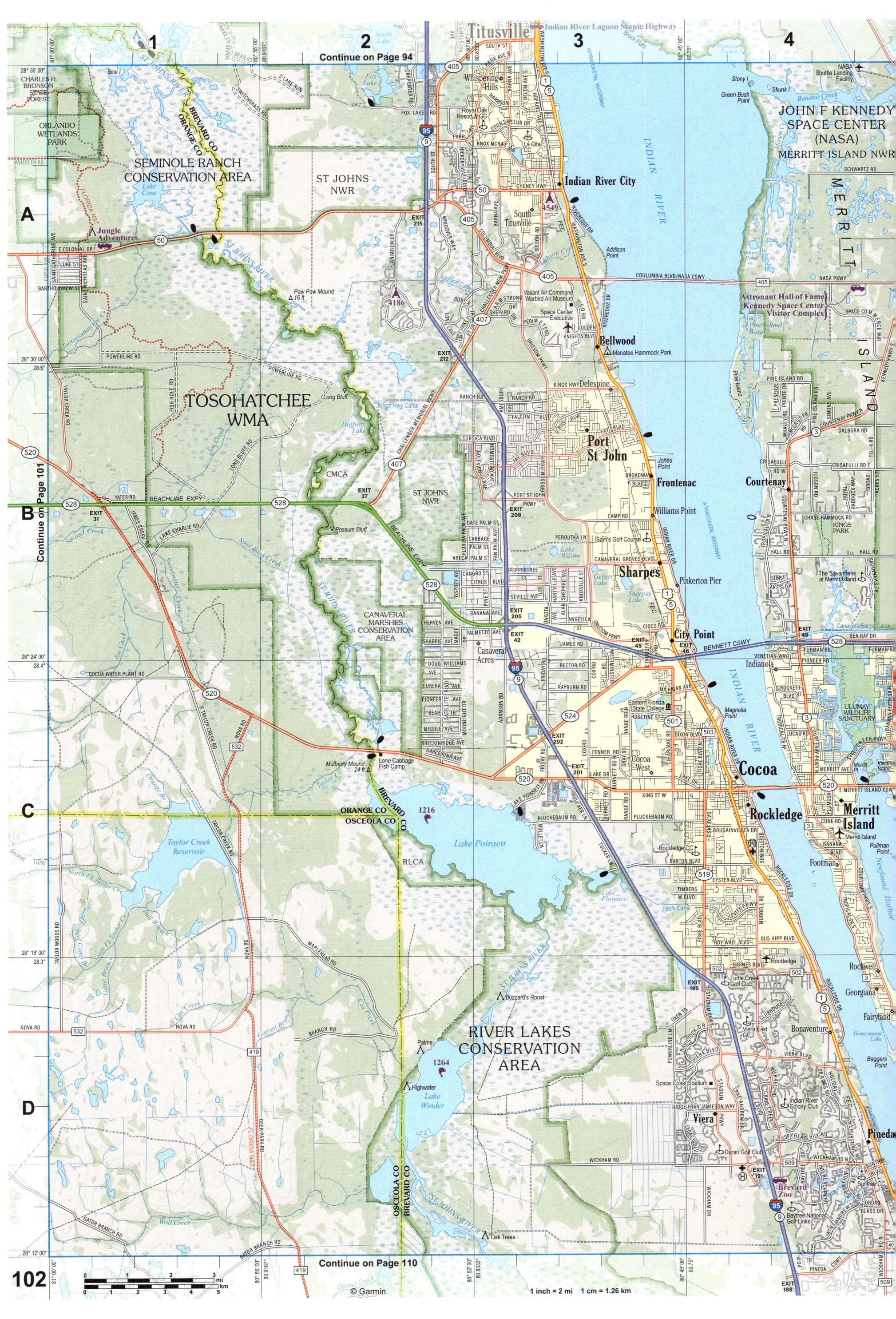

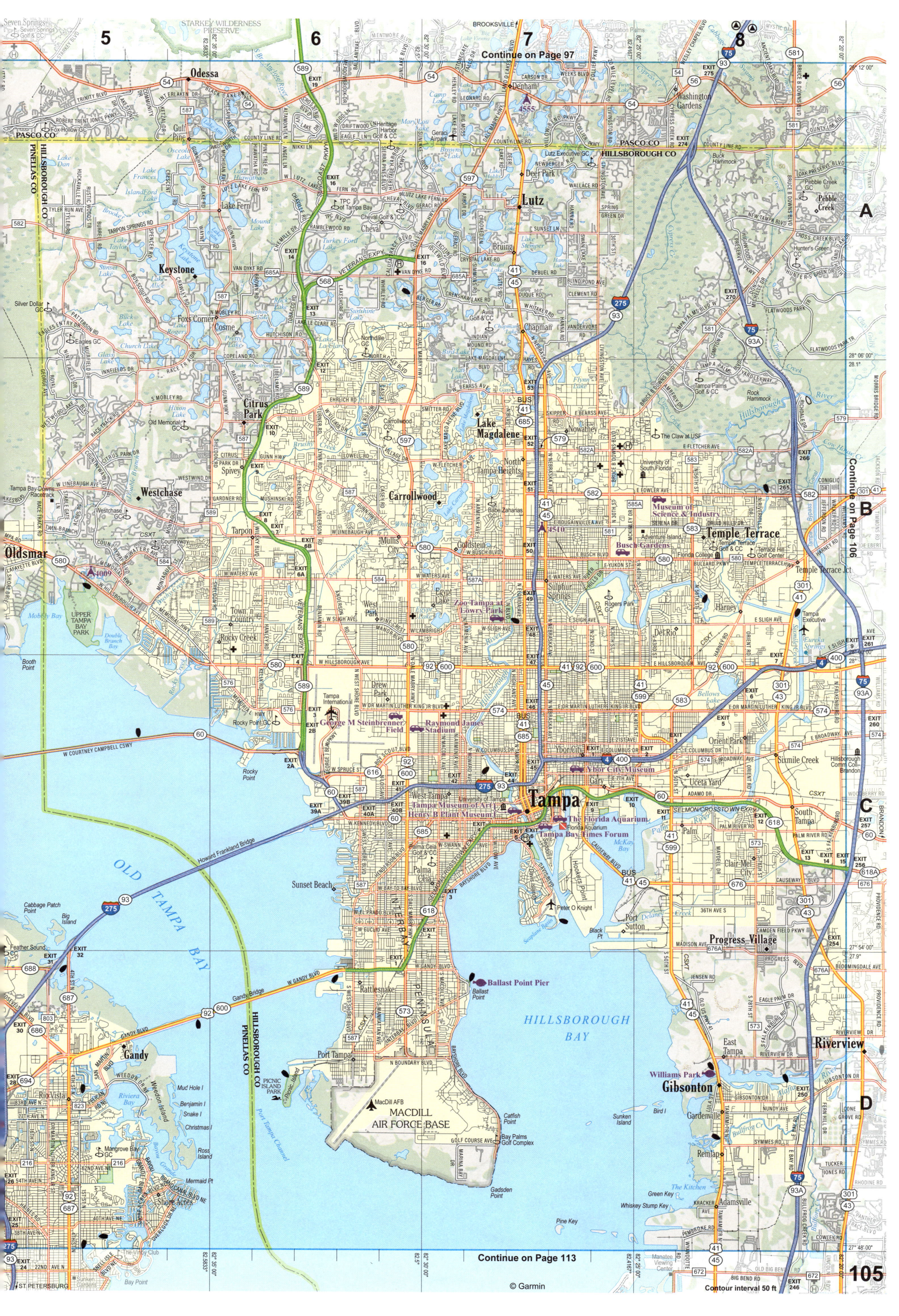

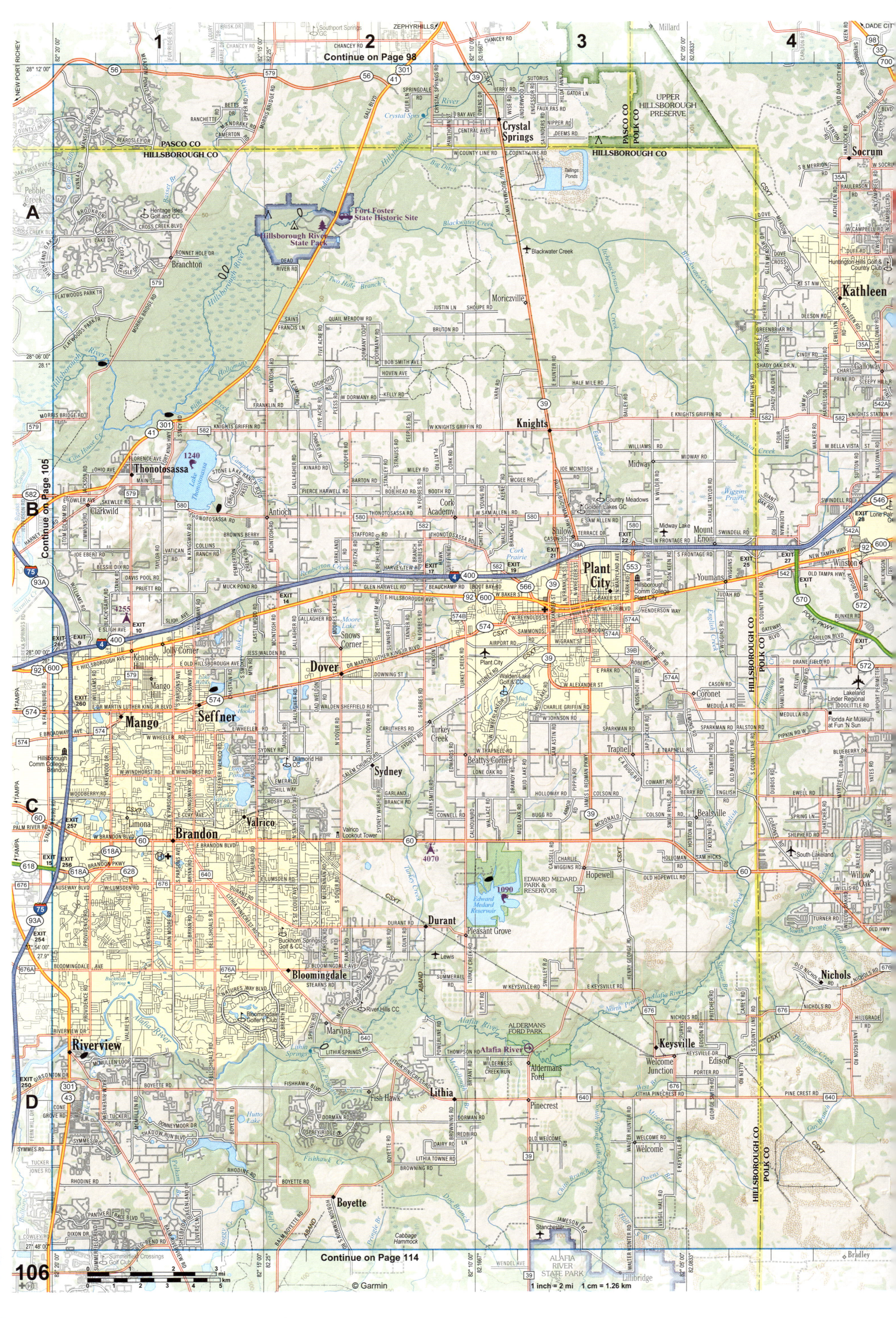

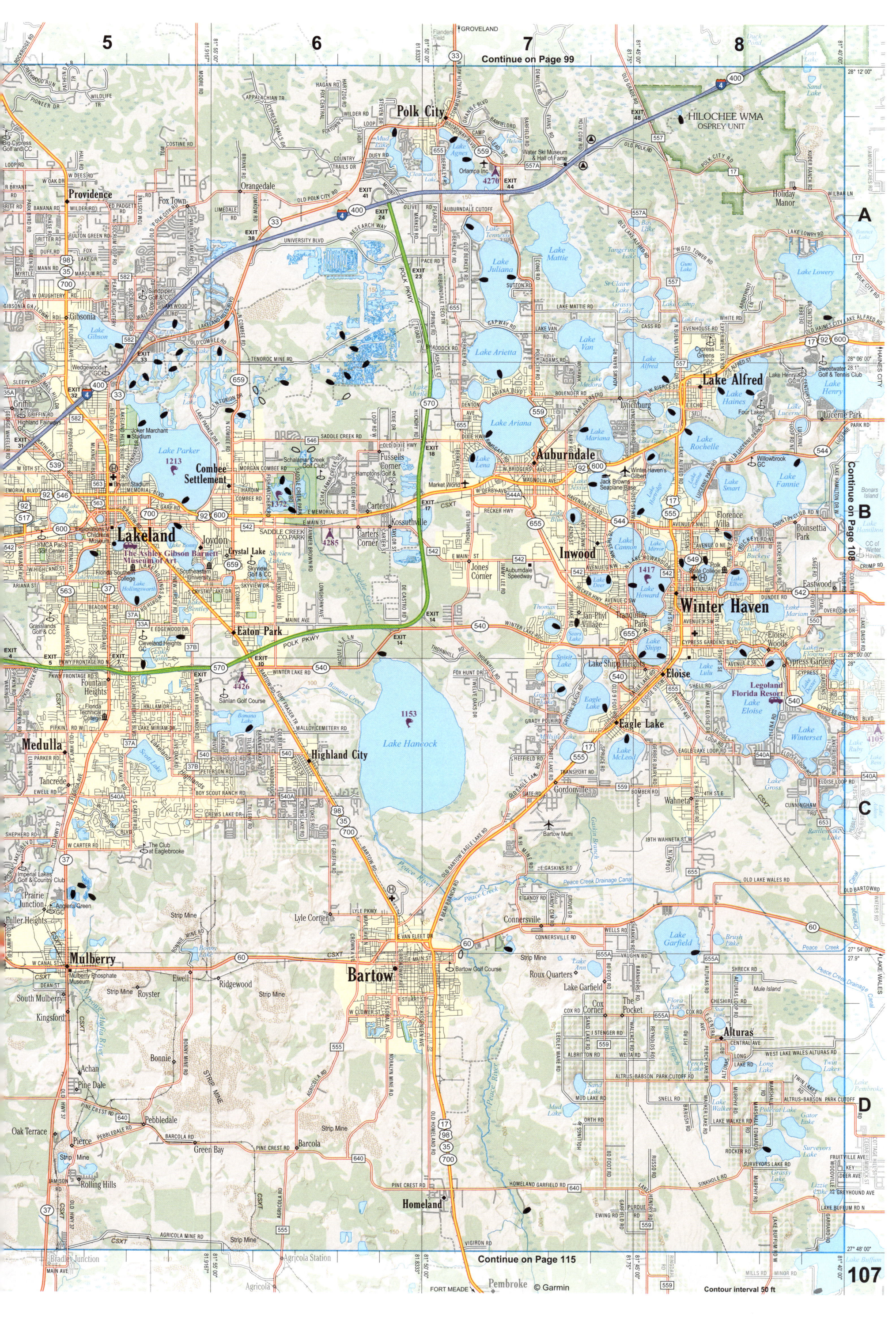

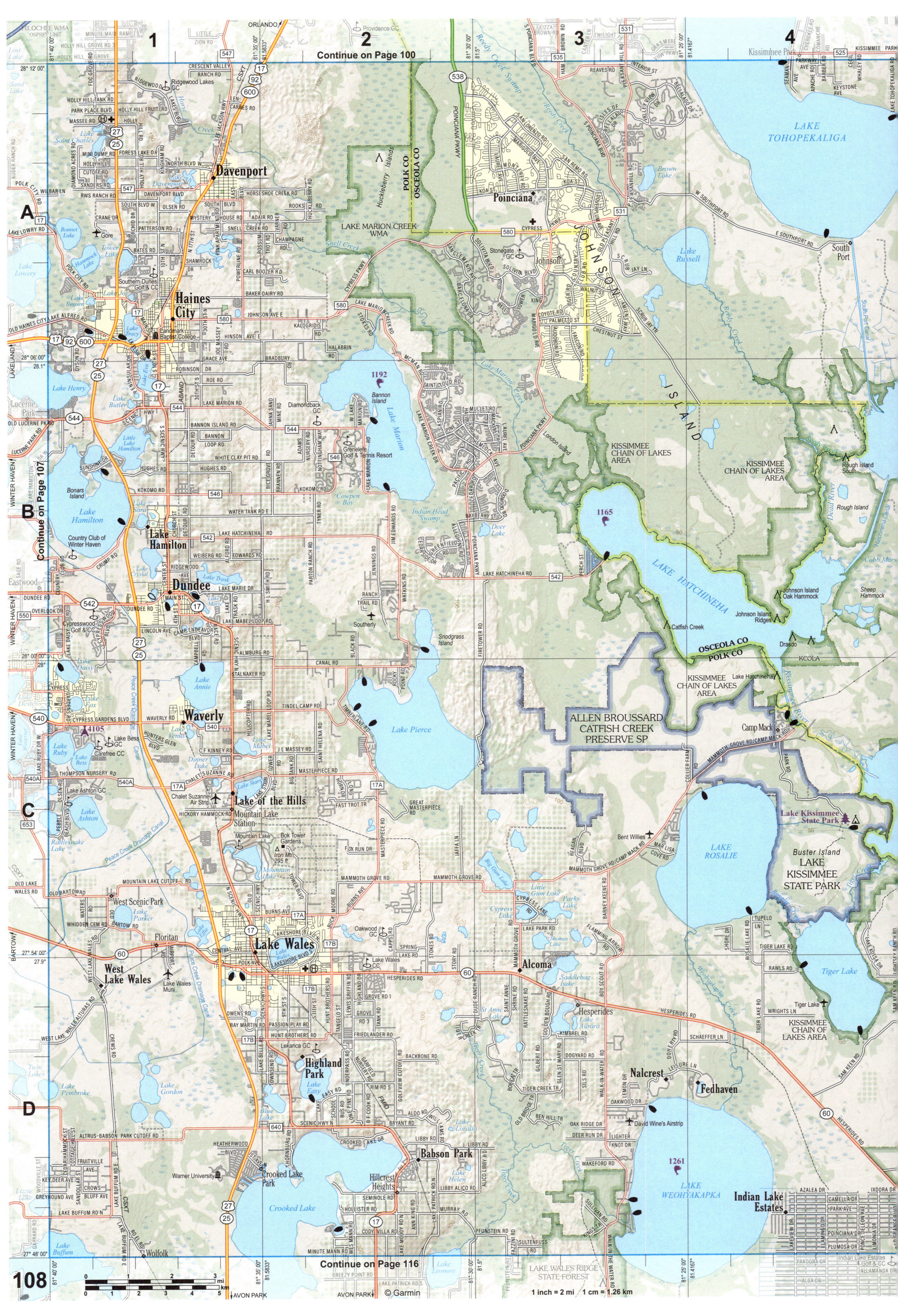

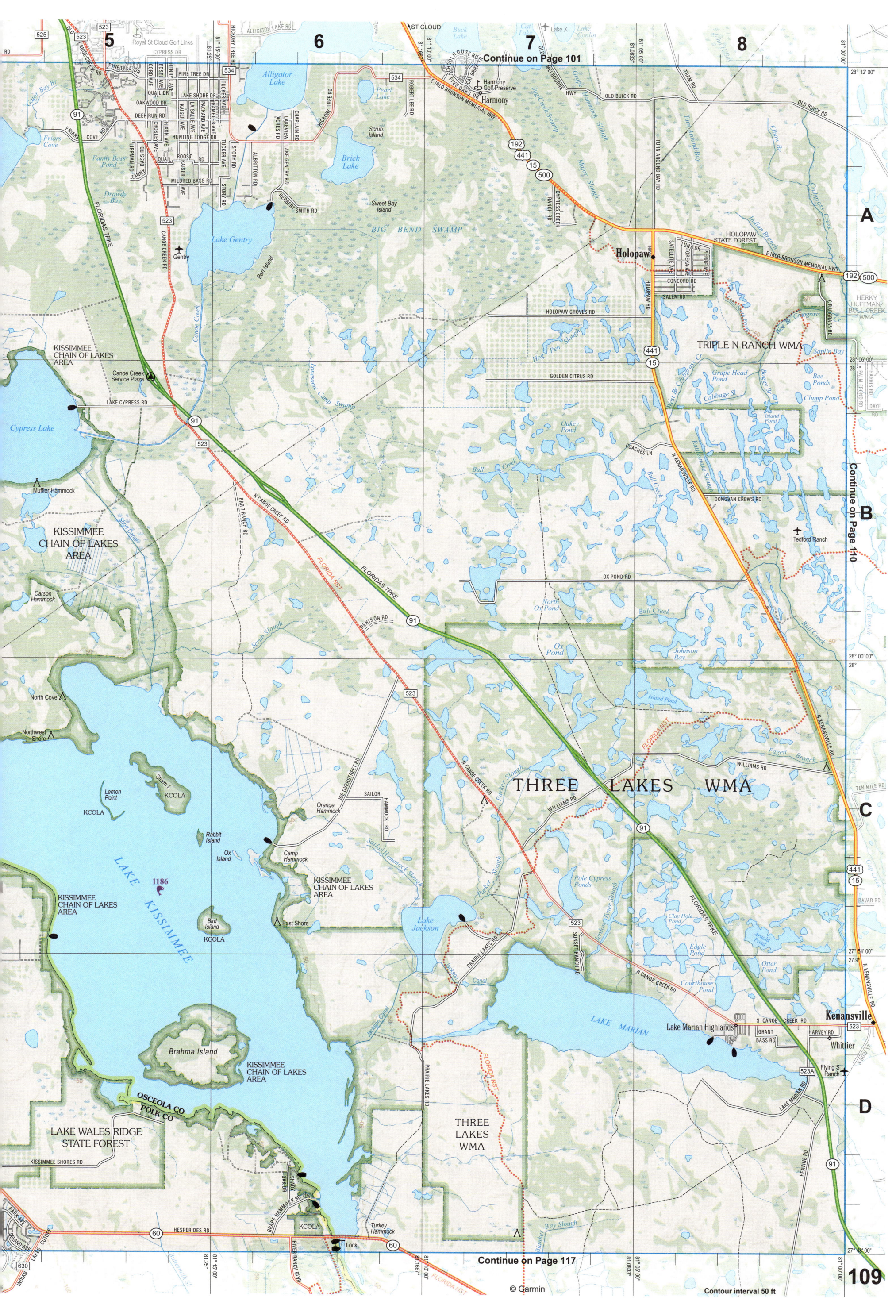

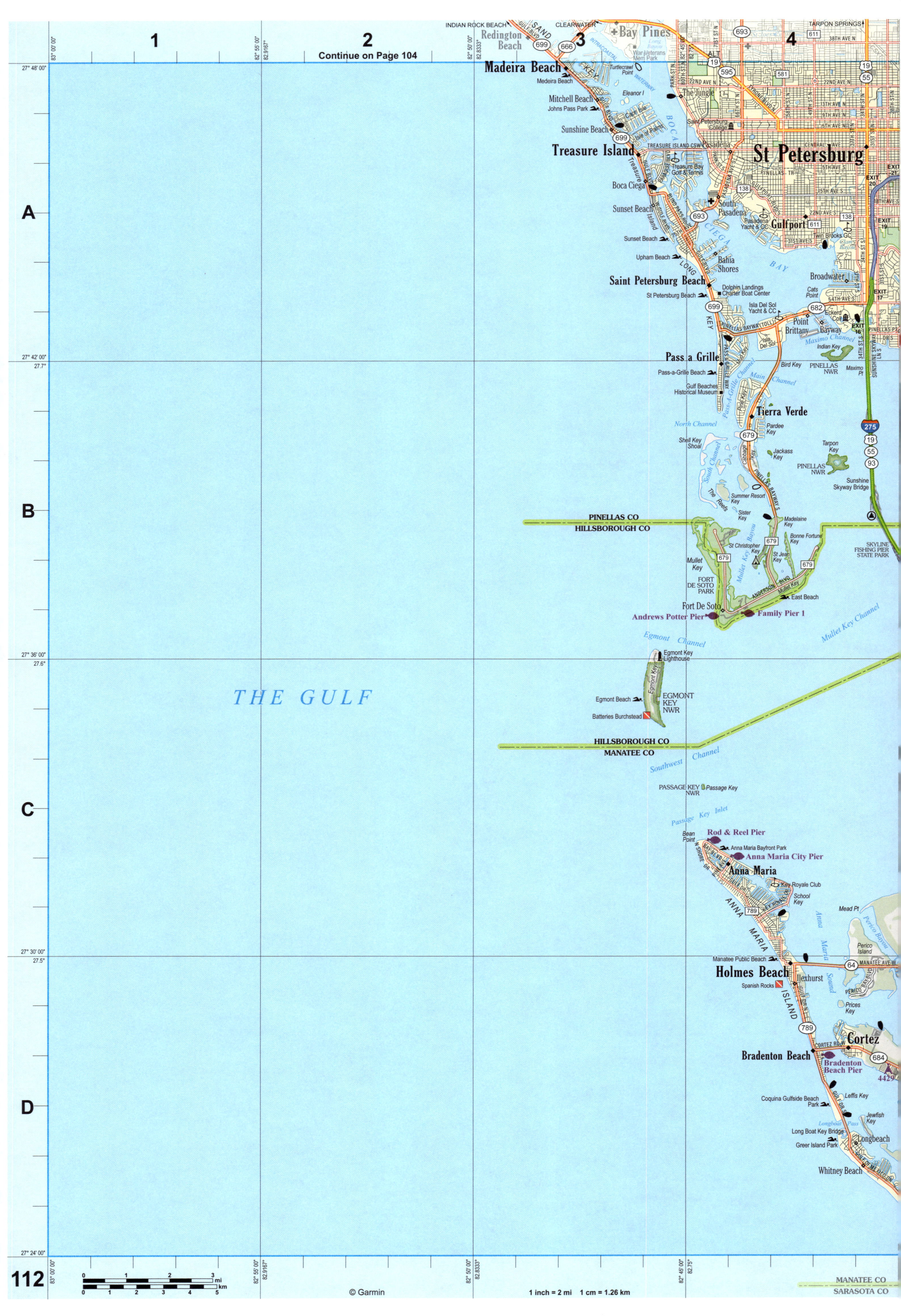

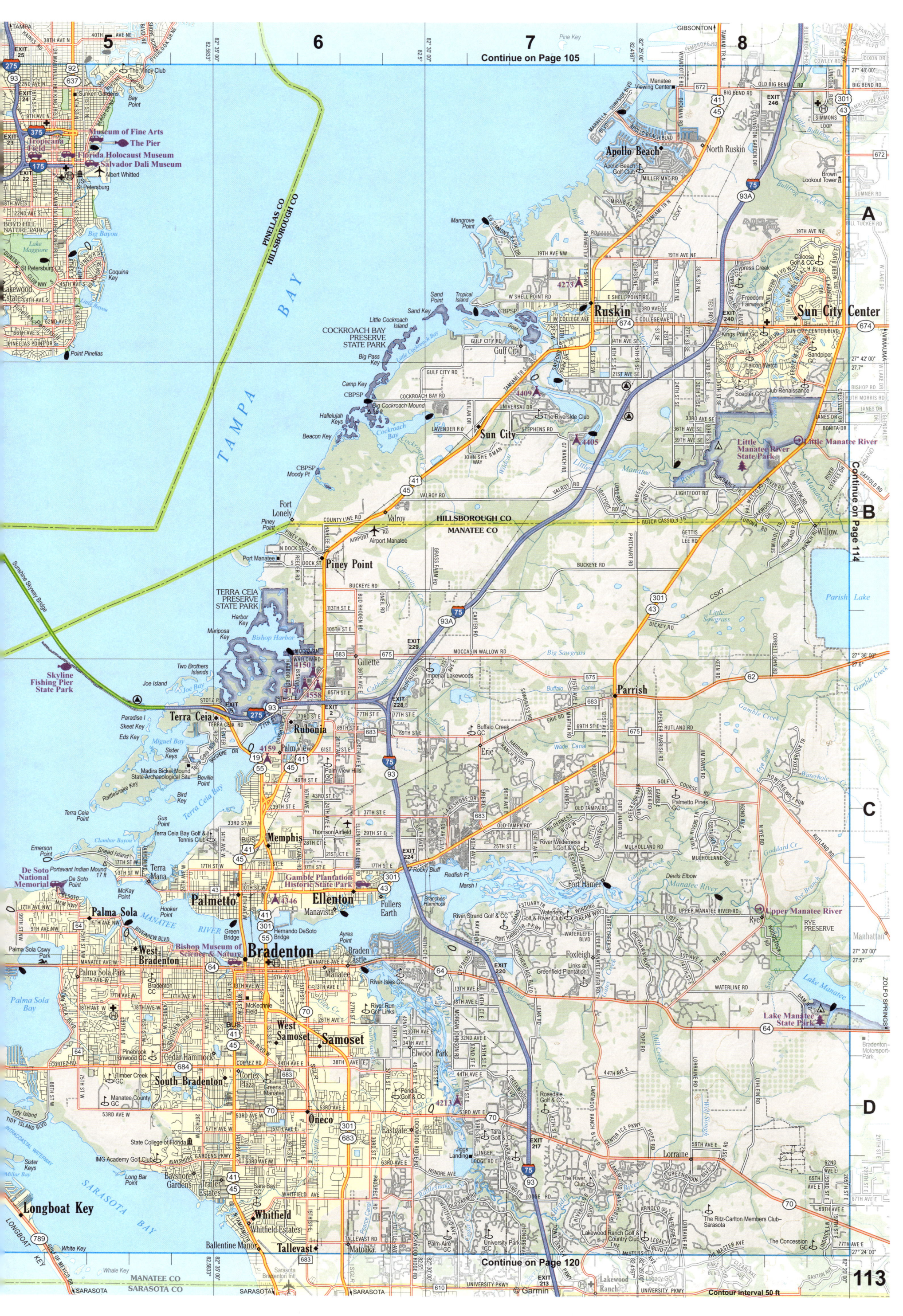

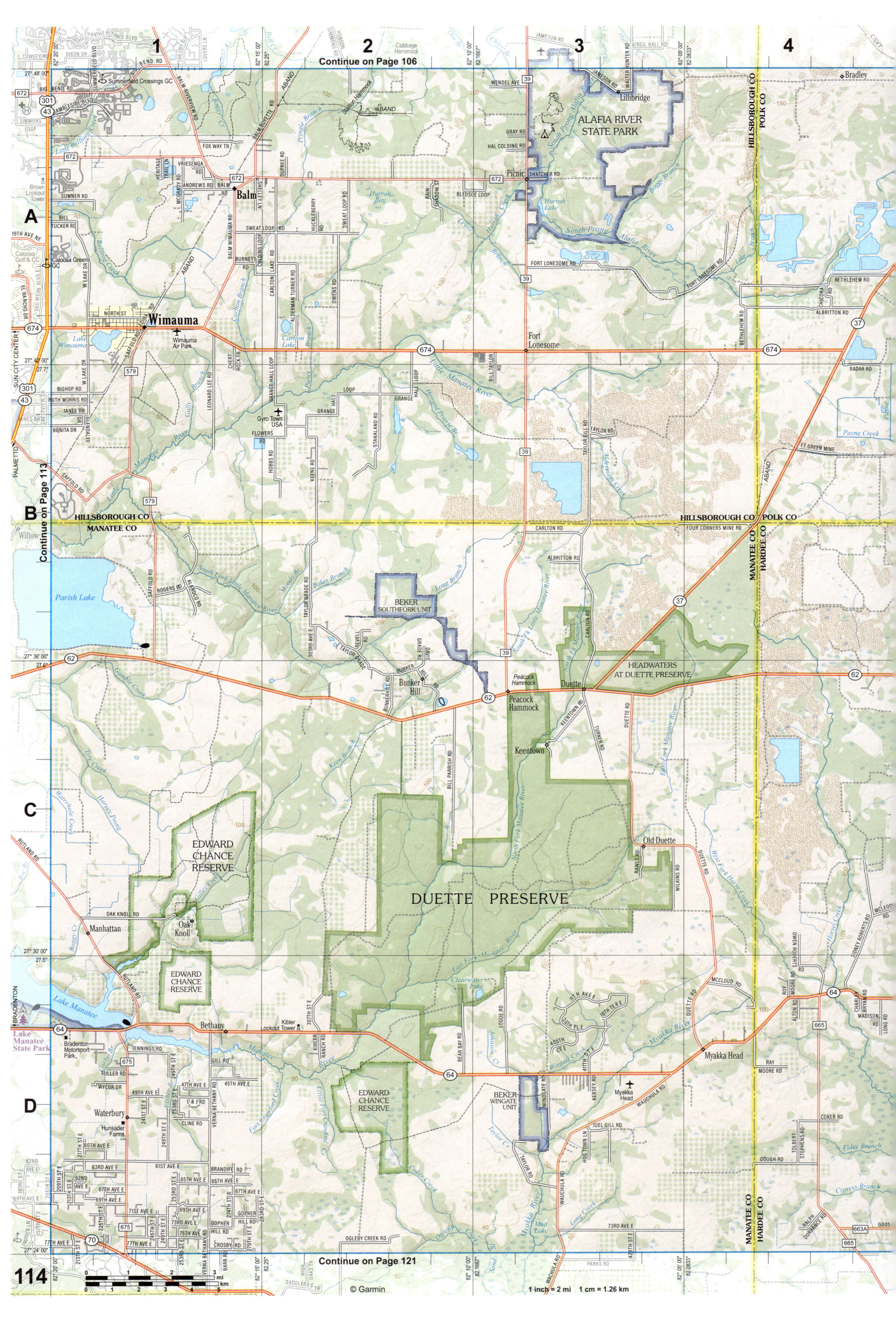

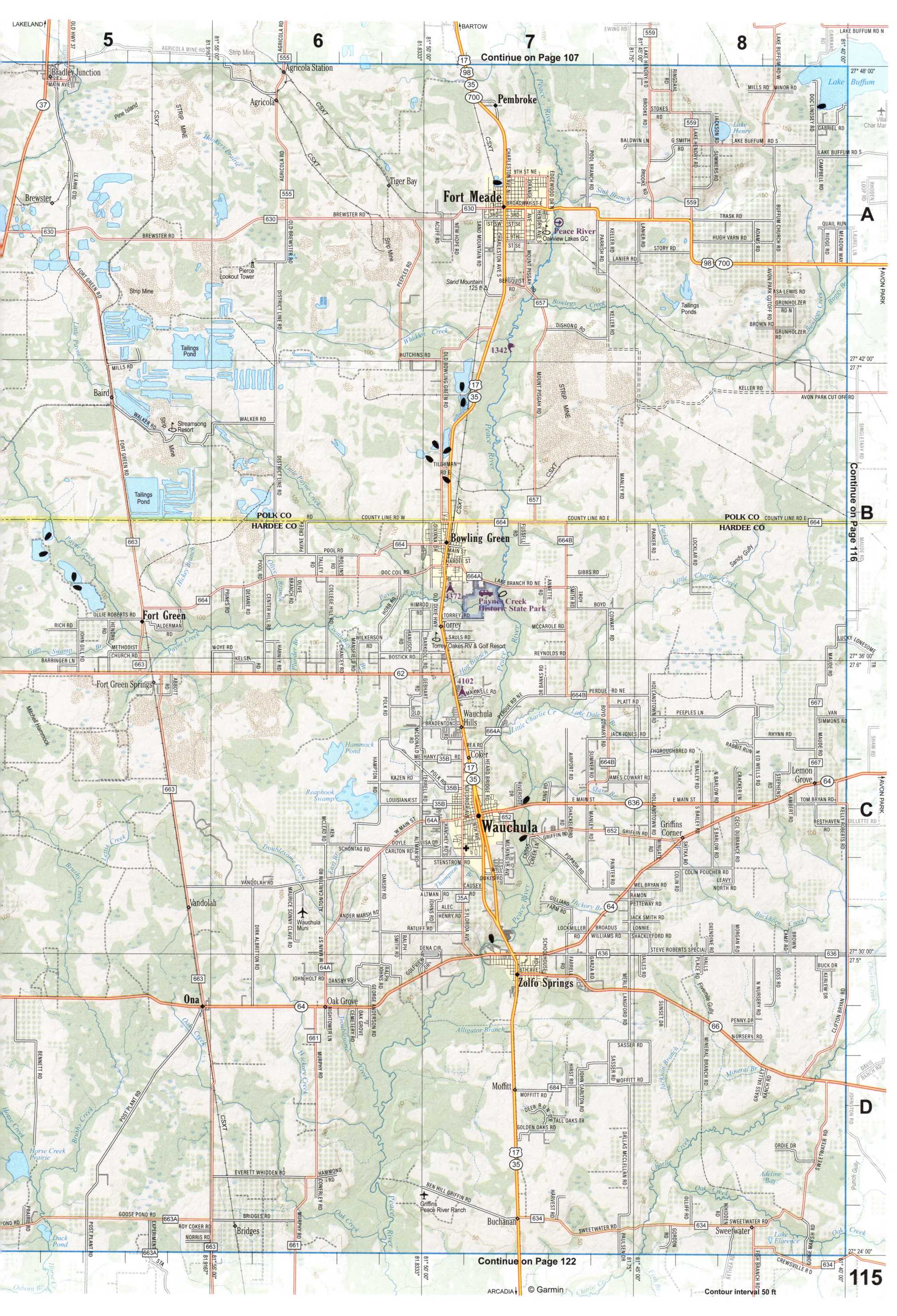

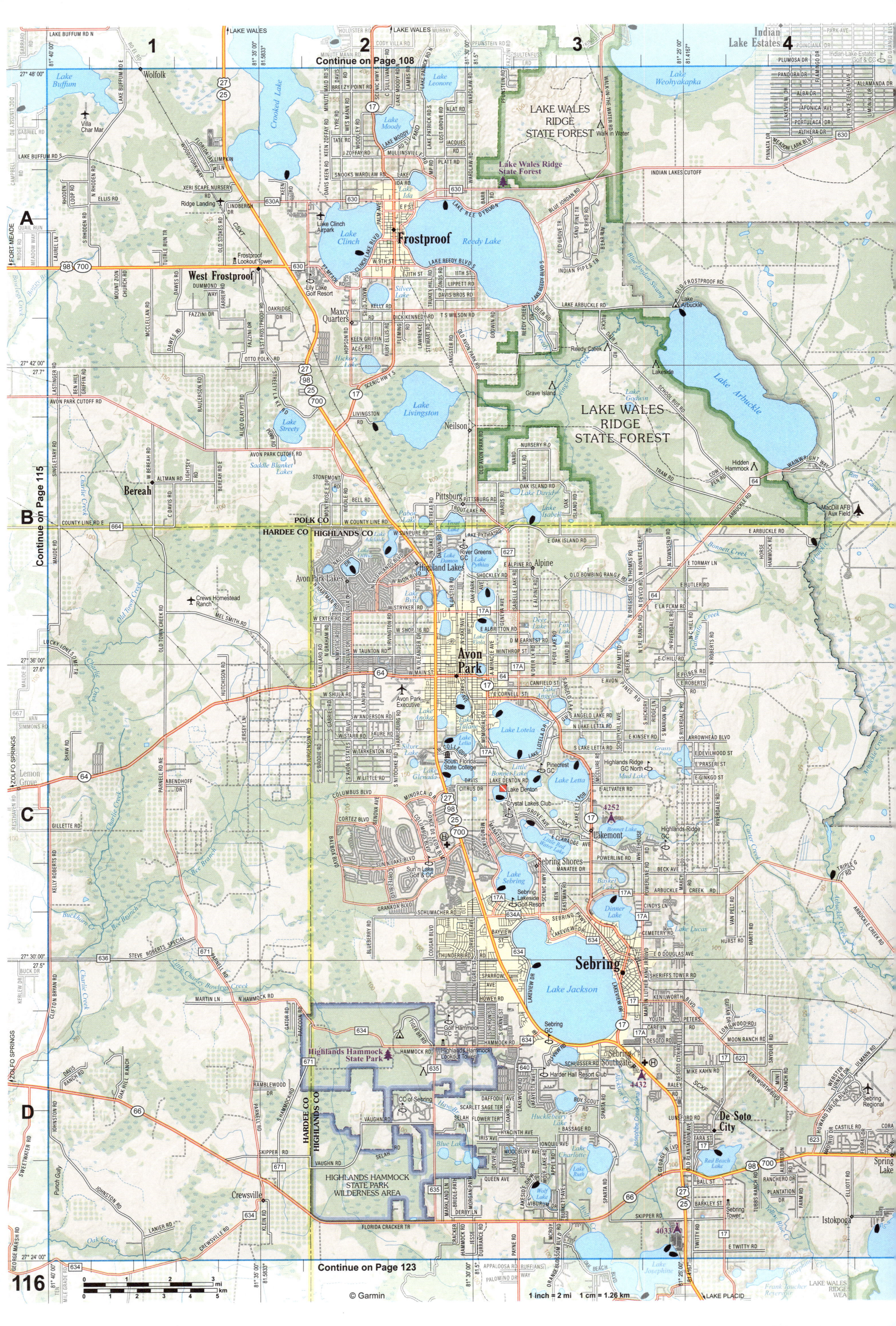

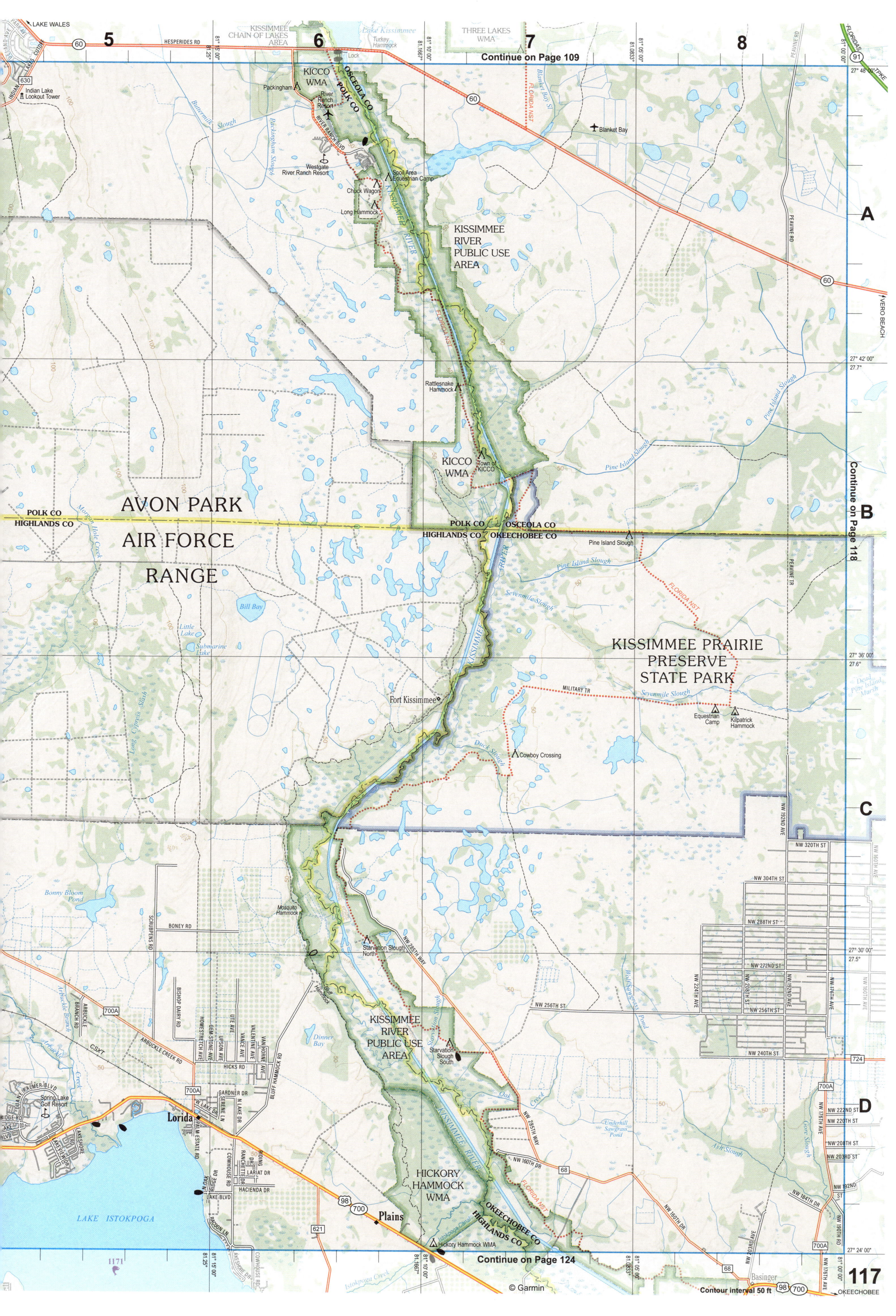

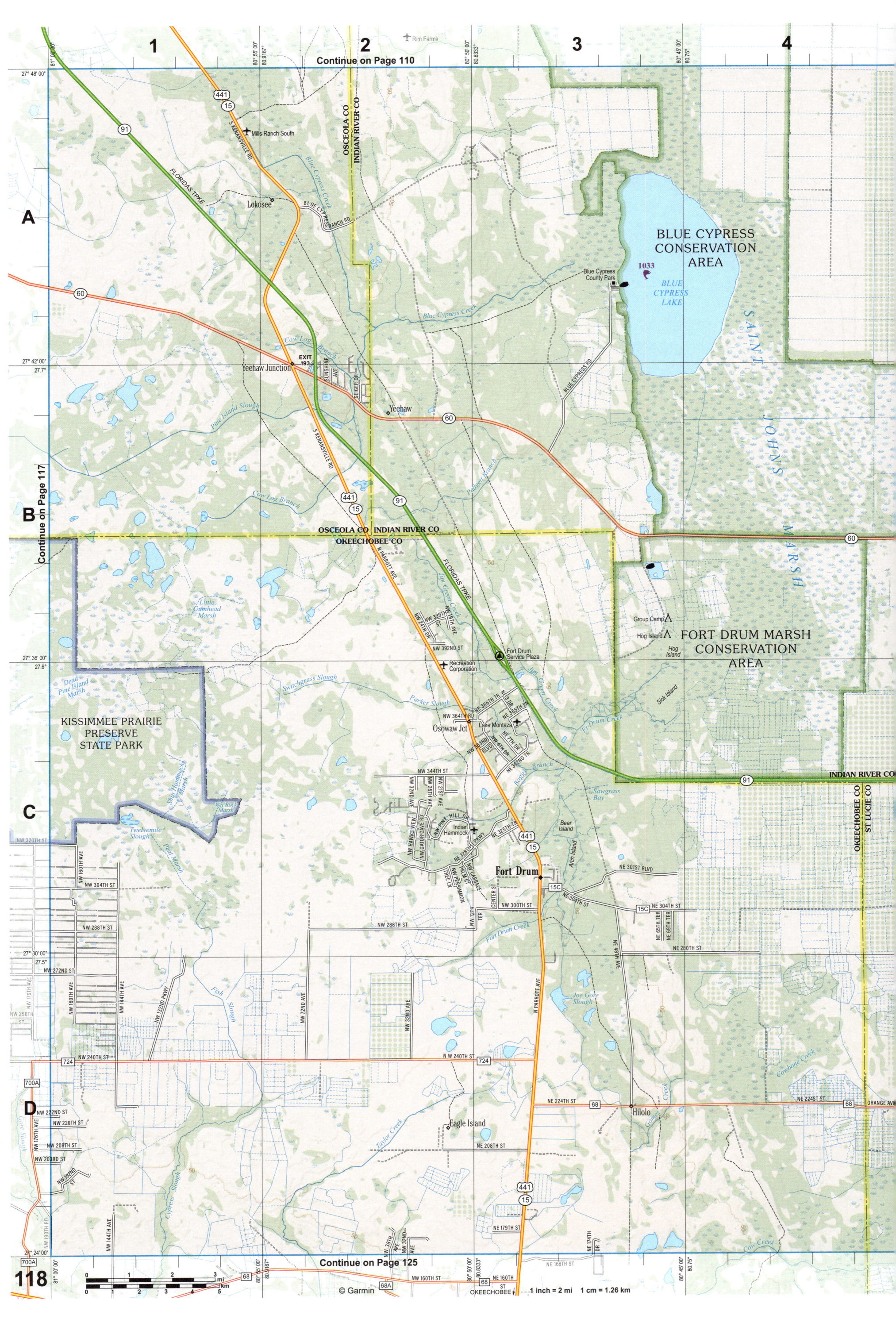

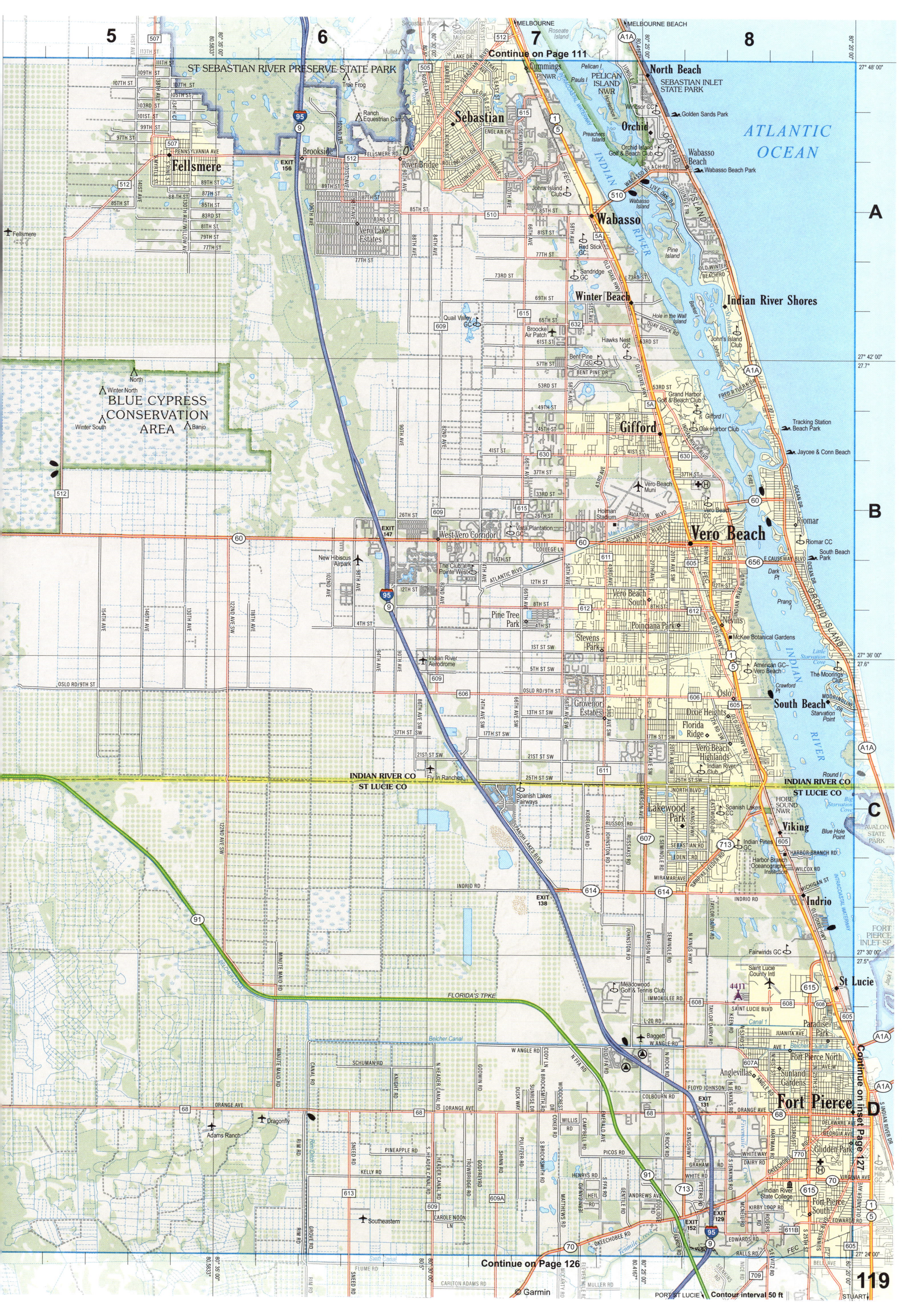

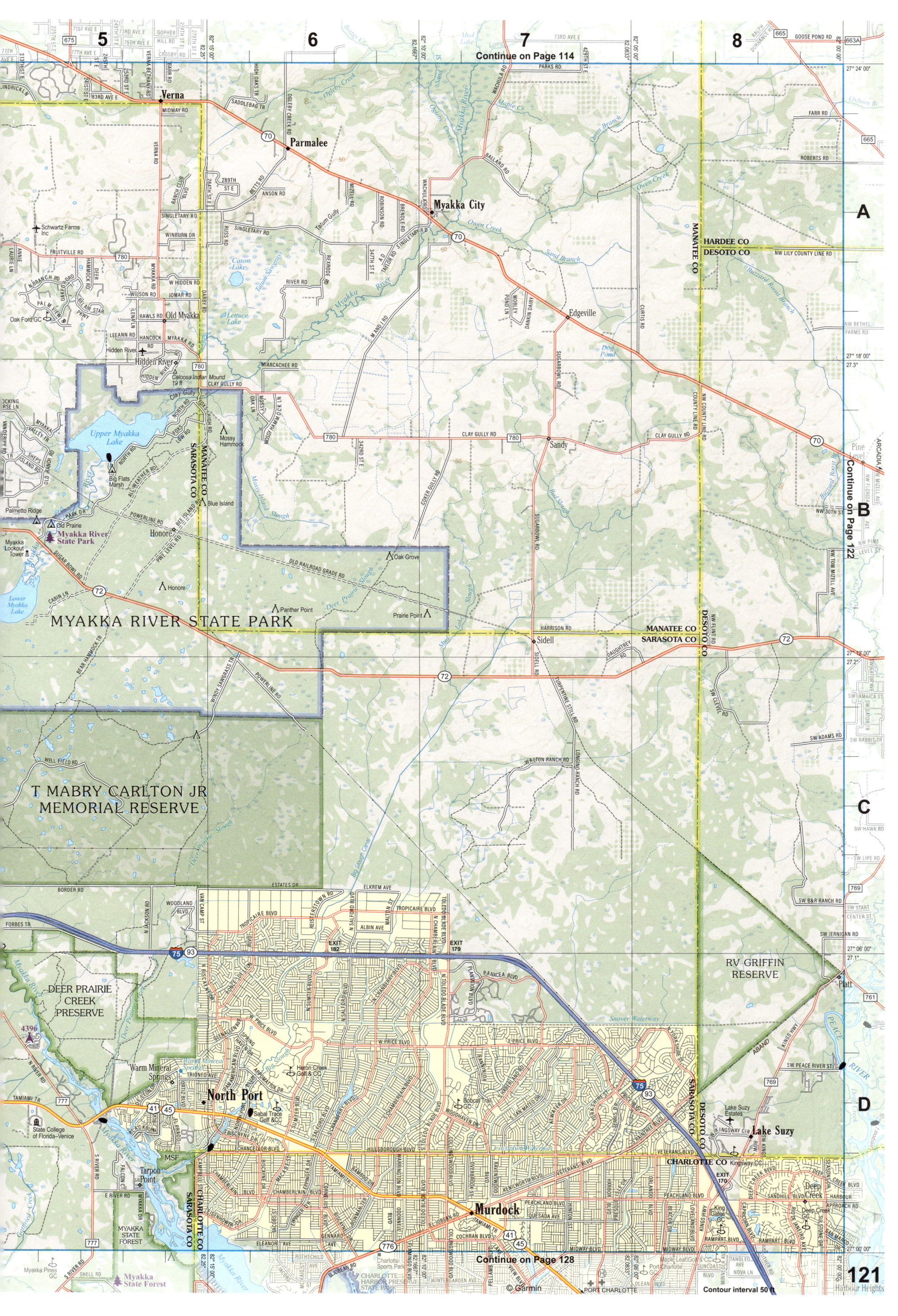

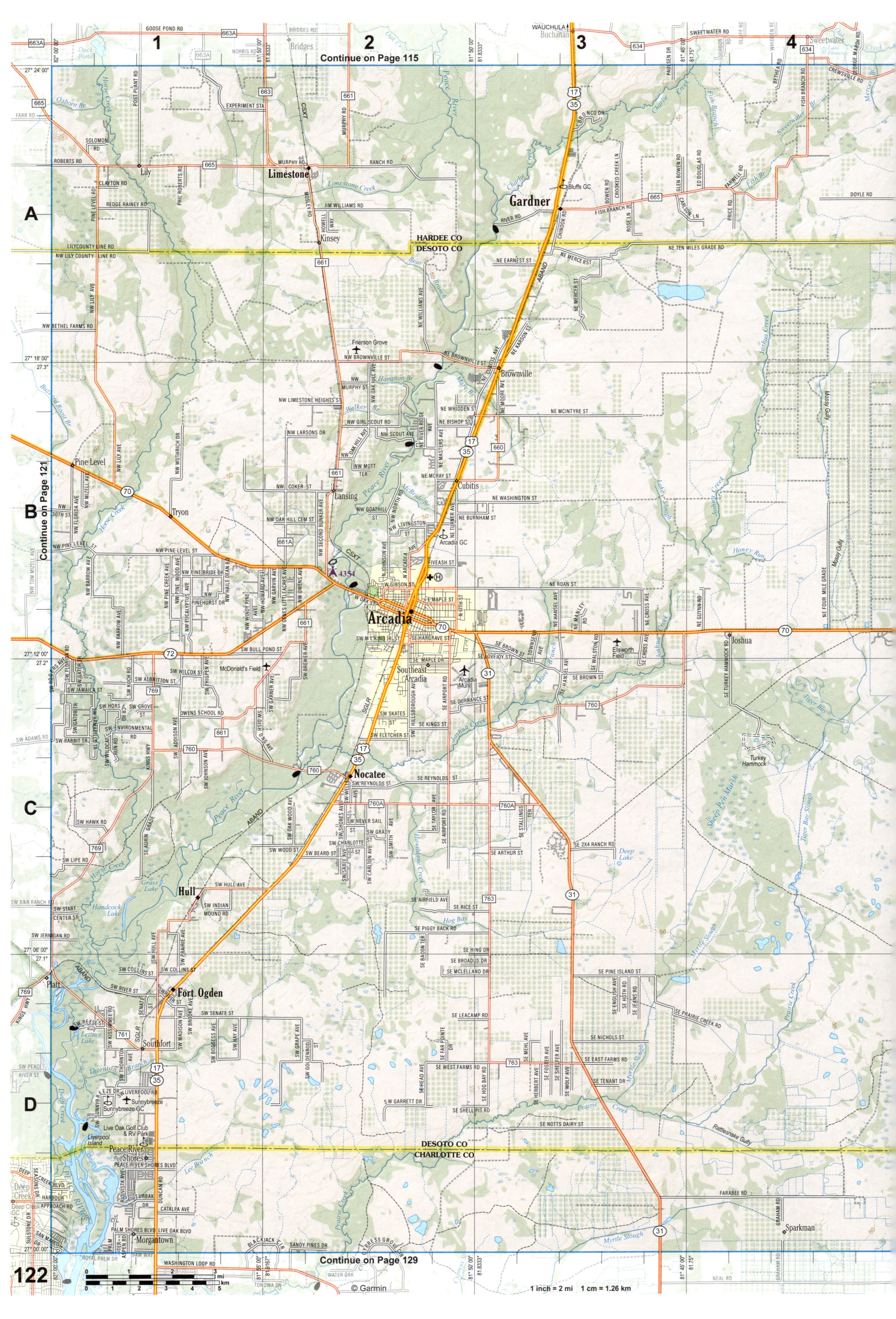

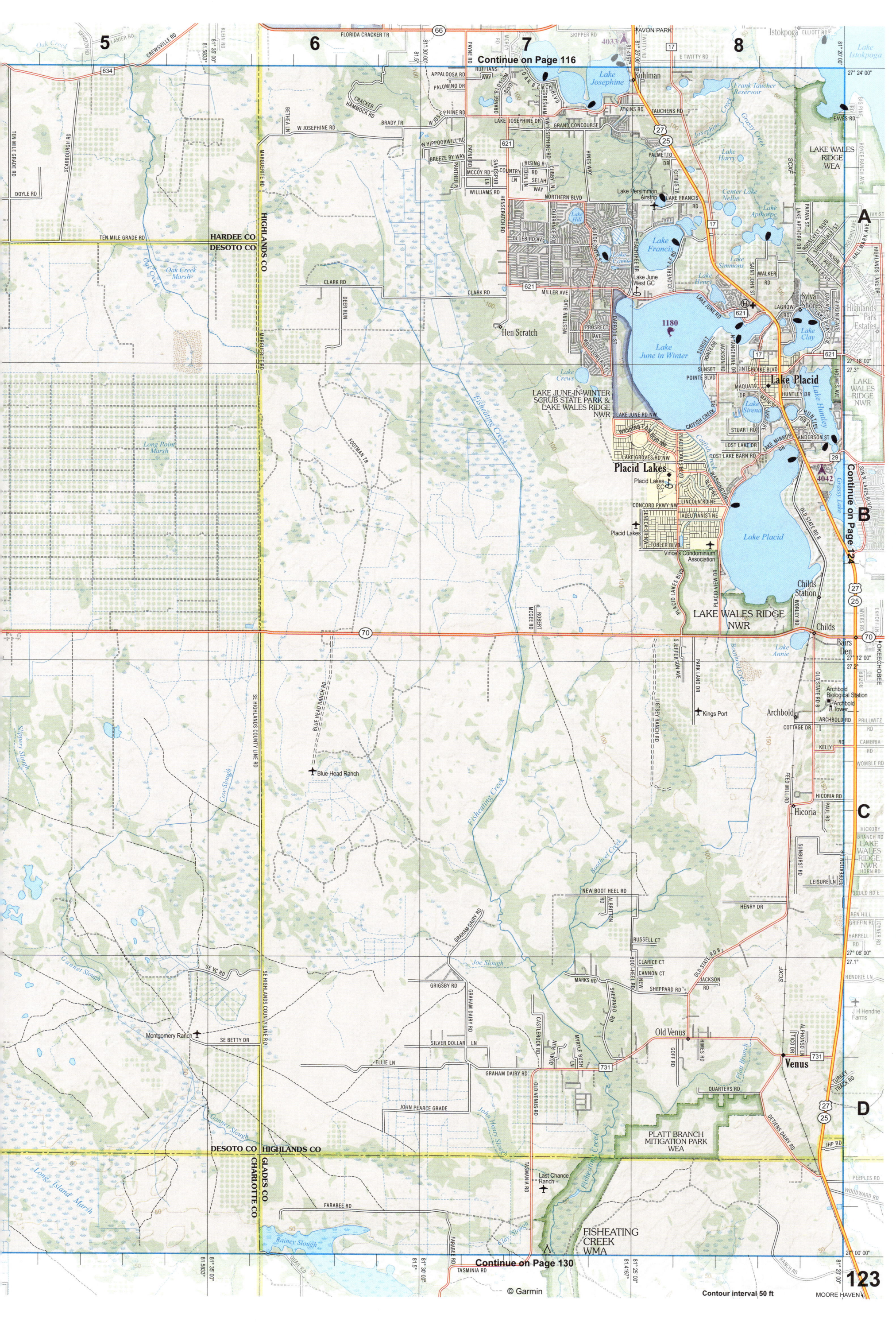

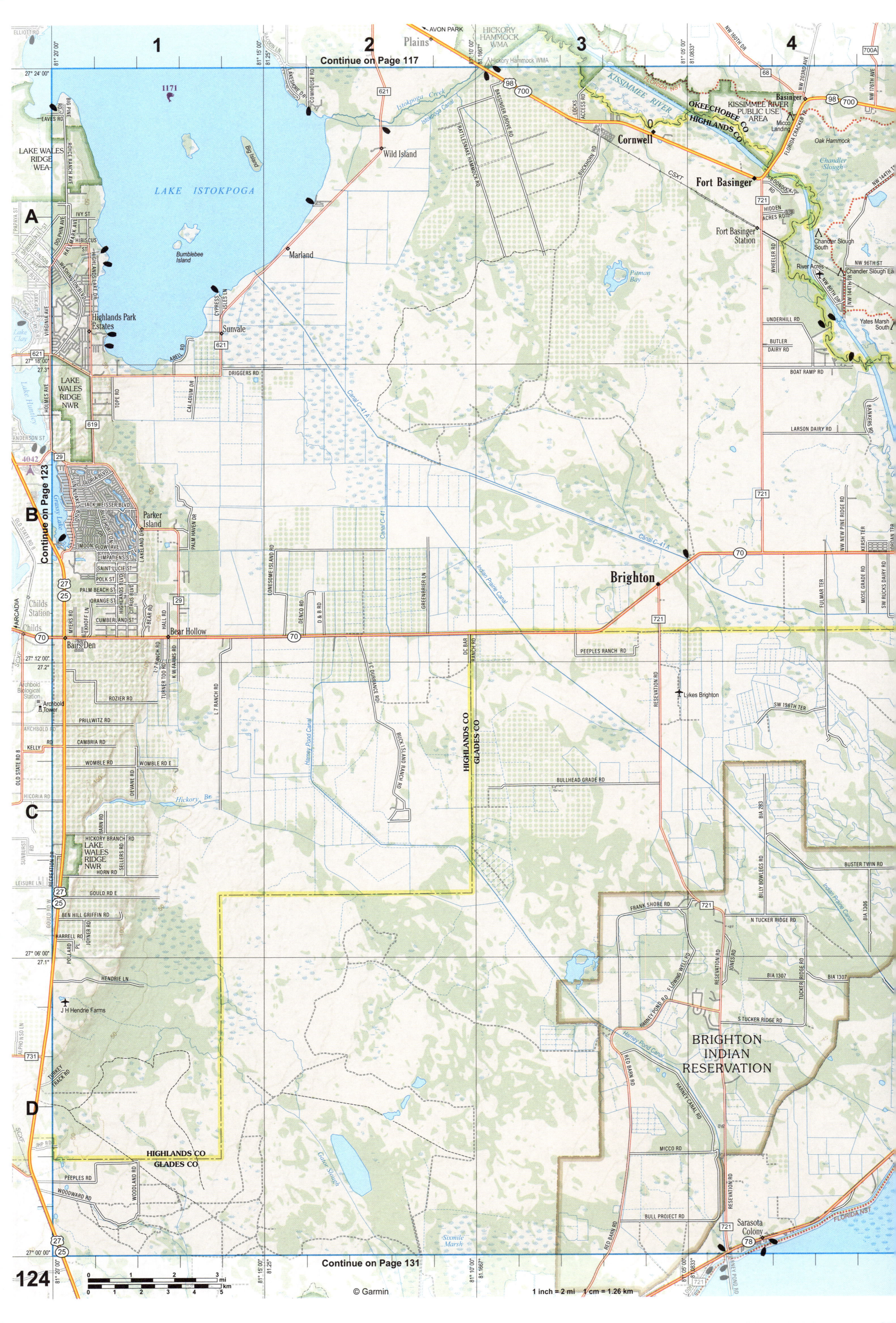

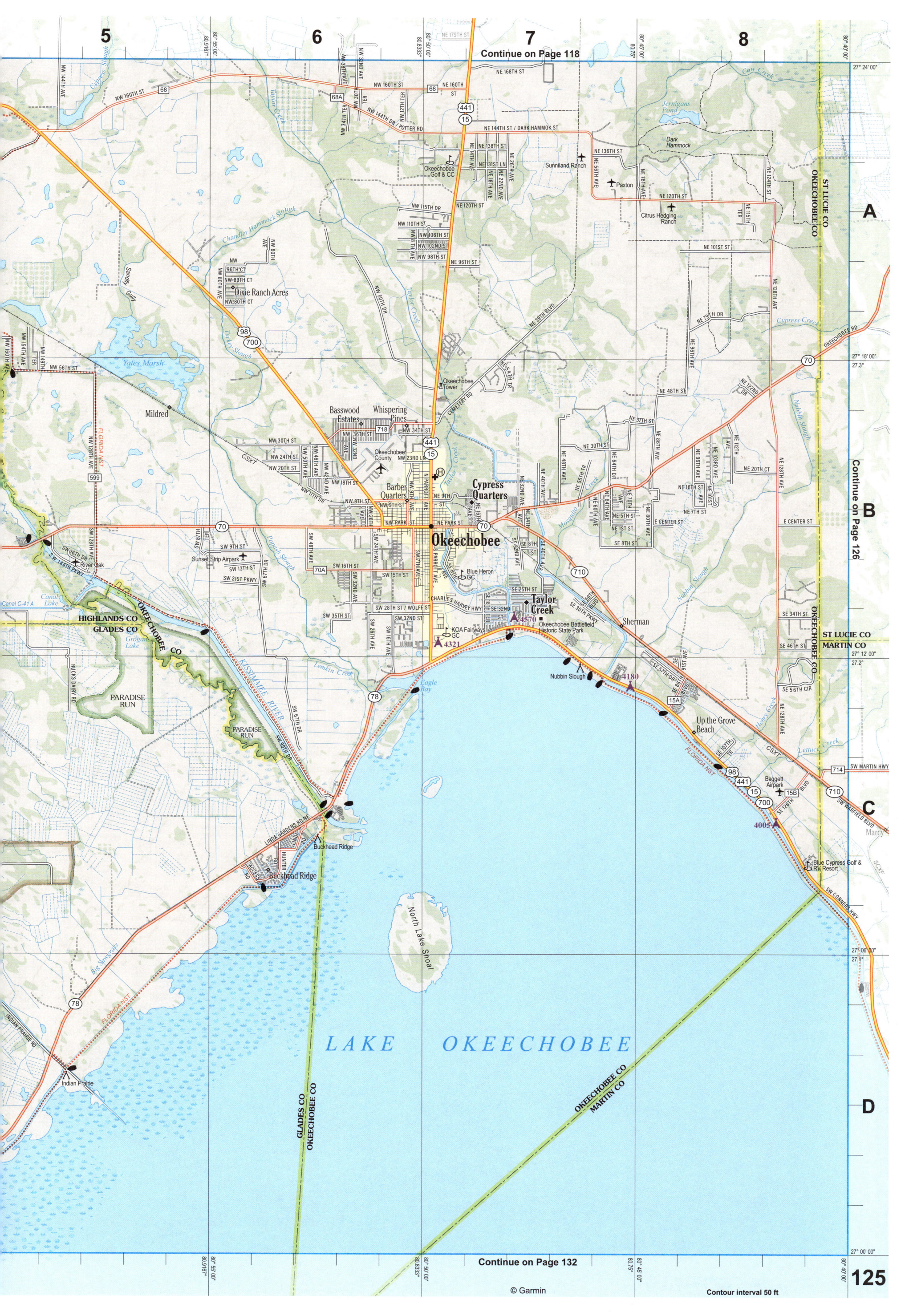

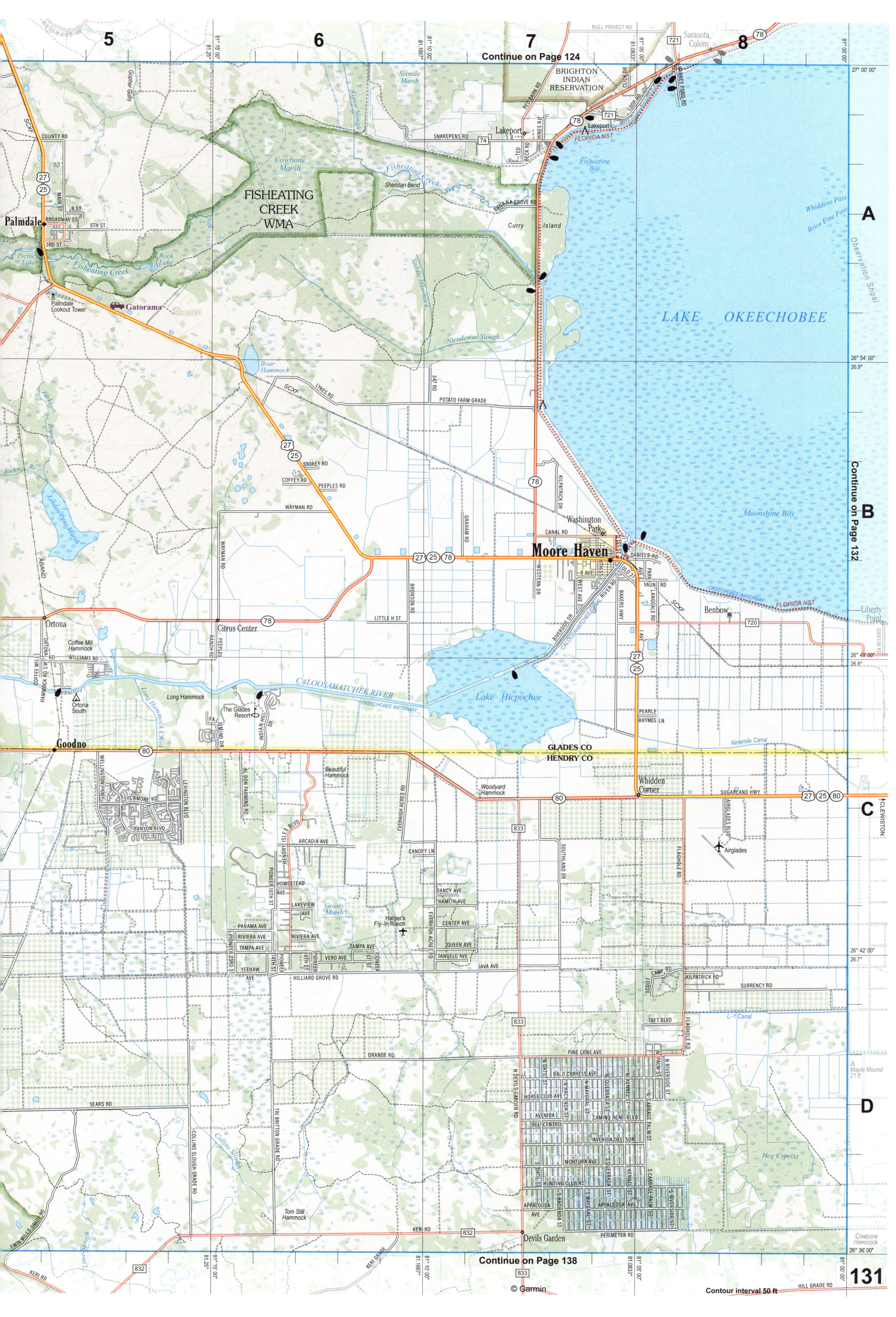

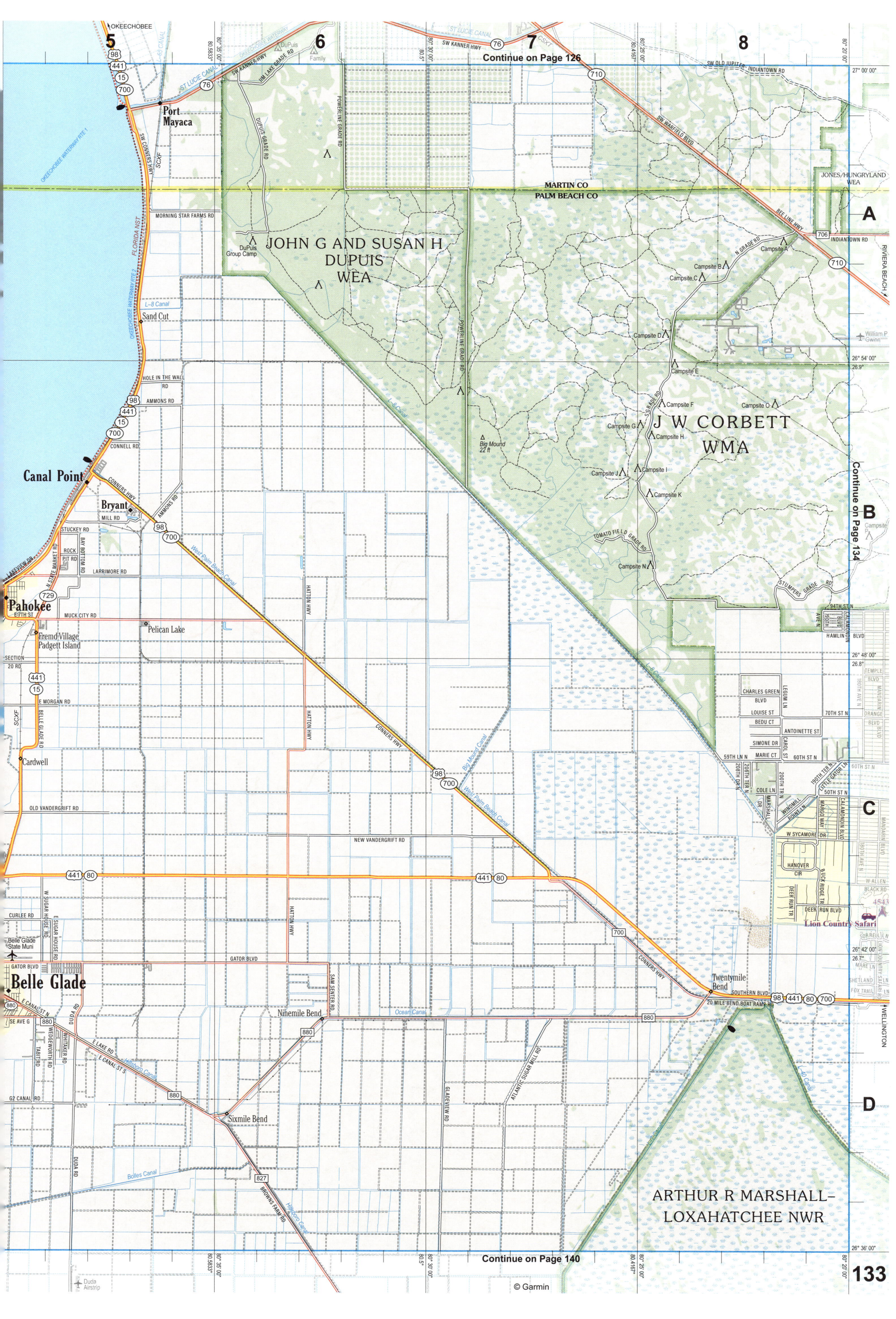

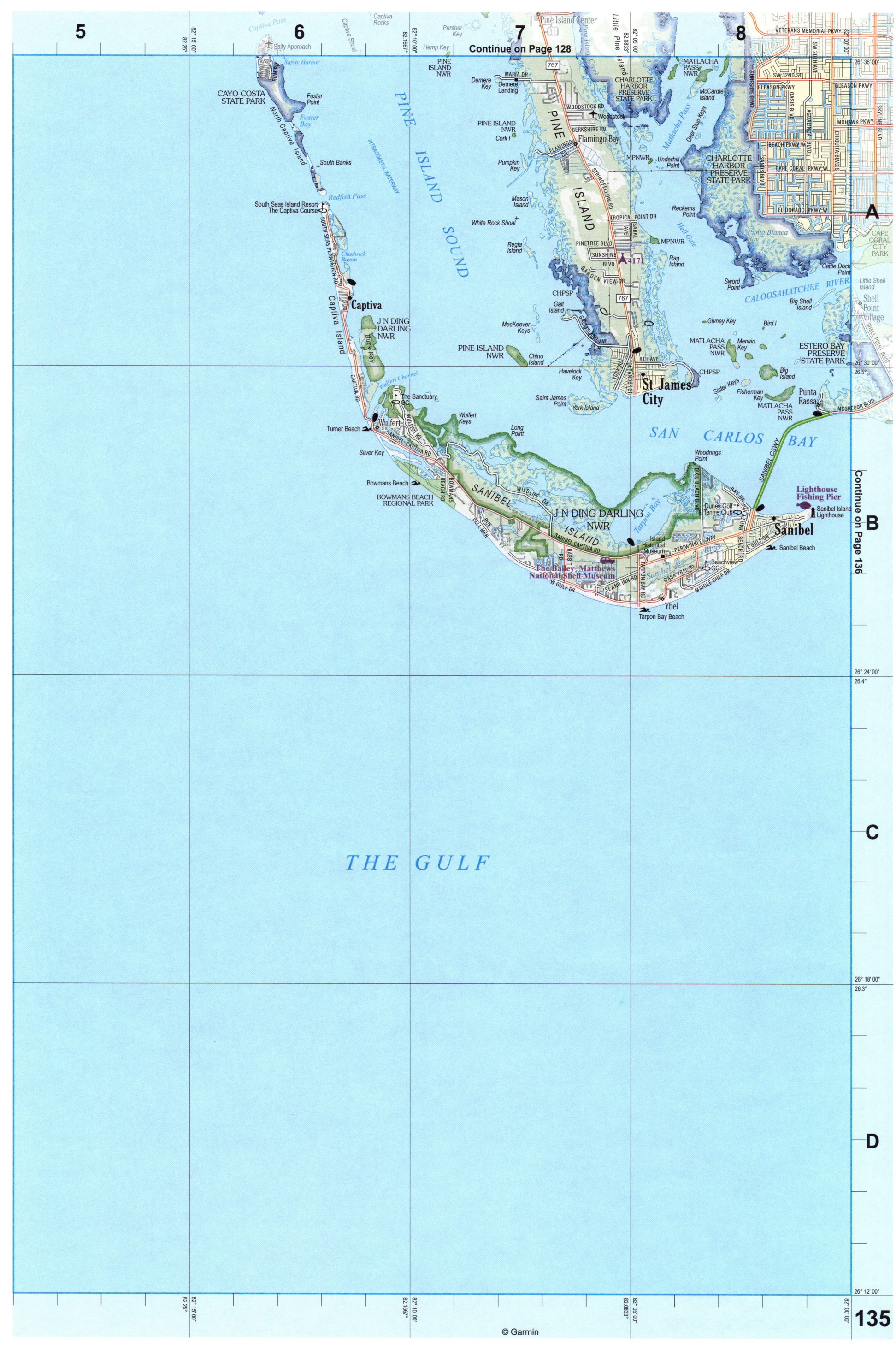

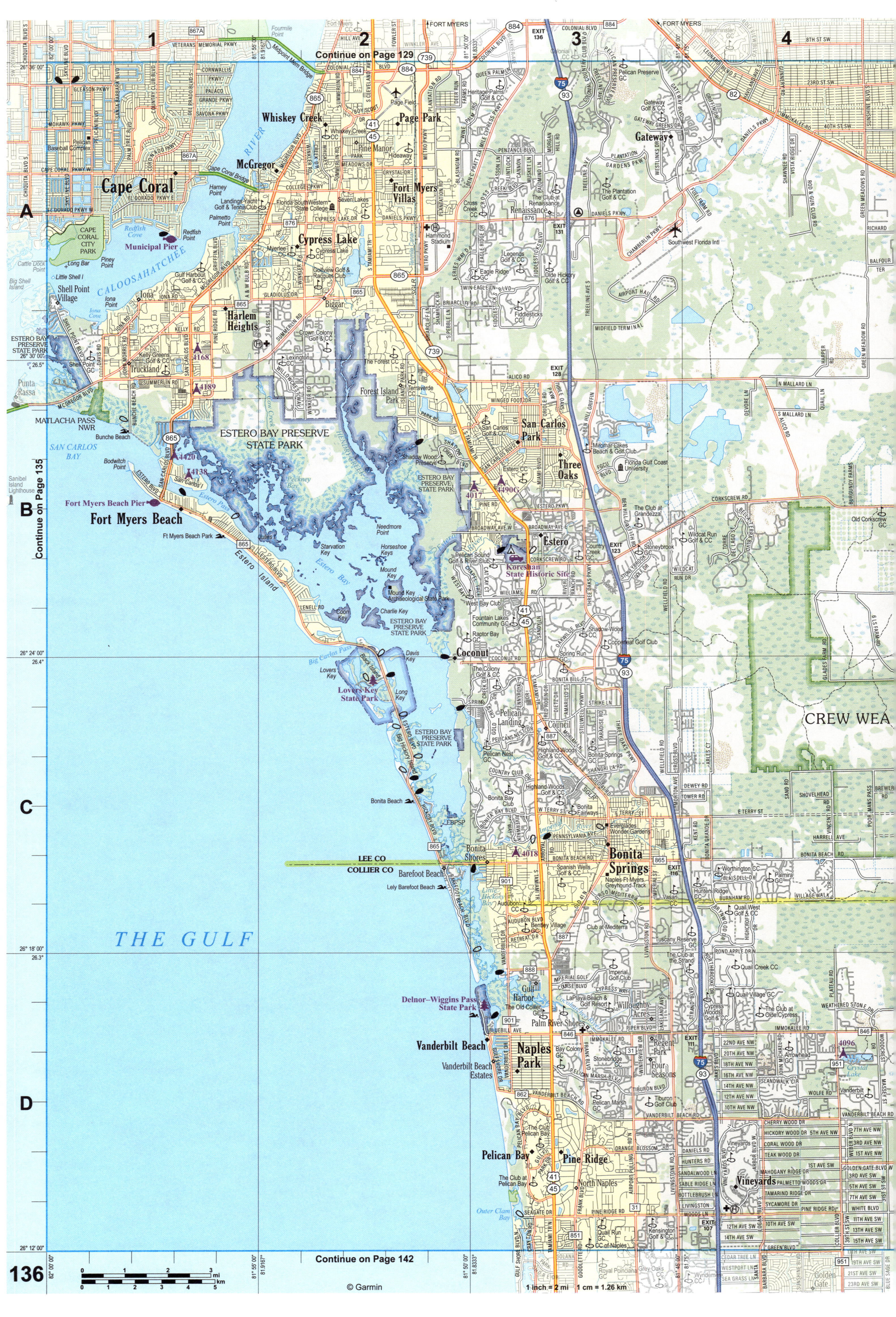

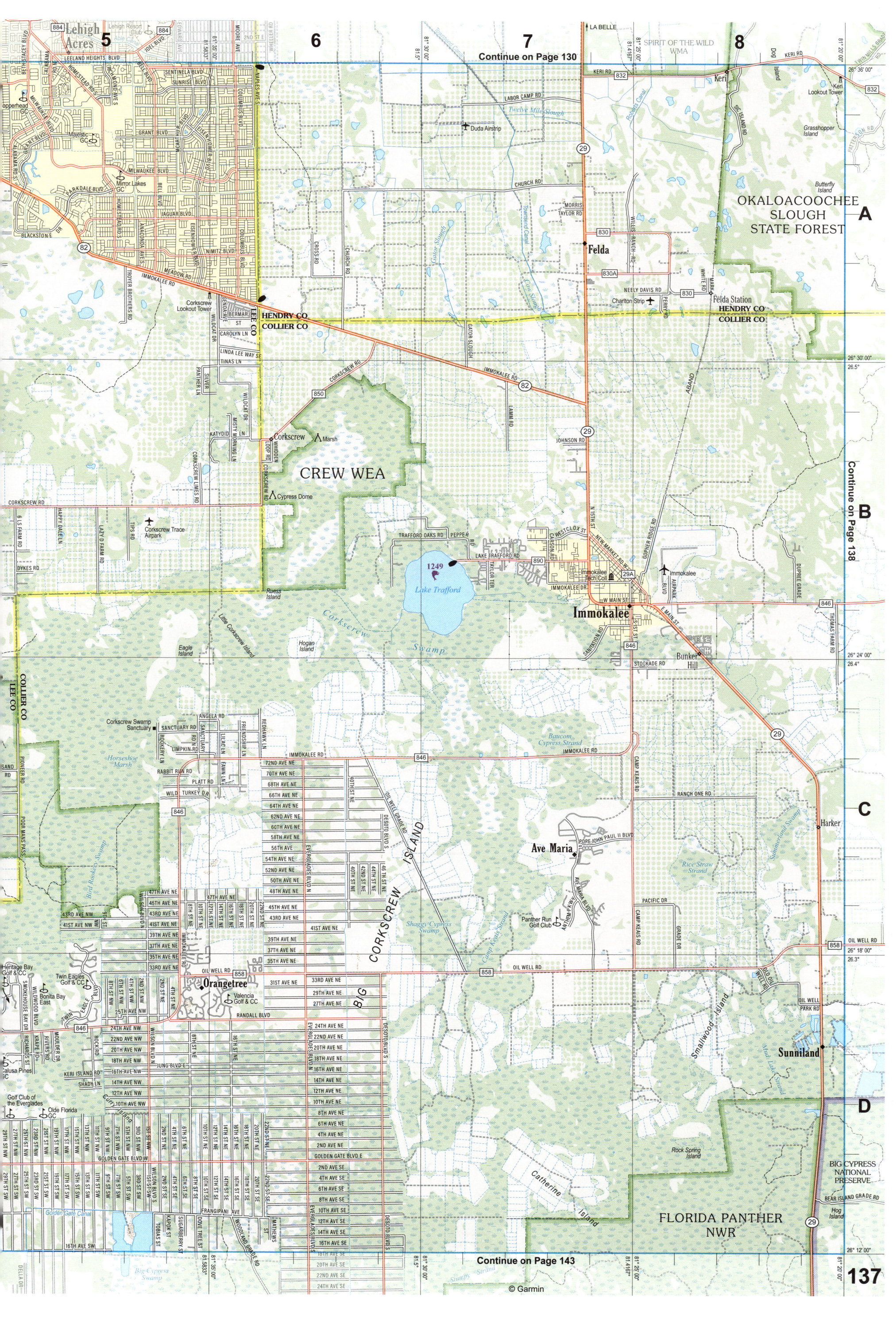

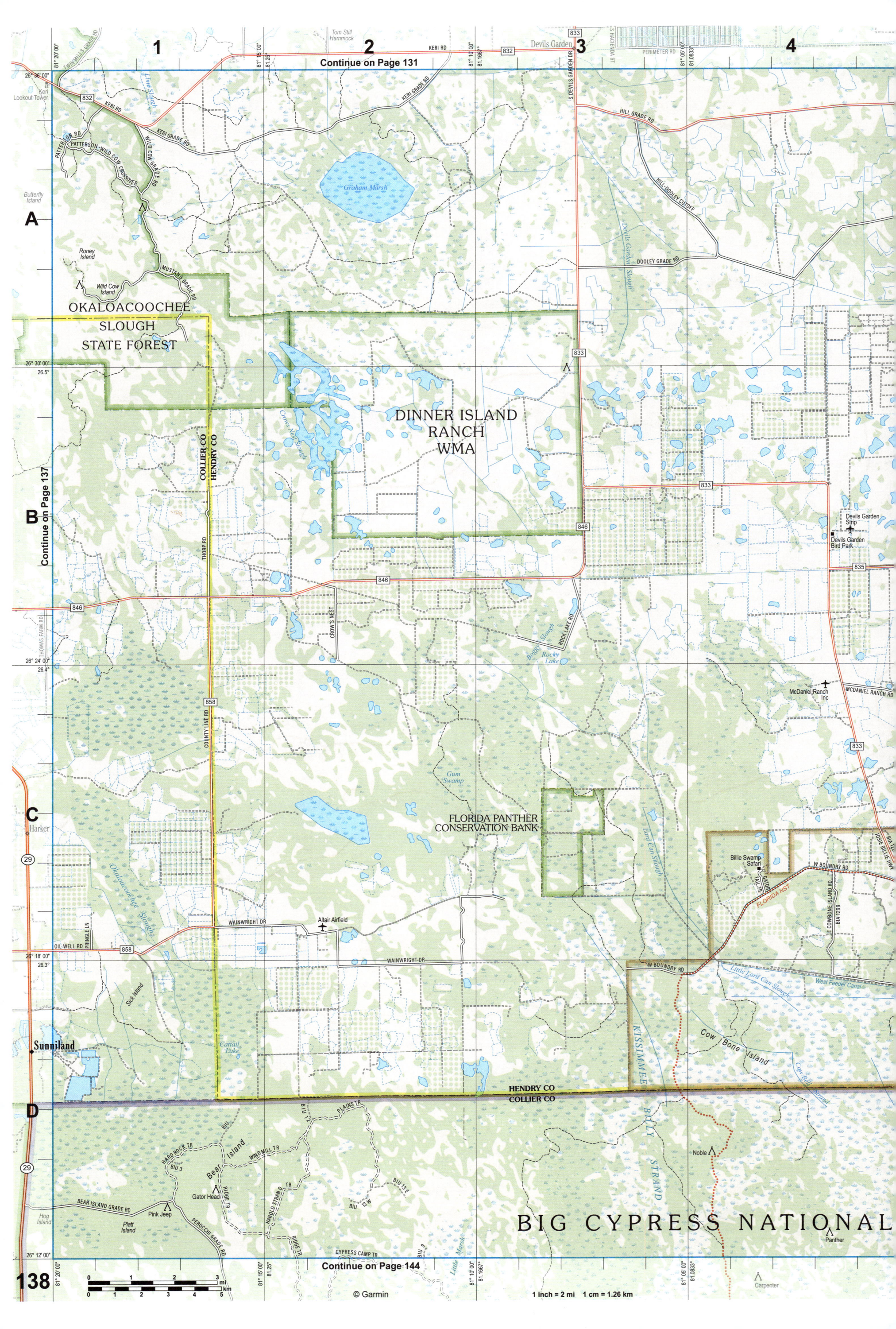

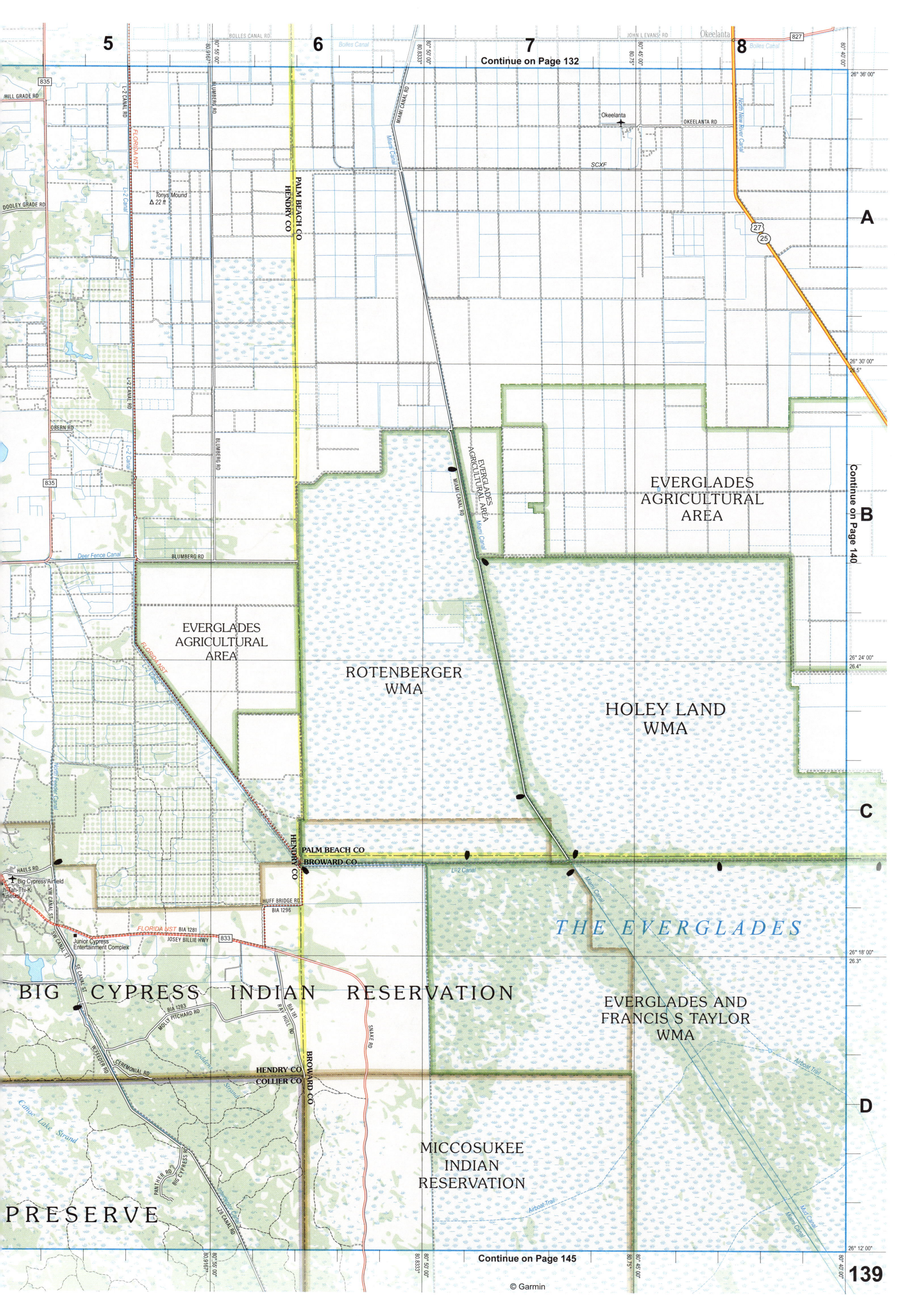

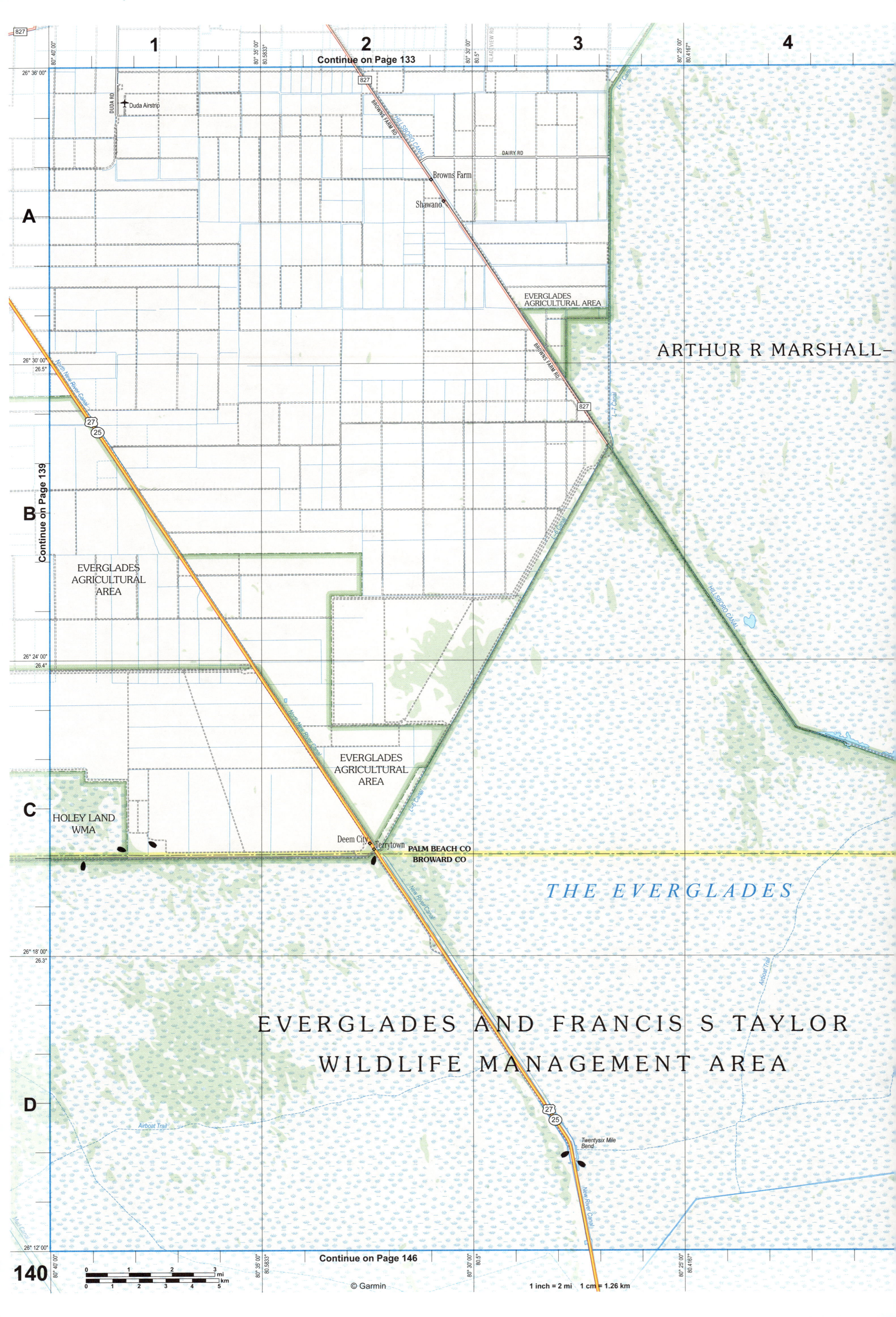

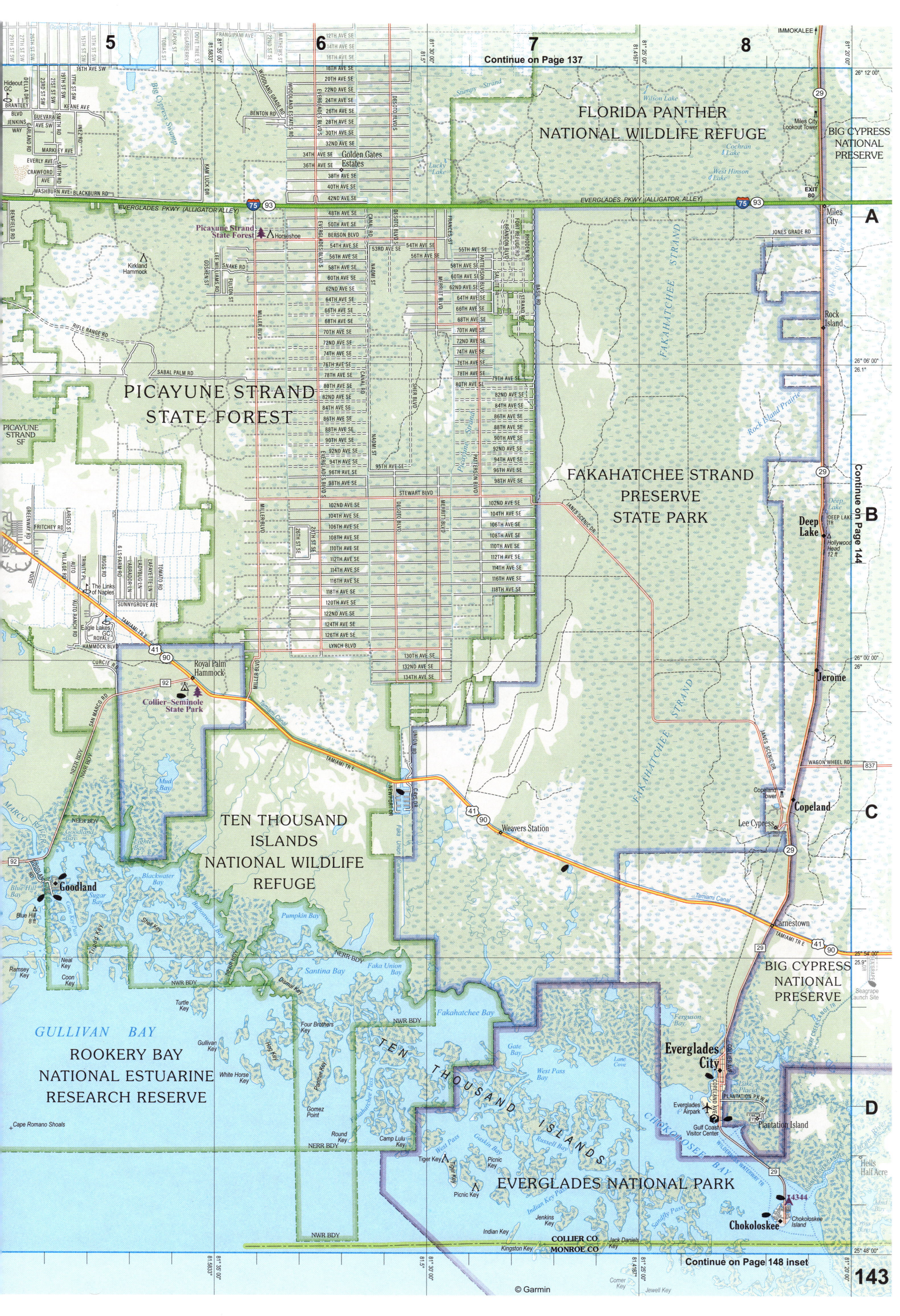

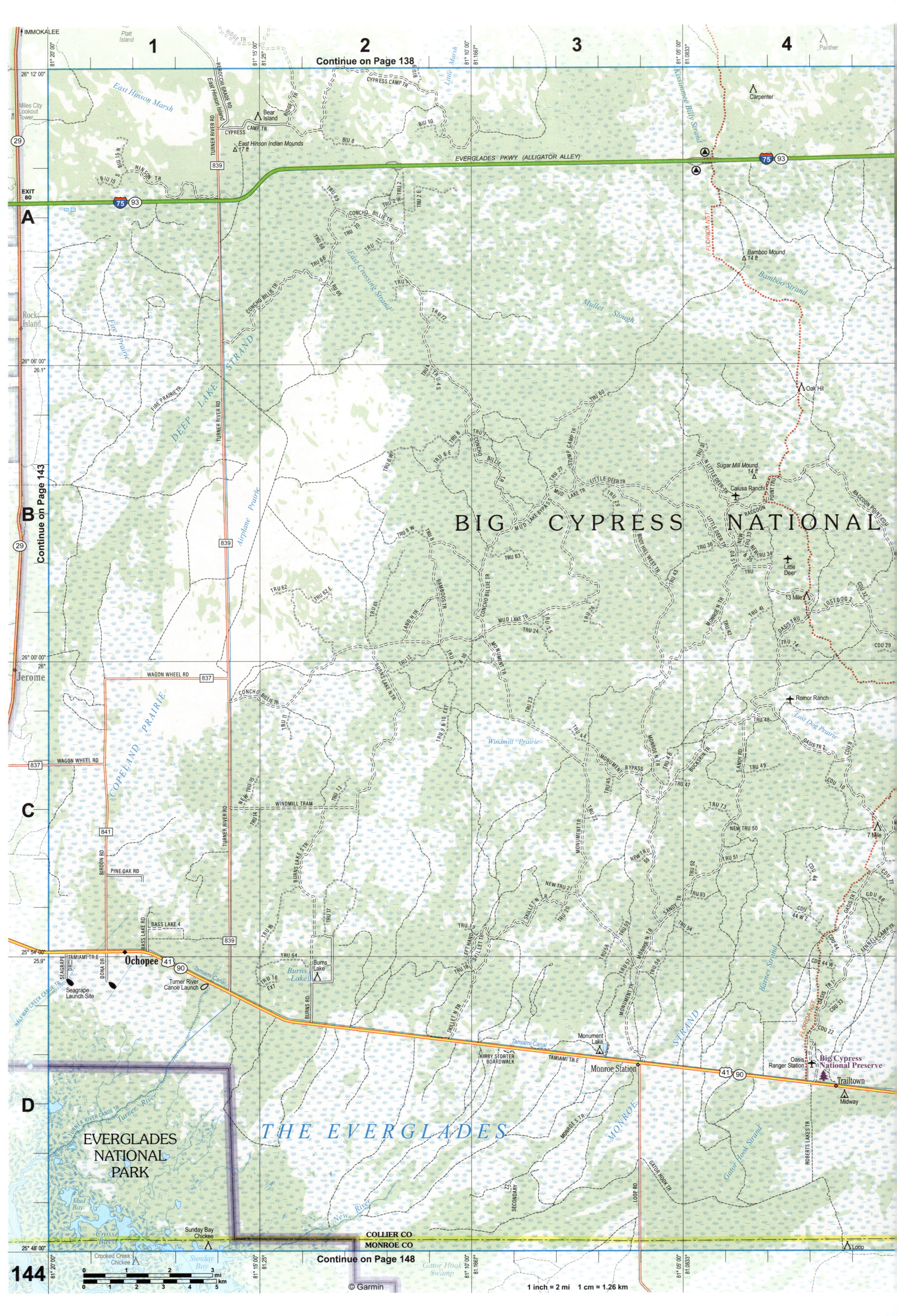

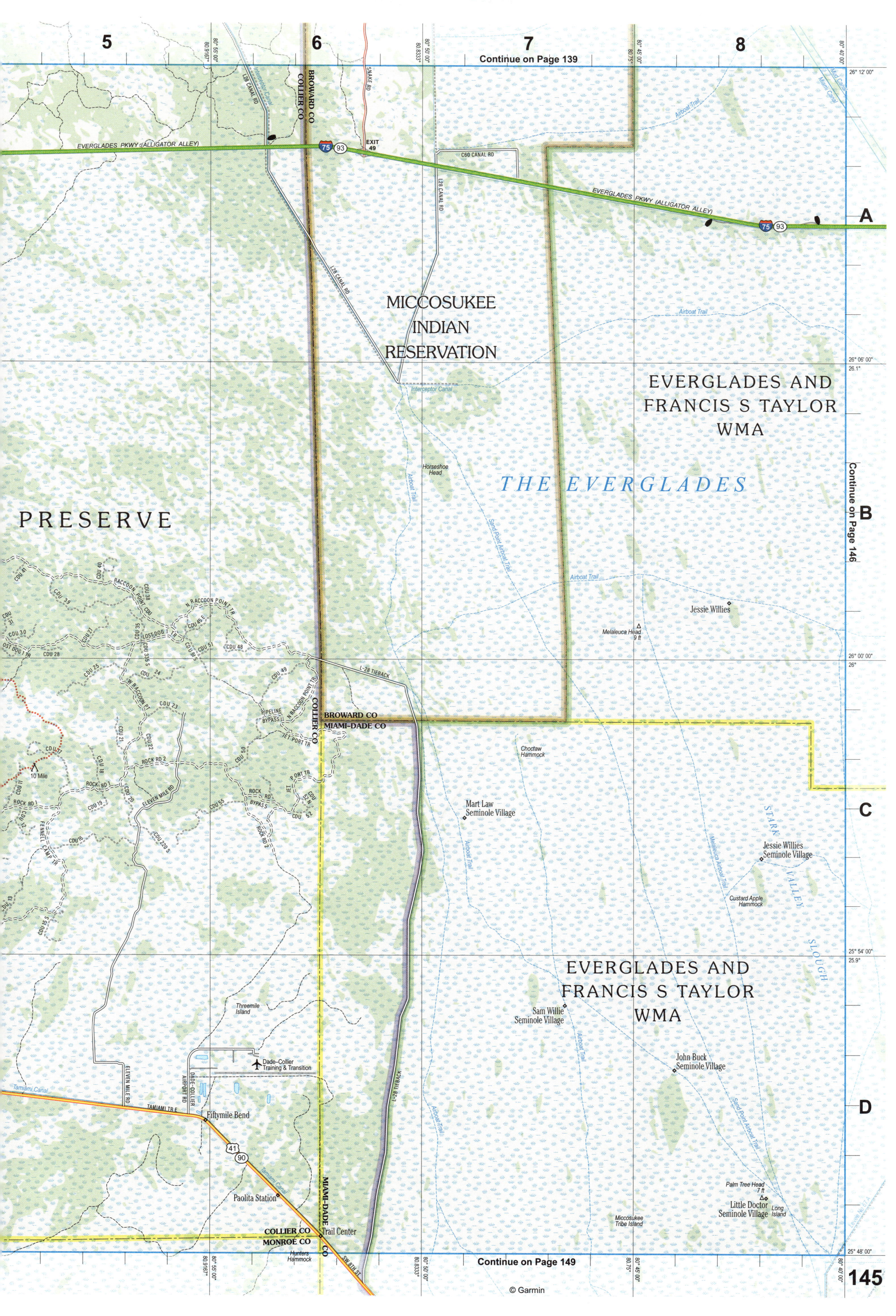

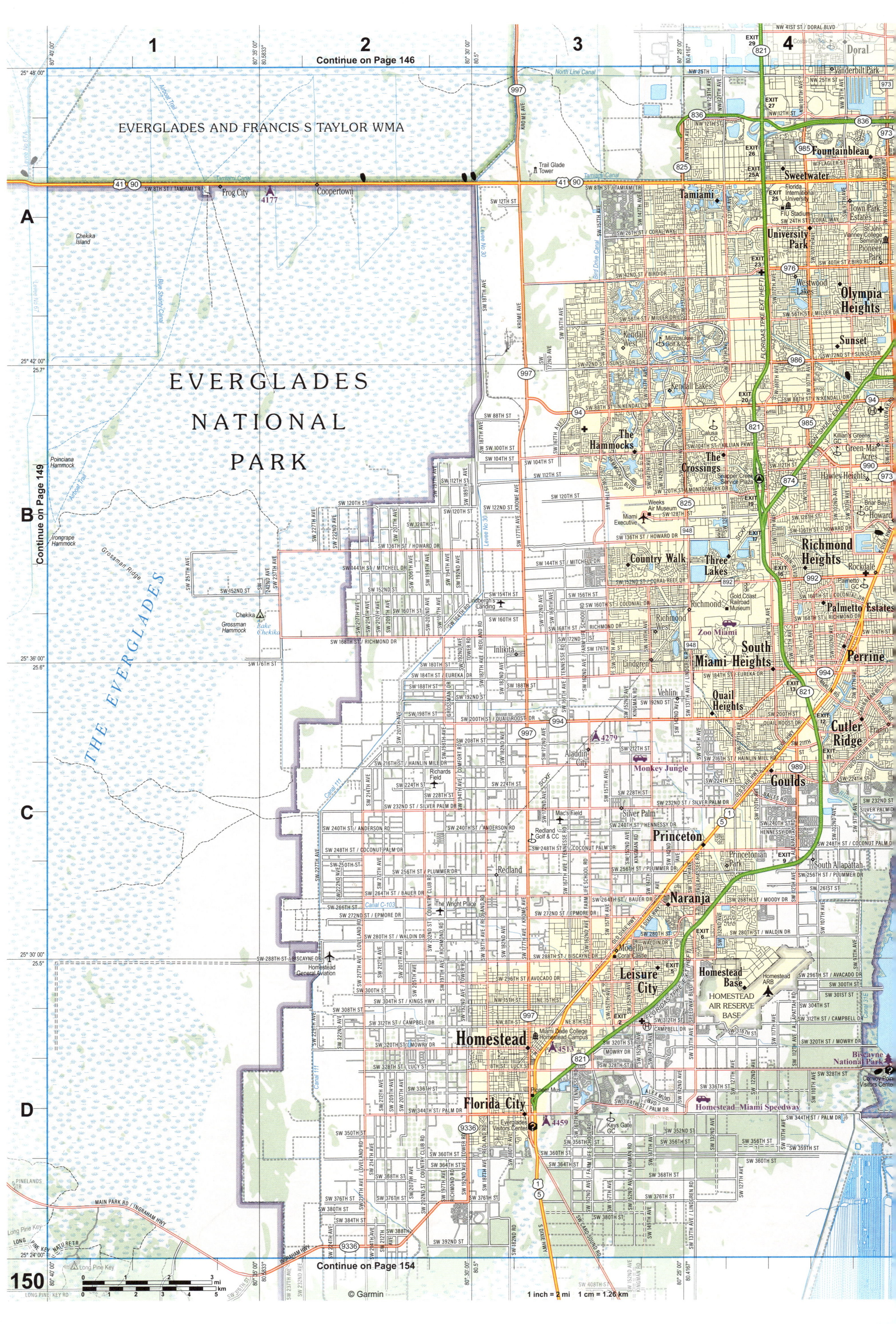

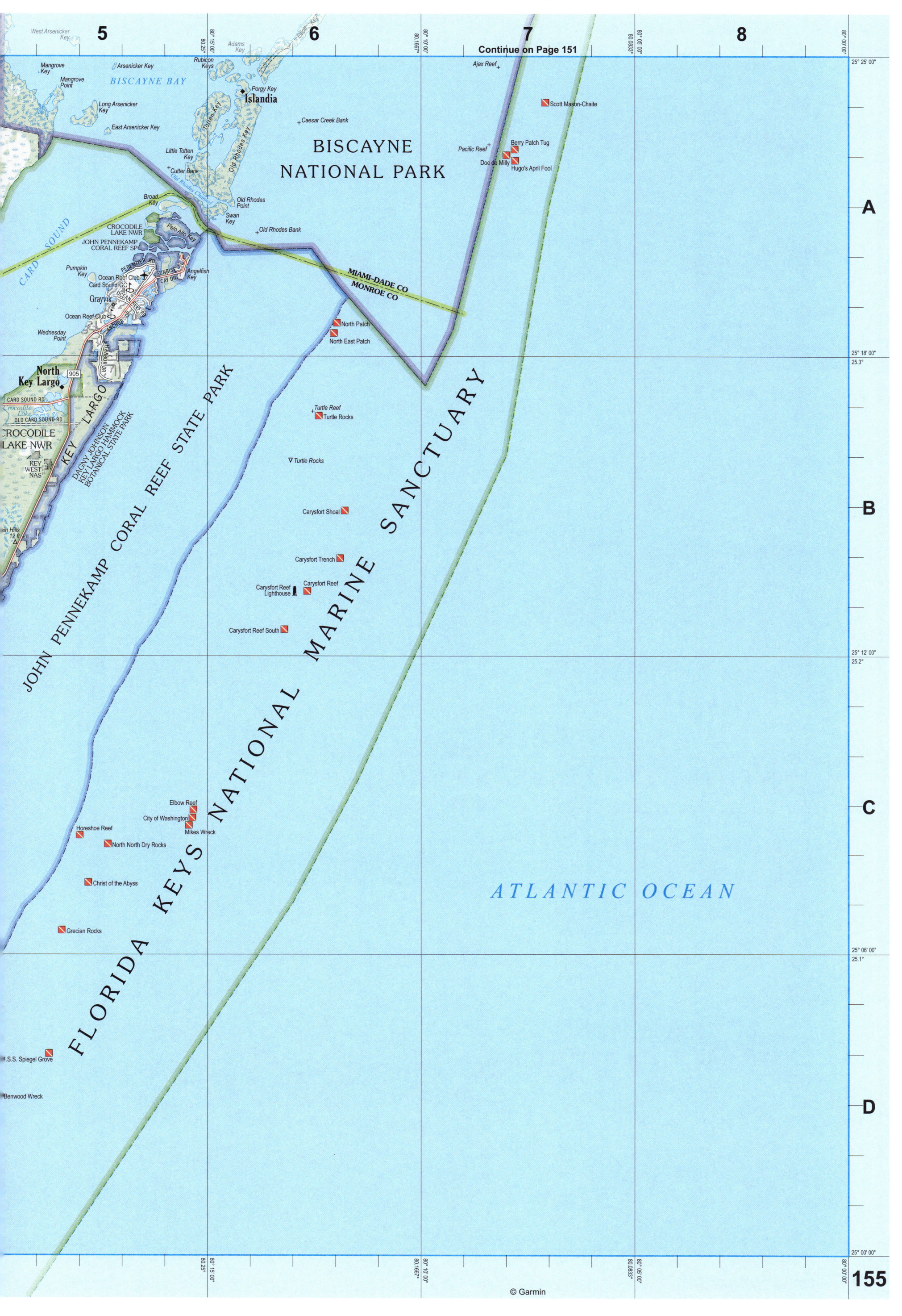

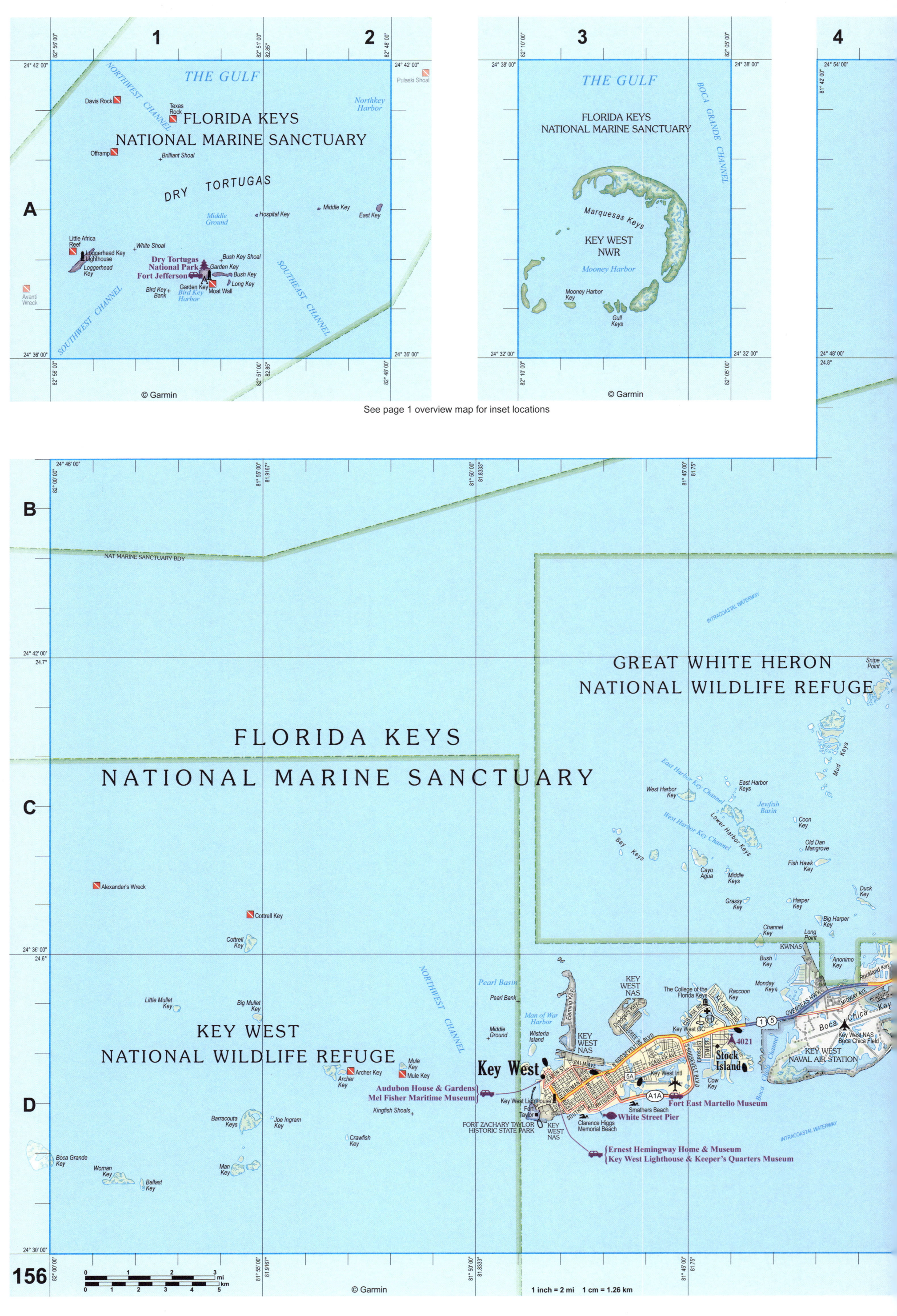

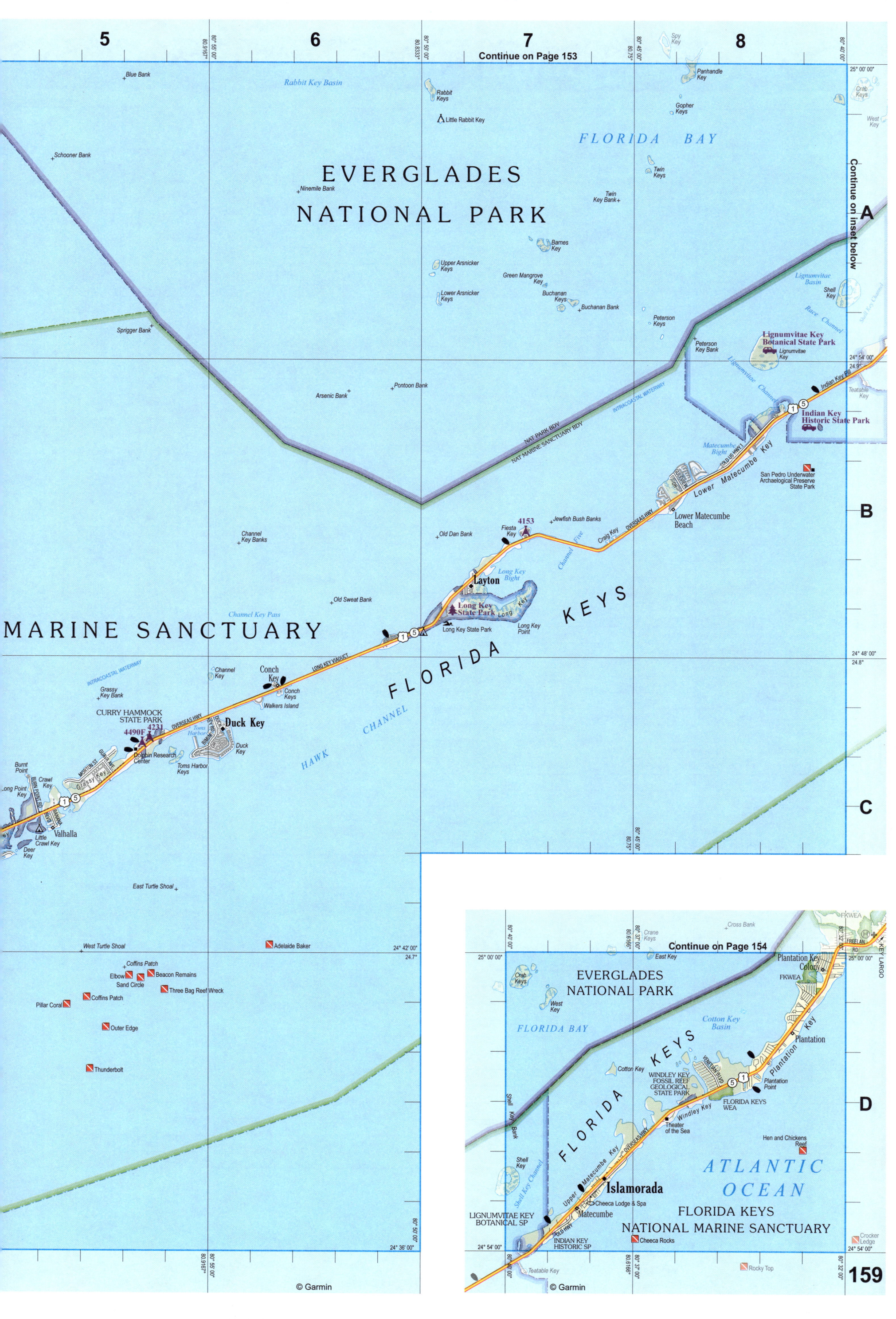

Campgrounds, continued from page 14

To locate campgrounds in this atlas, look on the appropriate map for the campground symbol and corresponding four-digit number. Listed are members of the Florida Association of RV Parks & Campgrounds. Public campgrounds, located on state and federal lands, can be identified by the symbol indicated in the Legend. For information on camping in these lands, see Recreation Areas.

NUMBER	NAME, LOCATION	PAGE & GRID	SITES	BEACH	BOAT RAMP	CAMPFIRES PERMITTED	FISHING	FULL HOOK-UPS	GROCERIES	LAUNDRY	ON-SITE RENTALS	PETS ON LEASH	PLAYGROUND	POOL	PROPANE	REC HALL	TENTERS WELCOME
4426	Sanlan RV & Golf Resort, Lakeland	107 C6	531					•		•		•		•	•	•	•
4429	Sarasota Bay RV Park, South Bradenton	112 D4	240		•			•		•		•		•		•	
4430	Scottish Traveler RV Park, Largo	104 D4	155					•		•		•				•	
4432	Sebring Grove RV Resort, Sebring	116 D3	110					•		•		•		•		•	
4435	Seminole Campground, Fort Myers	129 C7	129				•	•		•		•		•	•	•	•
4444	Sherwood Forest RV Resort, Palm Harbor	104 B3	107					•		•	•	•		•		•	•
4447	Sherwood Forest RV Resort, Kissimmee	100 C3	514					•		•	•	•	•	•	•	•	•
4450	Silver Lakes RV & Golf Resort, Naples	142 B4	560					•		•		•		•		•	
4453	Silver Springs RV Park, Silver Springs	83 B8	199					•		•		•		•		•	
4456	Smiling Gator RV Park & Storage, St. Augustine Beach	66 C4	50					•		•		•		•			
4459	Southern Comfort RV Resort, Florida City	150 D3	350					•		•		•		•		•	
4462	Spirit of Suwannee Music Park, Live Oak	48 C1	600		•	•	•	•		•		•	•	•	•	•	•
4465	Sportsman's Cove Resort, McIntosh	76 D2	49		•	•	•	•		•		•			•	•	•
4468	St. Augustine Beach KOA, St. Augustine Beach	67 D5	91				•	•	•	•	•	•	•	•	•	•	•
4471	St. John's Campground, Palatka	78 B1	31				•	•		•		•		•		•	•
4472	St Mary's River Campground, Hilliard	32 C1	51		•		•	•		•	•	•		•		•	•
4474	St. Petersburg/Madeira Beach KOA, St. Petersburg	104 D3	398				•	•		•	•	•	•	•	•	•	•
4477	Stage Stop Campground, Winter Garden	100 A1	248					•		•		•		•		•	
4480	Stagecoach RV Park, St. Augustine	66 C3	80					•		•		•		•		•	
4483	Starke/Gainesville NE KOA, Starke	64 C3	130					•		•	•	•	•	•		•	•
4486	Sugarloaf Key/Key West KOA, Sugarloaf Key	157 C6	145	•	•		•	•	•	•	•	•		•	•	•	•
4490	Sun Outdoors Sarasota, Sarasota	120 A3	800				•	•		•		•		•		•	
4490A	Sun Outdoors St. Augustine, St. Augustine	66 D4	176				•	•		•		•		•			
4490B	Sun Retreats Daytona Beach, Port Orange	86 C4	230					•		•		•		•		•	
4490C	Sun Retreats Dunedin, Dunedin	104 B3	239					•		•		•		•		•	
4490D	Sun Retreats Naples, Naples	142 A4	167					•	•	•		•		•			
4490E	Sun Retreats Orlando ChampionsGate, Davenport	100 D1	300					•		•		•		•		•	
4490F	Sun Outdoors Marathon, Marathon	159 C5	85		•		•	•		•		•		•		•	
4490G	Sun Retreats Estero Bay, Fort Myers	136 B3	300					•		•		•		•		•	
4492	Sun-N-Shade RV Resort, Punta Gorda	129 B5	191					•		•		•		•		•	
4493	Sunset King Lake RV Resort, DeFuniak Springs	19 C6	220		•	•	•	•		•		•		•		•	
4495	Sunshine Holiday Daytona, Ormond Beach	86 A3	602				•	•		•	•	•		•		•	
4496	Sunshine Holiday Ft. Lauderdale RV Resort, Fort Lauderdale	147 A6	130					•		•				•		•	
4498	Suwannee River Rendezvous, Mayo	61 B7	338		•		•	•		•	•	•		•		•	•
4501	Swan Lake Village & RV Resort, North Fort Myers	129 D6	104					•		•		•		•		•	
4504	Tallahassee East Campground, Monticello	45 B5	66				•	•		•		•		•		•	•
4507	Tallahassee RV Park, Tallahassee	44 B2	66					•		•		•				•	•
4510	Tampa RV Park, Tampa	105 B7	86					•		•		•		•		•	
4513	The Boardwalk RV Resort, Homestead	150 D3	145					•		•		•		•		•	
4514	The Campsites at Disney's Fort Wilderness Resort, Lake Buena Vista	100 B2	800				•	•	•	•	•	•	•	•		•	•
4520	Treasure by the Sea, Flagler Beach	79 C7	30	•		•	•	•		•		•		•		•	
4525	Tropical Palms Resort, Kissimmee	100 C2	343				•	•		•	•	•	•	•		•	•
4527	Tropical Waters RV Resort, Bokeelia	128 D3	145		•			•		•		•				•	
4531	Twelve Oaks RV Resort, Sanford	92 B4	247					•		•		•		•		•	
4532	Unhitched Garcon Point, Milton	35 A8	45			•	•	•		•		•		•		•	
4533	Unhitched Milton, Milton	17 D5	103			•	•	•		•		•		•		•	
4534	Upriver RV Resort, Fort Myers	129 C7	350		•		•	•		•		•		•		•	
4537	Villager RV Park, Wildwood	90 B4	108					•		•		•		•		•	
4539	Wandering Oaks RV Park, Milton	16 D4	40					•		•		•		•			
4540	West Jupiter RV Resort, Jupiter	134 A2	104			•	•	•		•		•		•		•	
4543	West Palm Beach/Lion Country Safari KOA, Loxahatchee	134 C1	233					•		•	•	•	•	•	•	•	•
4546	Whippoorwill Sportsman's Lodge, Quincy	43 B5	6		•	•	•	•		•		•					•
4549	Whispering Pines Mobile Home & RV Park, Titusville	102 A3	64					•		•		•		•		•	
4552	Whitey's Fish Camp, Orange Park	65 A8	40		•		•	•		•		•					
4553	Winter Garden RV Resort, Winter Garden	100 A1	368					•		•		•		•	•	•	
4555	Winter Quarters Pasco RV Resort, Lutz	105 A7	257					•		•		•		•		•	
4558	Winterset RV Resort, Palmetto	113 C6	221					•		•		•		•		•	
4561	Yacht Haven Park & Marina, Fort Lauderdale	147 B6	222					•		•		•		•		•	
4564	Yankee Traveler RV, Largo	104 D3	210					•		•		•		•		•	
4570	Zachary Taylor RV Resort, Okeechobee	125 B7	210		•		•	•		•		•		•		•	